D1806029

1

My
WALK
THROUGH
SHAME

My Walk through Shame

Sifelani Masamba

First published 2023

ISBN: 978-0-7961-0983-5

To the two souls whose love and affection towards me have always been expressed without measure – my girls;

Blessing, my first born who lived a short but meaningful life. Your indelible works, infectious smile and graceful conduct will remain to us priceless treasures.

Moreblessing, who now stands like a brand plucked from the fire. It is your presence that encourages me to summon the courage and energy to approach each new day and every new challenge with increasing willingness.

CONTENTS

7

Foreword

When our mutual friend Aaron connected me with Sifelani to help review his manuscript and provide publishing guidance to him, I thought as an ardent reader, it would take me a couple of days to read the book since I'm the kind that struggles to read the book and put it away to continue the next day – it haunts me to get to the last page in few sittings. With *My Walk Through Shame* I couldn't. As an empath, I found myself feeling every emotion and experience embodied in Sifelani's journey; I was transported to Unit M in the Harare Province of Zimbabwe, the dusty roads of Kenzamba, Regent House in Cape Town, the corridors of Red Cross Children's Hospital, right to the seat of the massive metal bird, Boeing enroute to Australia. There were tears that were shed, laughter bursted into, smiling hearts experienced, and a surge of courage and inspiration felt. I saw how resilient the human spirit is or rather can be.

My Walk Through Shame, will really help you walk your own walk. The book will help you walk to places within yourself that you may be afraid or feeling ashamed to visit alone. Sifelani is one talented writer whose storytelling ability transports you with images and get you glued up to every page because you never know what to expect, which makes his writing, seasoned with sarcasm and humour, therapeutic. Indeed, sharing one's story is not only a worthwhile endeavor for the storyteller, but also for us who hear those stories and feel less alone because of it. Like Michelle Obama in Becoming said: *Even when it's not pretty or perfect, even when it's more real than you want it to be. Your story is what you have, what you will always have. It is something to own.* And *My Walk Through Shame* will empower you to own yours.

-   **Kgadi Mmanakana**

Competitive Advantage Strategist, Speaker, and Author

Polokwane, South Africa

27 August 2023

Prologue

When I was a kid, there was a time I had no clue that food grows from the ground. From the time I became aware of my existence, I lived in the city and knew no other life, and my world was painted sorely in the marvels of the vibrant charming city life. My childish thoughts and actions where shaped by the world around me. It was that setting that planted in me a misconception that food comes from supermarket shelves.

Then, when I least suspected it, while I was still in the tender bloom of my existence, life gently spewed us out of the vibrancy of our familiar city surroundings and before I knew it, I found myself living in the rural area where we grew our own food and ate of the ground, and from the ground.

Despite that sudden change, our home remained a place where peace and love seemed supreme, and my parents where my world. Outside of my small world, nothing mattered and I never cared to worry.

Then life turned a sour page to usher us into another scripted chapter in which there was a radical turn of events. My parents parted ways and life threw us further into what felt like a valley, further away from civilization, and from that moment we found ourselves in a place where we wouldn't dare to dream. As we became aware of our surroundings, it became a taboo to envision or dream of a day out of the abyss. We found ourselves living far from civilization that I remember the coming and going of the bus being the only thing within reach that reminded us of a civilised society beyond our rustic realms.

Even though we could see the jumbo jet flying high in the sky above leaving a trail of cloud like smoke that stained the sky. It was hard from our point of view to imagine fellow human beings sitting in it, talking, eating while journeying to attend life affairs. I remember how it felt otherworldly to be ambitious, let alone daring to dream of a day we could be among the throngs seated and taking a trip in a jumbo jet, or picture myself traveling the world or dreaming with eyes open.

We grew up grinding in poverty, a life of fruitless toil in which fortune refused to work in our favour, our surroundings forbade us to dream or plan. Nonetheless we taught ourselves to view our glass as half full and cultivate attributes that have helped us crawl out of the bottomless pit to a world of possibilities.

From our humbling setting, we drew invaluable lessons that became tools useful to navigate life path which as ever, had been fraught with peril and adventure.

At every stage in my journey, it seemed like odds of a supernatural nature and the universe itself have been conspiring against me, throwing all sorts of obstacles. So, I learned to fight and overcome feelings of shame and despair. Even now, I haven't won accolades, but I can't help to celebrate every small stride especially in this life jungle in which I have been a nomad from the time my parents divorced.

Introduction

A milk and honey genesis

My preschool memories feel like a secret portal to a distant planet that isn't plagued by Earth's troubles. Oh how I long to journey back and be there in person and re-live those unforgettable moments. Unfortunately, that ability to wind back the clock is beyond me. Nevertheless, I still cherish with unbridled excitement the joy and those fond recollections of our time in Seke, the place where my wheel of life began to swing.

I have longed with no success to remember more beyond Seke. Despite my inability to recollect beyond my early years in unit M when I was just four years old, I treasure the simple pleasures of playing barefoot in the warm sunshine and hearing the laughter of my mom and fellow stay-at-home ladies gossiping over the fence to satisfy their curiosity in what I now feel was their rat race routine. The prominent sweet scent of blossoming flowers from our avocado and peach trees is forever rooted in my mind, a reminder of the innocence of my childhood spent in Seke.

All my recollections cannot go beyond this point and telling my life story takes off with my reminiscences of living at house 17248 in unit M, in Seke Chitungwiza. A house like all the typical government-built structures consisting of two rooms built of cement blocks. Inside, we had the infamous water system squat pan toilet, a concreted earthenware bowl in the floor that required you to squat as if you were using a pit latrine. Additionally, we had a high-level cistern that was raised to allow gravity to provide the necessary water pressure for flushing. At that time, we had no issues with this setup, as it was considered the best available option.

Our country Zimbabwe was still young, fresh from the liberation war that led to independence from the British a few years back. Young our country was, yet there were significant advances in the urban, like the availability of constant supply of electricity running in cables housed in conduits pinned to wall surfaces. Not forgetting the perennial supply of water running in pressurized galvanized steel pipes, ready to supply clean water at the slightest turn of the tap.

The house stood proudly on the corner, just two streets away from the main tarred road that marked the boundary between housing units and St. Aidens Primary School. As far as I was concerned, all of my memories of life on this planet began at this very house. It was the moment when I became aware of my existence, and everything that came before it was a hazy, distant dream that I could only rely on my parents to recount for me. They told me stories of our previous homes, like the one in Chegutu, which was still referred to by its colonial name of Hartley, or Gatoma, which was their colonial name for Kadoma. But to me, those places remained nothing more than fantastical imaginings, existing only in the stories my parents shared with me. Nonetheless, I cherished those stories and held onto them tightly, as they were a link to a past that I could only imagine, but never truly experience.

At that time, both of my older sisters were already attending St. Aidens School, while I spent most of my days at home with my mom and my aunt, Perisa. Auntie Perisa (Priscila) was my only childhood friend, my confidante, and my partner in crime. She would often take me to visit her friends who lived just two streets away from our humble abode. However, during these visits, I never touched any food or drink, as my mother had taught me to be cautious about accepting things from strangers. But one day, after much convincing from my beloved aunt, I finally gave in and ate something. I felt assured that my best friend and confidante would keep it a secret. However, upon leaving her friend's house, she made a complete fool of me by threatening to report me to my mom. I felt utterly scared and tricked, so I protested, vowing to tell Mommy the real story. From that moment on, my auntie bestowed upon me a special nickname - Mandikwatisa. She was the only one who called me that until she passed away.

While my auntie was my only trusted confidant, my trust towards her had limits. I would not allow her to bathe me, neither would I undress while she looked on. The only person who had the privilege of bathing me was none other than my mom. This only made sense, as she had been doing it since the day I was born. When we lived with Auntie, I knew she had kids, two boys, but I was too young to ask why her kids, Augustine and Truther were not with her. Above everything, we lived with no problems. Most of the time it was mainly Mom, Auntie, myself, my two elder sisters and my little sister who was still nursing. Daddy would return every month's end or holiday because he was an employee in civil construction.

Many relatives had not acquired houses in the city, my parents being among the few privileged that got from the government rent-to-buy houses. Our house did not only become a haven for our family, but relatives would come and go, some spending days, some weeks depending on what programs they had. Life seemed good and promising.

People looked progressive, many already expanding their houses and beautifying their homes. I don't think my parents felt any pressure because things looked promising especially to people that had jobs like my dad. Urban life looked promising and attractive, the environment in the city offered relaxation and tranquillity, the kind that is still felt in countries considered developed. The streets were nicely tarred and clean, and from end to end there was no sign of garbage. People never knew sewer drainage could get clogged and overflow. Words like overpopulated, potholes, and load shedding among others were never uttered even from the lips of the most educated or eloquent person.

Life in the city was nothing short of inviting, with its distinct charm setting it apart from any rural setting. The city nights were a spectacle to behold, with bright tower lights illuminating the streets from end to end.

For any forward-thinking student in a rural school, the desire to one day make it to the city and live a life of ease was almost palpable. The city promised endless opportunities and possibilities, and the overwhelming majority dreamed of being a part of it. As for me, until that stage in life, all I had known was city life, nonetheless, mom had always sung a beautiful chorus about another form of life in the rural area, an idea well sold to me that I longed to find my way to go and see the experience.

So, one day we packed our bags and headed to Guruve, and I never knew we were not coming back, and I never figured we were drifting into trouble.

Chapter 1

Unwanted change

It all started unexpectedly on a clear, sunny morning. I was just a young and well-fed boy, feeling content and blissful in our home, surrounded by a loving family. I never saw any lack in wants or needs, and I always supposed my glass as half full. However, one day, change paid us a sudden visit, and in the blink of an eye, our peaceful morning was turned into chaos.

Change had been stealthily lurking in the shadows until that day when it caught us completely off guard. Our father had arrived the previous evening, arriving when we were all asleep. So, upon waking up we anticipated a great day like the previous times, alas! The morning decided to set a different tone for our day, and in one day, our familiar surroundings transformed from a place of peace, joy, and happiness to one of uncertainty and fear.

I was now six, still trying to make sense of life, but the memories of that day have remained ever vivid in my mind. My dad was dear to me, I felt strong about him with a constant longing to see more of him because he stayed away because of work. Dad lived away from home most of the time because of the nature of his work, however, he made it definite to often come home at each month's end or at any given time.

In my judgment, which was perhaps the judgment of a small mind, all was flawless, and I felt satisfied, neither I nor my siblings sensed any danger out there, and never was I bothered to imagine an impending doom like a thick dark cloud hanging over our little family loaded and threatening to rain trouble, again no signs of any sort of trouble, not even the type that hides in the dark closet.

Forgive my ignorance which perhaps was a result of me being too minor to care or imagine the closed doors concealing any form of trouble, I had all the things I desired at my disposal. I mean, at that early age, worry never existed in my life curriculum, there was no room for it because my mother cared and made sure I was well clean and fed, while dad showered me with all kinds whenever he came home. My father possibly spoiled me somewhat during those early years.

From the faintest recollections of my childhood, while we lived in Seke unit M, I was still the only boy surrounded by girls. Daddy probably out of ignorance cultivated in me an inclination towards sweet things, and it got me into trouble so many times when Mom would return home to find me sitting with a pan full of sugar after a failed attempt to make sweets. Not forgetting also how Mom made sure to hide condensed milk, not only from me. Condensed milk was the biggest temptation for any kid to resist, but I was found at the forefront of it. All these and more were the things that meant the world to me.

Besides these little spoils, I had toys also, not so many of them, but only one at a time, as I could not have more than one or play with one for too long.

From these early days, one thing became clear, I began to exhibit a curious mentality, I could feel restless until I open that toy or break it apart to see what was inside it, and why it worked the way it did. This annoyed my parents, especially my father to the point where he stopped buying toys for me.

All things around our home according to my small mind made my life delightful. The only problem that interrupted my joy now and then was a terrible headache that used to hammer me to the point of bleeding profusely through the nose, it was a worry for Mom, and the same problem continued up until I was around 15-16 but eventually vanished.

We lived alright with less to no complaints and worries. Little did I know a day was coming in which settings would take a radical turn.

My guess then and now was, and still is; mom would have known things were descending to the steep, but I feel like she never foresaw the house she was building brick upon brick with much determination coming to a crash.

Because of the telling signs that were so obvious to her, she intelligently devised a way to prepare and trick us into the future, and I think she did a sterling job making sure what awaited us ahead would never stress us. Honestly, Mom had a clever way of preparing us for difficult times, this was not the first time she pre-programmed us into this kind of thing.

I remember how she used the same method when we were still in Seke Chitungwiza, Mom knew she was preparing to go and live in Guruve, so she sang praises about the goodness of life in Guruve and I for one could not wait to get there and live the experience.

Now we were living in Guruve rural where most of our relatives also lived. Our beloved home was nowhere near glamorous, only two simple small standalone structures, the bedroom in rectangular shape and a round hut kitchen, all built of backed farm brick with a thatched roof overhead. However, humble it was, yet it appealed to me as the best home ever. It's an impression that makes me agree that a home is more than just a building.

On that memorable day, my father asked me to run an errand in Kuraini, a nearby family compound where most of our relatives lived, he sent me to call his brother. Raini or Lane was a quick 15-minute walk. It was on my return when I sensed unmistakable signs of trouble, filling the whole atmosphere, instantly, a chill washed over me as I tried to make sense of the commotion.

The dark clouds that had been hovering over our seemingly perfect family finally let loose, unleashing a storm of epic proportions. The joy, peace, and happiness that we had treasured for so long were suddenly overwhelmed by invisible giants that seemed determined to just swallow everything in whole.

For as long as I could remember, my world had been filled with nothing but love, happiness, and peace. But on this day, I was introduced to a side of life that I had never known before - a world without the warmth and affection of my father. Before our very eyes, the love that had once held our family together was replaced by an epic silence, leaving us all to wonder if our lives would ever be the same again. What a way to be unleashed into a new life, a stark reminder to me how even the most perfect of families could be torn apart in an instant.

Just like that, my parents were separated, and we were all left aghast. I only came to understand the ultimate reason for my parent's separation when I went to Granny that same afternoon. Daddy had brought with him another woman, a fat one, sitting there, making sure my mom and the kids, five of us, immediately embark on a new journey like one we never anticipated. Surprisingly, my grandma seemed cool about it, that left Mom alienated.

Now that I am old, I understand that Mom soaked in so much from the days in Seke, and if I am right, her outburst on that day can be justified. I mean, she left city life for rural and decided to work with her own hands, and now Daddy was so daring to come and flaunt a new girlfriend before our mother.

So, to pave way for Daddy's new chapter, Mommy had no choice but to play the matriarchal role and lead us into a nomadic life journey, thus leaving Daddy to enjoy a new season of bliss in love. What a powerful woman Daddy's new love turned out to be, not giving care that six souls were now entering a journey into the unknown.

A journey that would ultimately strip us of dignity and cause us to appear less human but a team of strong workers. But as less human and vulnerable as we appeared before many, yet we saw ourselves at par with those that felt superior. A walk through shame. Nonetheless, a walk, a slow one though, and there was not another walk to talk, hence we braved the journey and began to inch through the journey of shame, daring to ride the many obstacles awaiting us in the way.

From that point onwards, it dawned on me that avoiding this shame walk was not an option, trying to avoid shame land would have been equal to denying self of destiny. Until and unless I walk it, the land of promise would remain with its green meadows and rivers of pleasure on the distant horizon.

That day, with its unforgettable events, marked the beginning of our never-ending troubles that seemed insurmountable, but we neither cared nor worry about the dangers and obstacles that lay ahead. Sometimes, I reminisce and glance back, while other times my thoughts focus ahead. One thing I've learned is that life constantly asks questions, and it never falls short of them. Even when I give my all, life doesn't relent. Therefore, I've stopped trying to provide answers.

Life is full of mysterious twists and turns, and you can't find the answers to life's relentless questions. Instead, when life bombarded us with questions. We in turn end up with countless unanswered questions that require simple yet profound answers.

Is life simply a vapour, a mist that dissipates into nothingness? Or a mystery at work from date of birth to date of death? Perhaps it's a persistent sickness whose only cure is death? Perhaps, life is an angry bull called Dilemma, with two deadly horns and we are trapped and tossed in between the horns with no escape in sight. Whichever way I chose, and whichever theory I chose to believe.

The quest for the simple answers or the desire to see the piecing together of the puzzle that makes life worth living, whichever way I choose, every single, simple meaningful thing that makes life beautiful remains elusive. And it seems like the more I walk further, the more I realize there's no need to keep searching behind closed doors when trouble is always staring me in the eye with a menacing grin, trouble big enough to take us through the year and beyond.

So, let me leave the more subliminal anxieties that lurk within me. I mean, why bother searching the inner room, when dilemma knows how to sniff me and locate me?

The events of that unforgettable day were so brief but bitter. Soon we were getting ready to leave. To me in particular, when we left Guruve for Sachuru, it felt like we were going to be better off, after all, mom's brothers according to the many good stories were so rich, they had many heads of cows from which they milked not less than 20L a day. That to me sounded like a lot of milk, having been used to the 500ml of sterilised milk, I could only picture what it can be like to have 20L milk every day. That sounded promising for a start. I couldn't wait to leave; I had my picture of the adventure ahead.

Our leaving was so sudden. These dramas took place a few days before school commenced. I saw my classmates and never informed them I was leaving in a day; they were older than me, and in fighting, I wouldn't stand a chance. I had always played second best to all of them, but not on this day when I knew they would not be seeing me in a very long time, if not at all. I stood there while arrogantly speaking to the two guys.

Next, I picked up a large rock and charged at them, they looked in between terrified and perplexed, of course they had all the reasons to get astounded, this was the first time they had ever seen me exhibiting such levels of arrogance. They knew me as that timid boy who at any point was willing to lose an argument for the sake of peace, now it was my time to unleash the rudeness within me as a means of revenge to my bullish friends. That day they found no answer to my insolence but only ran away, nonetheless shouting from a distance, giving a promise to deal with me on the first day of school.

I don't know what my fate would have been. Imagine if for some reason, probably a reconciliation between my parents, or a change for any reason, imagine if we had stayed. So, after this, I prayed for leaving without failure. But I surely did not know what I was praying for. Thank goodness there was no turning back, all was set, everything packed and only waiting for the next morning to say bye to Guruve.

Then the excitement, the exuberance of a 6-year-old who had just registered a journey in his mind kicked in. The mere thought of embarking on a journey through town would leave me positively giddy with excitement. I can still recall the Goosebumps that would run down my arms, and the flutter of butterflies in my stomach as I anticipated the adventure ahead. Sometimes, my anticipation would even manifest in vivid overnight hallucinations, where the sound of an approaching bus would ring in my ears with such clarity that I would awaken from my slumber to listen more closely. Despite the fact that the night was still young and there was no actual bus in sight, I was often plagued by these auditory hallucinations that seemed all too real.

I certainly cannot be the only one who can relate to this experience, a lot of my fellas who had the privilege of living in an area where the bus is the prominent vehicle that passes by can share this experience. It was not necessarily that longing to be in the bus and watch the trees rushing backwards that brought about that appetite for travelling. But it was mainly this thing, a major one that kept us on our toes, pushing our anxiety levels to the limits, nothing other than the longing for a cold Coke accompanied by that candy coated in pink cream, the candy was commonplace on many bus terminus around Zimbabwe.

That candy cake remains legendary for causing the young and the old to salivate just by looking at it. Even bees could not help but gather around that candy for its cream to the point of making people uncomfortable because of their numbers. I don't know of any person who did not love the combination of Coke and candy. It was indeed difficult for anyone to overcome the ever-inviting candy. So, who were we not to love pink creamed candy?

In our hearts, we considered it a crime against humanity for any parent to fail to buy their kids pink creamed Candy. It felt like a sad day seeing the candy man waving it over and over while you salivate. Even the coke was so strong and felt like it could resuscitate the fainted, but surprisingly it invited you back for more, it had the sharp sensational taste that felt like a thousand needles hitting against your tongue and mouth causing your tears to fill your eyes on the first sip. It also had that long-lasting tingling after-effect that calls for your return.

Ah, those were the days of the family-size bottle, how surprising that a family could share a 1.5L and be satisfied. Nowadays you probably need a barrel to keep everyone happy. Those things caused us less sleep and made the clock tick so slowly all night, we were children and doing things only children do.

Finally, after a long night, dawn was upon us, while it was still dark, Mom had the previous day arranged and hired an Ox-drawn cart to ferry the portable things of her belongings and all our clothing, arriving early at Mudhindo to catch the first-morning bus. Everything happened so quick, soon we were on the bus, looking through the windows hoping to see someone we knew, but there was no familiar face to wave goodbye to.

Then, the bus began to move slowly, gradually picking speed, past Nyanhunzi which is only a kilometre from Mudhindo, I kept watching through the window, the maize fields, the round thatched red-brick huts, even the houses closer to the road in Nyanhunzi Hwadaya where our cousins, Abedi and Collins lived, I saw all these objects and structures rushing back towards

Mudhindo, I was later told the trees were not running, it's called an optical illusion.

Soon there were no more fields, neither were there any houses to see, but only green little trees and tall grass rushing back, this time all rushing much faster as our bus picked more speed. Before we knew it, we were descending towards a low area approaching Mukuvadze bridge in the Mavare river, then past the bridge, I could hear the change of sound and a slight pushback against my seat as the driver threw the bus into a lower gear to go past a steady incline, climbing Mukuvadze incline into a narrow-tarred road, setting the bus towards Rafingora through the many commercial farms whose impressive tobacco, Maize and wheat fields also rushed backwards towards Mudhindo as the bus reached travelling speed, tearing away from the second home we ever knew.

While the bus was carrying us from one trouble to the unknown, one could not fail to take notice of the conductor of the bus wearing a strong brown leather bag shoulder crossed by its strong leather belt to have it rested on his right hip while he executed his duty of collecting money and recording in a duplicated ticket book. The man looked conscious of the movements and shaking that required him to keep steadying himself to remain standing.

He comfortably staggered nonstop time and again to keep to terms with the movements as he continually collects money while writing in the ticket book making sure every passenger got served. We were truly on our way; it was goodbye to Guruve as we went off to live at our Mom's ancestral home.

The following morning we awoke to a new life, a new environment, in a semi-primitive location, surrounded by all new faces, many of the elderly knew us by names and they all seemed excited at our appearance on the scene, probably because they assumed we were only visiting. Once we began to settle, we looked forward to all the goodness Mom used to sing. But, despite the glamorization and romanticizing of the adventure that lay ahead, the experiences that awaited us were far from fairy tales, life was waiting with open jaws and a bucket full of misery.

How foolish I expected to swim through the sea of life expecting an easy and quick swim to the shore. Experience is truly the best teacher, the Sea gets rougher and angry, and there is a pushback against every forward effort, swells become high and boisterous, threatening to send you crushing to the bottom of the sea. To make it to the shore, you have to keep making strokes, one after the other, a stroke of hope followed by a kick of faith and belief. In many cases in life, perception is the guy that carries you to leave you mid-ocean and you have to find your way to the shore

Chapter 2

Our survival

The upbringing of my siblings and I was branded by such hardships. For some reason or no reason, almost all the things that we touched turned out sour, and for that reason, our meals were almost exclusively sour things. Sour things for a meal could be an underestimation, there were many days, evenings, and mornings when our hunt failed us and we would wish to have sour things, those days I vividly recall were many, all these things and many, we learned to normalize. Normalizing such was good for us so that we could accept our situation, live within our means, and not bother anyone. It's not like we did not wish for the finer things of life or daydream about them, we, like all sane persons, had it in our hearts and our wishes to someday sit down and enjoy the goodness that life affords, but while we normalized it, we tried to tread between the balance in order for us to not be content and settle in mediocrity.

Each new day we woke up with hope and enthusiasm to keep trying, but, for one reason or the other, things did not go according to our wishes despite the hard work and effort of our mom. So, we did what was good for us, we minded our business, and we minded it so well. Despite all the problems that kept hammering us, there were surprising, yet laudable, decent attributes that can be credited to the whole family, but mostly to Mom for the way she brought us up.

We never had gloomy moments in our family. Secondly, we were not known in society for the wrong reasons, never in a single day was there an ill report, and never was one of us caught stealing or gate-crashing dinner meals. Mom had a way and a secret – she modelled us without sitting down to lecture us. Without sitting us down in the lecture room she taught us to see value in ourselves and return dignity even when we sat crammed up and entangled in poverty and meaninglessness. I really wouldn't mind tapping into her gift, hopefully, I have such attributes. I don't know.

Without any formal education, Mom was able to model us into knowing the way to live in dignity, how to behave when we visit, and most importantly we were taught how to maintain correct body language when we had visitors at home. It was a punishable offense to linger around and become a distraction while visitors were eating or talking. We were discouraged to look visitors in the face especially while they ate. Hence, we preferred to play outside until they get done eating, she also taught us how we should not look strangers in the eye when travelling on the bus, especially while someone was eating. For this reason, it became natural for me to shy away from making eye contact, and you know this habit became a struggle to overcome, the time I began to meet with people from the white and business community.

While I consider avoiding eye contact as a sign of respect, it is in other sectors considered rude and a sign of disrespect. There were times we would encounter strangers with a tendency of tempting kids with food, and as such, the policy was always not to stretch my hand and accept, but to turn my gaze and look Mom in the face and it would be up to her to throw back at me the look of approval. While in other instances I would just look away as a sign that I was not interested in their food. Also important was mom could only approve if she got satisfied, we were not admiring someone's food. But temptation or not, food was never a bait to me because I had learned since childhood that we only eat at home. Then there was one crucial golden rule that all of us knew – that was to read mom's body language, to be able to understand that look and the message behind the look.

For instance, there were moments Mommy felt if we lingered around, we might end up getting tempted to look visitors in the eye, so without speaking, she would give a look that says go and play outside, and silently we would go. Then there were other moments when she disliked your behaviour before visitors, Mommy would give you a communicating stare that says: "I will deal with you once visitors are gone." So, at times you knew your fate before it came. Nonetheless we also knew when she threw out a sympathetic look, and we also had our ways of driving her into a good mood.

Many of these values we held dear to were never acquired through classroom teachings, but rather through the transfer of wisdom from those who came before us. These values played central in shaping us into a family, and at large a society of well-behaved kids.

For instance, we grew up eating together in one big dish like plate, transforming our mealtime into a contest of the fittest. Despite the competition for sustenance, we were instilled with the knowledge and understanding not to cross set rules and boundaries. When we partook the traditional meal of Sadza and meat, it was customary that girls ate together and the same for boys. Here we observed old age customs and traditions that governed our conduct. One such custom dictated that when it came to picking of meat, we followed the guidance to do it in the order of birthright. The eldest among us had the privilege to pick first and the rest followed in chronological order. But it didn't stop there, on wrapping up the meal another rule played to the advantage of the younger ones. The eldest was expected to surrender his portion first, and in that order one by one all would surrender until the youngest is left. This was done to ensure that the young ones were not left hungry as they found it hard to keep up with the older ones. That way we looked after each other and made sure none among us was left starving despite the competition. What a way to teach selflessness.

All these values we lived by while we were among the most disadvantaged in our community.

I remember how we would cook Sadza while there was no relish and sometimes found ourselves only boiling Salt, or simply dissolving it in warm water and taking that as an alternative to stew or soup. Many times when we found ourselves doing this, we'd tease each other by encouraging one another to imagine we were eating a delicious chicken. We ate such without complaining or murmuring and we had a way to keep our spirits high as if we had all we desired in this life. This we usually did after exhausting all self-sustaining methods taught to us, I mean we knew all sorts of trees that could give us food and all sorts of insects that could be turned into food, some that lived in trees, some like grasshoppers in grass and plants while others could be dug. Other extreme instances were the days we found ourselves going for certain tree leaves that could be cooked and turned into okra. On such days we found ourselves each with their cup drinking that slippery semi-liquid juice. That would be that and we would go to sleep, though sometimes waking up several times in the night due to the emptiness of the stomach.

That is always the case with every hardship. We quickly learned how to navigate our way through the storm. Our circumstances called us to engage that extra gear for the rough terrain, talk of all ways on how to trap a mouse, survival tactics, catch a bird, and freshwater fishing. I became cunning in many of those, knowing that many times it was that catch that would be the difference between eating and no meal.

There were many things we would do to either catch something breathing or other things, you may speak of mushrooms during the rainy season, hunting birds using various methods, to the dry season when we used methods to catch birds when they drink at the water hole.

The dry season also allowed us to have a day of feasting on fish. We would continually watch those water holes as they diminish in volume daily until a certain point. It was at that stage when the water is not deep to the knee height. Then in our numbers, we would begin to do all sorts to steer the water to unsettle any fish. The vulnerable creatures would then come to the surface, and we would catch every fish we could afford to. Sometimes it was fish enough to last us days.

One other thing, a catch did another trick also for me besides making sure we ate at dinner, it brought a bit of respect from my rivals who happened to be my two elder sisters. Knowing they were looking forward to something from me, all the friction and constant conflict would go away, and they knew how to find a way to call my name distinctly, making us all to forget yesterday's fights. But fights or no fights, catching or not, we stayed restrained from other people's business. Talking of self-restraining; there was always an inviting temptation to eat next door, and there had always been someone making deliberate moves to show off the better side of things, the "we are better than you" kind of thing. I see that human behaviour has not changed a lot, only times vary, it was hard then as kids to detain ourselves from the temptation of eating next door.

Showing off as we now see it in the era of Instagram is not a new thing, only the methods of showing off have changed as well as the things people brag about. Kids and adults alike would make it a point to know the message reaches a neighbour when they eat chicken or puts on a new summer shirt or that viscous dress after a cotton sale, yeah, it was indeed a big deal those days just as it is now with certain things.

Having tea and buttered bread was considered a privilege equal to the modern-day showing off of happy pictures in an expensive restaurant, a great-looking car or whatever thing one perceives of great value making it worthy to brag about, especially those that were able to have tea and butter daily.

Imagine those were the things to die for, and your family consistently failed to afford these things for many days unto months, when you only had salt and maize meal and matches to light the fire.

At times we found ourselves embarrassingly asking for fire next door or making sure the fire never dies, just like the ever-burning fire of the altar of sacrifice in the Old Testament sanctuary. Fire was very important because of the role it played, a role which stood central in our lives especially winter nights when we had little see-through blankets insufficient to keep us warm through the memorable calm freezing winter nights. We were still small, so, together with our sisters, we slept in that round hut which was commonly our kitchen.

The fire was kept alive all night, I mean, who can forget how the Mopani tree makes the hottest, the best fire you can think of.

I remember the days we used to boil veggies in salt, as they came from the garden, rape, Covo, and tsunga during the dry season while in rain season people would drop all gardening activities and focus on the field.

So, from the field it was given, the mind knew the time of Muboora is upon us, the season of Okra, both from the field and the wild. While it may sound like sticking with healthy eating, you know, too much of anything becomes monotonous they say, and it truly is. I remember how we grew to detest muboora and Derere re Nyenje, just the sight of their dark green colour would make you want to run away. When these have become your norm, except for the few times when we would kill a Chicken, we used to call it the game changer, even the sisters knew automatically on a chicken day they had to change the Sadza pot from a smaller to a bigger one.

Such were the experiences around us, when you haven't tasted cooking oil for three months or more. It was difficult as a child to resist the enticement of a delicious meal next door. When that aroma so inviting cuts through the blowing thin air towards our home. A well-fried chicken or brown-looking fat cooks sending into the air that invite and the taste buds at that point couldn't help but crave and yearn and made you feel like you couldn't wait to sink your teeth into such. That was a lot of temptation for any hungry kid to resist, the same pressure could equal how you feel as a grown person when your friends and Church mates are constantly posting on Facebook fulfilments, happy pictures, new nicely trimmed suits or their second house in a nice quiet suburb painting a picture that everything is going so well, while you still wondering and wrestling with basic monthly bills.

In those old days, there were certain things replicated throughout the community, poor or otherwise. Ah, those were the good old days! I can almost smell the scent of Chimugondiya soap which was a staple in every household in our community. It was the ultimate multi-purpose soap that served as a laundry detergent, dishwashing soap, and even a bathing soap. And who could forget the times when Geisha soap was a luxury item that doubled as a lotion when Vaseline was not available.

But let's be honest, using soap as a lotion was not without its challenges. On hot and humid days, or when it rained, the soap would get reactivated by sweat or water, leaving you feeling sticky and uncomfortable. Looking back now, it's hard to imagine using soap as a substitute for lotion, but back then, it was a common practice. Thankfully, I never had to resort to using margarine or grease as a lotion. Just the thought of it makes me cringe! Instead, I opted for cooking oil.

Despite the challenges, those were the simpler times. And despite the prevailing competition, there was a sense of community and togetherness that we still strive to hold on until today.

One day we saw our classmate after applying Margarine how flies mistook him for a meal and lingered around him for the scent of Margarine probably. It's true we had nothing but we somehow managed to draw our lines and bothered neither neighbours nor relatives. Even though some neighbours and relatives were hospitable and minded not a dinner crash, we simply stayed home, minded our business, and we minded it so well.

Above all, we stayed humble, or should I say life humbled us and we simply obliged, preferring to indulge in sour things or tasty hard-shelled insects in their diverse kinds or such as the meal we could afford at that particular time. Experimenting even with termites, specifically the solder termite, termites left a lasting impression within my memory, I mean, how could I forget their razor-sharp hooks and their smell which made us list them on the bottom of our food chain?

We kept ourselves restrained that way, however, we were not entirely alienated, for there were people now and then who stretched an olive branch towards us. Whoever pitied us, we appreciated much, for there were also those days when certain neighbours or relatives would give us filtered water from the milk after they separated and sifted thick milk from the watery part to their desired thickness. So instead of throwing away or feeding such entirely to dogs, they remembered us.

Chapter 3

The way we lived

Summer evenings were a favourite of us all, for the love of gathering around the crackling fire outside, basking in its warmth while we talked all sorts and laughed our lungs out. Besides talking all sorts and fairy tales, we loved to stargaze while competing on who sees the highest number of moving stars, we called them Rockets.

I mean, when I reminisce upon this, I think of the beauty of a cloudless, dark grey, primitive night sky with its starry array across the heaven, staring back at us, some stars shining brightest while many seemed distant and faint, with others looking too crowded and tiny, resembling the colour of milk. We later learnt of the Milky Way galaxy and the complexity of the universe we call home. These things we taught ourselves and became a delightful part of our evenings. Every time we saw the sun disappearing into the colourful horizon, our minds also slowly switched from the day mode which in itself did not fall short of numerous, vigorous activities.

As the clear-skied dark summer night approached, the outside fireplace became the typical gathering spot. We gathered there not only for the warmth and crackle of the fire but also for our love and appreciation of the magnificent arrays of the Milky Way, especially its countless faintest stars. Often, we found ourselves simply lying face up, gazing at the awe-inspiring night sky, inhaling, and exhaling the pure countryside air, untainted by foul miasma or the scent and contamination of industrial fumes. What a magical night experience it was to gaze up at the stars, pondering their mysteries and marvelling at their beauty. It was a remedy for the soul, a balm that soothed our minds and emotions.

The feeling was indescribable as if we were melting in the presence of something greater than ourselves.

However, there were a few things that could bring uneasiness among us, and send us to early bed, especially when our mother was not around and the nights were dark – the piercing hoot sound of an owl or the howling of a jackal from a distant, a sound that would send shivers down our spines and even send the village dogs into a frenzy. These sounds were associated with bad things, and our elders warned us to be careful when we heard them. Despite the fear their sounds brought, there was also a sense of awe to the superstitious proclamations by these creatures. We knew that they were a part of the natural world, but their cries were never a delight but a cause for worry and panic to our little hearts. And so, at other times we would huddle together, listening to their sounds in the night while taking comfort in each other's presence.

Last but not least was a rare sting by a scorpion. Any of these would stymie our delight and see us going to sleep immediately. Some nights were filled with singing and tambourine lessons, mom taught us the melodies she sang as a youth in the Salvation Army. The endless traditional fairy tales as well were a crucial   part of our evening gatherings and mom had a mesmeric way of storytelling that kept us on the edge. We surely never ran short of activity.

A clear full moon brought a temptation hard to let pass, making us forget the fireplace, many times we engaged in countless hide and seek even late into the night. On a night like this, our voices would penetrate the clear night air through the neighbouring homes. I tell you, that was a temptation more enticing than the aroma of fried brown fat cook, hard to resist for kids living nearby, causing them to show up unannounced and dive straight into the night fun, making it even more exciting, and many times the noise deafening. What an energetic bunch we were. I do have a permanent mark from an injury during the hide- and-seek games.

There were also nights, away from the fire and from the home, on Mom's permission we could go to Jiti gatherings. These were traditional gatherings hosted by a family in preparation for a day when they do certain rituals on the grave of someone who would have died the previous year. Now the Jiti gatherings would start two weeks ahead of the day and it was mainly singing and dancing to the tune of song and drums, mainly boys and girls mixing up in dance inside a ring formed by the singing bunch. But these outings were very restricted, hence we spent most of our evenings at home by the fire.

Another exciting activity besides talking, clapping, singing, and teasing each other was the days when we could roast green mealies. This led to more fun and teasing when it became a competition on who roasted the best vs the worst. These nights would become even more favourable towards harvesting season especially after a good rainy season, despite the area being more of a subsistence community, during this time of the year food was never in extreme scarcity.

There were many things we could do around the fire. We were never short of entertainment; or activity, gloomy days were a rare thing in our syllabus, we were the fun, and we were the entertainment. If anything, the fireplace truly has a special place in my heart and probably in my siblings, if not many Africans who grew up in the same environment. It, the fireplace, is symbolic. it's symbolic as an instrument of unity, it's where our lives, and our values, were shaped and moulded.

Growing up I noticed in other homes where they had a father figure, grandpas, and even uncles, they would have two fireplaces. The one inside the round-bigger hut or kitchen would be mainly for women and girls while the one outside or under a thatched gazebo was for men and boys. But ours was a different setup, I was the eldest male in the family, and we had but one fireplace where we all gathered.

I don't know what would have become of our lives if one was to take the fireplace away. If I were to choose between the fireplace and the entertainment dominant on TV, I would without a doubt go back to gather around this all-powerful spot. No matter where life takes me, I feel like my way of thinking, my behaviour, and eating remains fixed in those humble dearest places of my childhood.

When I reminisce back to the time of my childhood, tough as it were, with meals characterized by sour things and dark greens boiled in salt, to no food at other times, there's a part of me that feels I could go back, or rather there's a part of me which lives there. Sour things to some extent remain part of the things I prefer, and I see in this age people clamouring to attend lectures on how to eat healthily.

One day I sat there and listened, what I heard were praises to the teaching, the knowledge so considered lifesaving. In these seminars, they teach people to prefer the things that we grew up eating. They call these foods healthy organic food, so, in this regard, I thank my tough upbringing, and it feels like it wasn't all bad, there are good things to be cherished. It's not a bad thing at all to find myself reliving certain experiences and getting to appreciate the positives that came with our suffering.

In life, there are things priceless, food among many, that we get to despise because of various typecasts according to how our thinking have been programmed. Take a look at how we associate many rural African lifestyles, and cultures with poverty. Some foods we now despise are relegated down the food chart simply because the taste could be too distant from the Western delicacies, true that could be, our test buds have been programmed to interpret anything sweet as delicious. Not only that but in other instances humans chose to agree and sing praise to other foods and drinks simply because taste buds can also at times be trained to accept bitter as delicious. So, when we eat in most cases, there are two things we aim to gratify; at times we indulge to gratify taste even when that thing is of no benefit. The other one is when people indulge in bitter drinks seeking intoxication, I have never heard anyone who drinks such things complain of taste.

Despite the suffering, our desire for a better life never waned, and we refused to settle for poverty. We knew that there was green grass on the other side. Despite our circumstances, we never regretted being ourselves. We chose to remain a group of happy kids who were learning to navigate the challenges of life. Although things were tough, we refused to let hardship break our spirits or bring any dreariness or gloom into our lives. We didn't worry about what tomorrow held.

Working your way out of a background like ours was no small feat. However, when surrounded or dominated by certain circumstances, moving forward might be your only choice.

One other thing of extreme positivity in growing under such an environment is, if you are a person of an optimistic mentality, life here teaches you not to be terrified by anything. From the smallest issues of life to even attempting mountains.

Coming from this setting still plays positive today, when I begin to lose my grip on courage, I require no motivational talk, neither do I go seek for heart-warming pep talk, my motivation is my upbringing, each time I feel like I'm losing steam, I simply look back and retreat to a cocoon of my upbringing. In other instances, I simply revisit some of those most courageous moments that propelled me to certain levels. From such, I awaken the positive energy that would have been going to sleep, and I simply find renewed energy to carry on. Judging from where I come from, I look back and recount my steps, and, my whole being agrees it's been a long shot, even though some may seem to have accomplished better than I have done, I simply remind myself that our journeys started from different starting points, and we race to finish and not to outdo each other.

Though at times I look and see how some from my present circles seem to have an advantage over me in quantifiable belongings, I also take valuable time to search within me and ask the definition of true riches. I am of the impression that true riches is having such things that are hard to find, and these are called treasures. This understanding has helped me to strive not to be better than anyone but to try and make each coming day better than yesterday. Yes, courageous I get to be and have come across many things, yet I know very little about life and continually seek to learn new things each passing day.

In my relentless pursuit to improve each passing day, I have encountered missteps, mistakes, and moments of embarrassment.

I have stumbled, fallen, endured ridicule, and battled with feelings of discouragement. Despite these challenges, I have always found the resolve to rise from adversity and push forward. Crucially, even in the face of life's unrelenting brutality towards myself and my siblings, we have always chosen to adopt a positive outlook. We have consistently viewed our cup as half-full, and this mindset has instilled within me a set of values that are truly priceless.

As I survey the world around me, I am struck by the pervasive sense of lack that seems to afflict so many individuals. It is abundantly clear that certain values, such as integrity, compassion, and love, cannot be bought with even the greatest wealth.

Reflecting on my past, I am filled with remorse for the days when I was consumed by envy and resentment towards those who seemed to have more than I did. But as I have come to understand the true nature of these intangible values, I have learned to cherish the richness within me. Regardless of my circumstances, I have steadfastly refused to allow my spirit to be broken. I continue to strive for material success, but I do so with the knowledge that it is my inner fortitude that truly matters.

I am determined to maintain this mentality, even in the face of the relentless negativity that pervades so much of the world. I will not be swayed by the voice of pessimism that emanates from the pulpit of despair, preaching doom and despair, instead, I will continue to hold fast to the values that truly matter.

Chapter 4

Understanding mom

Growing up, my family had an unspoken rule that we all tacitly understood. Despite the singing, talking, teasing, and occasional squabbles between my two older sisters and I, there was one thing that remained abundantly clear: our mother was not a character to be trifled with when it came to teasing. As a family, we all knew that even the slightest joke could quickly turn the mood sour and send us all to bed early.

One particular evening, my sisters – who were often the instigators of such teasing, tried to make light of our mother's pronunciation of a word. She had mentioned someone who had successfully passed their O-level exams, but my sisters found humour in the way she pronounced "levelling" as "levelling with a ruler." Amused by their own wit, my sisters erupted in laughter in front of my mother. But her stern expression quickly extinguished their mirth. She refused to allow the teasing to continue and immediately extinguished their laughter as instant as it had started. It was a clear reminder that, in our home, certain things were off-limits, and that our mother was not one to be trifled with.

As the laughter from my sister's failed attempt at teasing our mother subsided, I couldn't help but slip away to a place where I finally exploded as I released the chuckles I had been suppressing. Despite the carefreeness that often filled our home, we all understood that certain topics were off-limits. Teasing our mother or making her feel uneducated was simply not acceptable. We knew that doing so would only serve to sour the mood and invite her wrath. Above all, we recognized that our mother's painful memories of her separation from my father had the power to wound her deeply. It was something that weighed heavily on her spirit, and we did everything in our power to avoid reminding her of it. In our home, we recognized the importance of respecting each other's boundaries and sensitivities.

Whenever my Mom reminisced even on the good recollections, she would talk until she gets to the unpleasantly ugly side of the story. Beginning with the good memories down the line, sometimes relating the good side of our dad, then she would narrate how my father's relatives played influential in the demise of her marriage. Ultimately, she would arrive at that day when everything fell apart, a day that we also witnessed.

That was my mom, and we could do nothing to change it. But I guess it was a good thing that she could talk to us, you know it is highly damaging to keep things within, so I believe by talking it out she released a lot of harmful emotions. A few times she would even sob. Those moments would usually evoke feelings of empathy within me, especially when I remember that day when only one person stood with Mom while the rest supported Dad.

Despite all these, a happy family we remained, and life went on, and the least we could all do was to give her some headache, so we became a bunch of happy and well-behaved kids and that made it easy to keep a jovial mood around the home. We carried on that way year after year, continually sticking together as strong workers and a happy bunch. God remained present and sustained us through all situations.

We kept this blazing hope that it was possible to make it one day, for that reason we never considered ourselves inferior.

One fact remained true, that is, despite our courage to face hardships, life continued to be ruthless, without mercy or pity, but we only had one choice, and the choice was to face whatever life would throw in our way. We stayed ready to catch the kitchen sink if life was to throw it at us.

Chapter 5

Settling into new hardships

Sachuru, a place located in the Sanyati area of Mashonaland West, is a humble and lesser-known part of Zimbabwe. It is situated near the town of Kadoma and is considered to be a less privileged area, though no longer backwards now than it was in the past. Despite its lack of popularity, Sachuru is an equally important part of Zimbabwe, with its unique character and charm. It may be characterised as primitive to a certain extent, but this only adds to its authenticity and appeal. For me, Sachuru holds a special place in my heart as it is where my mother grew up.

When we first arrived, I was filled with excitement and anticipation, eager to explore this new and unfamiliar place. As I began to explore Sachuru, I was struck by its beauty and simplicity. The landscape was breath-taking, with rolling hills covered in dense bushes as far as the eye could see. The people were friendly and welcoming, and the traditions and customs were unlike anything I had ever experienced before. Overall, Sachuru is a special place that holds a unique place in the hearts of those who know it. While it may not be widely recognized or celebrated, it is an important part of Zimbabwe's rich cultural heritage.

My mother's family is a fascinating tapestry of history and culture, woven together through generations of marriages, extended family, and the legacy of their ancestors. My grandfather, a man of many wives, had a large and sprawling family that included relatives from his father's siblings, all of whom formed part of a complex and intricate family tree. At the root of this tree was the man himself, Sachuru, their great-great-grandfather, a legendary figure whose name still echoes through the generations. As the family grew and expanded, they faced a choice to opt to adopt Zvauya and Hwatetepa as a surname, the two names are from the two descendants of Sachuru. Some chose Zvauya, while others opted for Hwatetepa. The reasons behind these choices are lost to time, but the result was a family split between two names, each with its unique character but anchored and bound together by culture, values, and traditions.

Despite this division, my mother's family remained united and proud of their heritage. They were the chiefs of the Sachuru area, a place named after their great-grandfather and a testament to their deep roots in the land. It is said that they were the first to arrive in the area, and their impact on the region is still felt to this day. From their colourful history to their vibrant present, my mother's family is a true testament to the power of family and the enduring legacy of our ancestors.

The air was thick with excitement and anticipation as we arrived. My uncles greeted us with open arms, their smiles wide and their laughter infectious. We had come unannounced, but it seemed as though they had been expecting us all along. As the sun rose on our first morning there, however, the mood shifted. My mother's face was drawn and serious as she delivered the news of the tragic end to her marriage. The energy levels dropped like a rock, and even my uncles' enthusiasm couldn't mask the solemnity of the moment.

As a child, I didn't fully understand the weight of what had happened, but I knew that something was different. I had always assumed that people would love us unconditionally, but now I realized that life was more complex than that. Despite the sadness that hung in the air, I couldn't help but be struck by the beauty of my mother's home country. This was my second time visiting, but the first time I was too young to remember anything. Now, with a curious mind and a thirst for knowledge, I took note of everything around me. One thing that stood out was the dense forest that surrounded us, a stark contrast to the barren landscapes of Guruve,

Dambaza, Chikwirandaombera, and Mudhindo. In those places, people used cow dung for firewood, but here resources were abundant. It was a small difference, but it made me realize just how much variation there could be from one place to another. I have to admit, that was my first time to see such dense bushes, trees so many that it was hard to see houses at the next homestead only fifty meters away. Because of the denseness of the bushes around, I also took notice that the nights here were thicker and dark than what we were accustomed to.

So, the darker and more imposing the Sachuru night, and as the case is always, the more the sky reveals more stars than you had seen before.

Another thing that stood self- imposing in these dark nights was the various sounds of night birds and certain small animals doing what was naturally their way of living. The sky was so high yet it drew my attention with its inviting spectacle above us as it imposed its presence making me feel like we remain alive at its mercy. This was the place we learned to star gaze, wondering. What if the sky comes tumbling down? Was it solid? Would it crash us? Were those stars and moon attached to the sky? Oh suspended! How so? Such were the questions we tossed around.

This was also the first time we found ourselves gathering around a fire outside. I mean, why not? When you have the inviting temptation of dry dead wood in abundance scattered all around the bushes closer home.

What a contrast to Guruve, people there cannot afford to have a fire whereby they simply sit around without cooking. Firewood is hard to find in the Guruve Dambaza area, so nobody wants to sit around a cow dung fire. I remember many times while we were kids in Guruve, we often made the mistake of boiling water or cooking porridge using cow dung fire, what a terrible mistake, as we get to school, the whole class could tell from the smell as soon as you enter the classroom. The smoke gives your clothes a very strong smell that lingers for days to come.

The second thing that could catch one's attention without failure in Sachuru was the way people spoke. I was at that point ignorant of the existence of various Shona dialects, let alone language in its variety. Kore-Kore is the dialect common in that area, while Guruve and other parts around the central province of Mashonaland consider themselves the true and original Shona speakers, or Zezuru as they are known, because they feel like the real deal, they belittle and make a mockery of the likes of Kore-

Kore and Shangwe and in turn, the mocked tribes seem to harbour within them elements of inferiority complex.

Mom spoke differently, probably her Kore-kore got diluted because of the many years she spent among the Zezuru speaking, but once settled there she began to slowly slip back into speaking like her relatives especially when she was among them. Some also spoke a different kind which I later understood is prevalent in Masvingo. My other uncles of school-going age told me these were the Vitori people, and I found their way of speaking more outstanding than the Kore-kore. These two struck me in a way that put me a little off, so I had to teach myself to remain in the same lane as it is spoken in Guruve, maybe that superior mentality had also taken a grip on me while that young.

As we made our way to school on our first day in Sachuru, I was struck by the third and most remarkable difference between Nyaunde School and our previous schools. It was beyond any picture of a school I had in mind, as I looked upon the school structures that loomed ahead of us. Having come from Mucherengi Primary, and with my sisters having attended St Aidens Primary in Seke Chitungwiza, I was accustomed to decently built schools that could accommodate a large number of students. But what I saw at Nyaunde Primary in Sachuru dampened my enthusiasm. The classrooms were built using a mixture of clay and ant hill, with Mopani wood providing the framework. Each classroom was small, with only a single class per grade and up to thirty kids in attendance. The benches were fixed, made out of either wood or stone and motor, and they complimented the rustic charm of the surroundings.

As I took my seat in the classroom, I realised how much I still needed to know about the area. This was a place that had been shaped by the land and the people who called it home, making use of what was at their disposal at the time. Sitting on the benches always resulted in clothes being covered in dust, but the girls had a solution to this problem. During Friday afternoon's general work, they would smear fresh cow dung mixed with water on the floors. Once it had dried, they would apply chlorophyll made from crushed green leaves of a particular plant. Despite the pungent odour of cow dung and chlorophyll, these memories of Fridays remain vivid in my mind. It felt like a homecoming of sorts, as we settled into our surroundings. Though I longed for Mucherengi School and St. Aidens, it is Nyaunde that holds a special place in my heart. Not because it was glamorous, but because the time spent there and the experience entrenched in me lessons of value. It is truly a place with so much to tell and remember.

When looking at schools like Nyaunde, it is truly awe-inspiring to imagine the level of tenacity required for students to envision themselves as engineers, accountants, inventors, footballers, cricketers, and more. These remote schools present a unique challenge, as it often takes a tremendous amount of effort to rise above the circumstances and achieve success. The students who attend these schools possess a remarkable level of grit and perseverance.

The obstacles they face are many, yet surprisingly a few continue to strive towards their goals and pursue their dreams with unwavering determination. However, it is important to recognize that their journey is not an easy one. It requires a significant amount of hard work, long time, dedication, and sacrifice. Life had taken us there and we had to acclimatize and do what it demanded. Without a plan or promise, we waited for the sun to rise each new day and with hope, determination, and courage we carried on, living each day as it came.

New school it was for my sisters and I, and we were newcomers, looking different and drawing the attention of many because of our green uniforms from our previous school.

To be honest, when I began attending kindergarten and ultimately primary at Mucherengi in Guruve, I was never one of those brilliant kids, nor did I understand why we were forced to go to school. It felt like we were being frog-marched without any knowledge of why we had to do it. I was now in a new school, still unclear why I had to be bothered to wake up every day and march to school, nonetheless, I just had to follow the orders and do what others were doing.

Somehow, naturally, things began to shape up, first and the second term in grade two, the results came as a surprise to me that I had done well, I remember on the school closing day they had a tendency of gathering the whole school to announce how children had performed starting with grade one, meaning by the end of the day, the whole school would know who passed or failed. As the last day of school rolled around in my second term at Nyaunde in grade two, I found myself in an unexpected situation. I couldn't quite recall the details, but I knew I wasn't at school on the closing day. It wasn't a deliberate choice - I think my uncle had convinced me to stay and help pick cotton from his field instead. As it turned out, my uncle's cotton field was located close to the road used by other kids to go to school.

So, there I was, working away in the field, feeling a little embarrassed as I watched my classmates pass by on their way home. I thought about hiding, but it was too late - they had already spotted me. To my surprise, they called out to me in excitement, letting me know that I had come second in my class!

It was a bittersweet moment - I was thrilled to have done well in school, but I couldn't help feeling a little envious of my classmates who were able to attend the last day of school. That changed my perception towards my ability, and my interest towards school began to germinate within me. From this point I found myself getting considered a top student in my grade, only falling short of taking the first position because of Fadzai, a brilliant girl that scooped 100 marks whenever I got 96 or 98, she was extremely gifted intellectually, a very quiet girl without any friends, not even sharing in any discussion, be it school work or other things. Fadzi only spoke when asked by a teacher, she was one person I gave up trying to understand. From this point, I began to deliberately make efforts toward school while at the end of each term looking forward to good results.

At the same School, I furthermore established myself in sport and became a top runner, and after getting impressed by my performance, the teachers picked me up the following year to give soccer a try. I did not disappoint, having only been picked because of my speed and athletic abilities. I was a boy of prodigious physique, I also did really well in soccer and began to play for the school team.

Admitting that on my first day of soccer training, I felt overwhelmed and struggled to even touch the ball is not something to be ashamed of. Soccer is a team sport that relies on passing and manoeuvring opponents, but at this particular training, the focus was not on passing. Instead, most kids were either dribbling or kicking the ball forward.

It is important to acknowledge that learning a new sport, especially in a new environment, can be challenging. It takes time, patience, and practice to develop the skills necessary to succeed. In this case, the training approach may have been different from what I was used to, but with time and effort, I was able to adapt and improve. The defenders were the guiltiest part. How hard it was for me to play sandwiched by two centre-backs whose job was simply to kick the ball back as far as they could. But with time we began to learn to pass the ball around and play as a team.

One cool thing about Nyaunde was the distance between my uncle's place which we considered home. So close one could easily walk during break time and be back to school in time, but the only problem was that my uncle was not the coolest uncle you could think of.

He was probably a bitter person, though bitterness may be a word towards my uncle, but I really don't know how to describe Uncle Biggie. He was blessed with appetite, food s e e m e d to be his first love above everything, especially meat.

He stayed agitated and ready to punish for any small and at times no reason or for reasons that made him feel good. It wasn't great at all living with him.

But his portrayal of fierce countenance failed to break us, we kept our spirits high and maintained our happy hour happy evening custom.

Because of my uncle's conduct, Mom decided we were better off living on our own.

We ultimately left my uncle's place because of the growing hostility, especially towards me, he developed a tendency of spanking me daily, always finding a reason to do so, a problem that carried on even with other kids after I left, he had that thing within him that always found faults in other people.

He lived on and passed away when I was a grown man. I remember years towards his death he had diminished miserably in stature, standing by my side, he looked inferior, and I wondered what was eating him, I picked my lessons about treating others even the little ones.

It is an honourable thing to treat people with respect and dignity because it is the right thing to do. Time does justice to everything under the sun and with the passing of seasons, everything has its beginning, zenith, and sunset. Before you know it, even mighty kingdoms crumble paving way to even inferior ones. Imagine being that person who gets remembered for inflicting scars. Sometimes the scars and the memories are still vivid, also because, under the sun, time and chance do happen to all, you may never know when the upside turns down.

So, for me the news that we were going to be living on our own felt like I had been hit by a ton load of goodness, I could taste the sweetness of relief before we even get to taste the experiences awaiting us. At least we were distancing ourselves from the antagonism surrounding my uncle's home, away from the belittlement and the hard work in his field with nothing to show, not even a single book or pen.

All the promises and goodness of heart my mom promised turned out to be the opposite side of the coin, especially from his immediate brother. Yes, we became independent, but it didn't mean things turned easy, it meant only an emotional relief. We still had to work hard in our now new field and do extra work in the fields of other people that were better than us. We needed the basics including books and a few things.

Thank God we left, hard it remained, but at least this time success and failure were squarely on us. This called for us to learn to double our efforts, and we quickly learned how to do many things to help Mom, it was a requirement from life that we learnt to fend for ourselves because we needed books and all that school required. So, we worked in other people's fields for books, and sometimes it was food for work, we had no choice but to do these things for us to get even money for fees, we did it for us to eat. Every step of the way we worked for the things that mattered in our lives, and we learned and treasured the value of little things in life that many consider rights and privileges.

Looking back, I can only say our situation slowly stripped us of our dignity. In the eyes of many, we probably appeared less human, but only a bunch of strong workers. Some people took advantage of our vulnerability. I remember a time we worked in the fields after certain ladies promised Mom some goodies. The deal was to do the hard work and receive clothes for my two sisters. That was a motivation to undertake the work with energy and willing hearts, only to be disappointed after work. The ladies did not hold back, they delivered their side of the promise. But obviously to our disappointment, because the clothes were too big, my sisters were just kids, those ladies simply took from their old wardrobe. You can imagine an old heavy lady giving eleven- and twelve-years kids her old clothes after three days of hard work.

These encounters were many, some called us to labour for food, some for books while some would pay cash. It appeared to us people were taking us for a team of strong workers, the work was always three or more times the reward and at other times the so-called reward was worth nothing.

With such things on the increase, Mom kept pushing for a way to breakthrough and looking for ways that could pull us out of our dire situation – a situation that kept us feeling like we could do better and longed for an opportunity to put our efforts into our things, being independent, and doing our things.

Chapter 6

In pursuit of fortune

Mom carried on with her continual efforts in research until she stumbled upon information that in Mupfure River, people were digging gold and making money.

So, with much determination and hope for a breakthrough, we wasted no time, Mom took me to Mupfure River. It had to be me because I was the eldest boy at home, the first and second-born being girls. This reason caused me to understand the responsibilities and what was required of me. And that requirement was a call to man up and manning up caused me to sleep less at night while that young, knowing I had fewer choices.

When Mom told me of the adventure ahead, I had in my imagination a picture of better things ahead. I was as much purposed as her in my heart, so the adventure seemed less of a tall order to me. With that enthusiasm and much hope of seeing life taking a turn for the good, we took off for gold panning along the Mupfure river banks, Gold was not yet a common subject in Zimbabwe within communities and very few knew or talked about it. But we went to discover for ourselves, both Mom and I were not even sure such a thing was happening, we only embarked on the adventure because the information came from people Mom trusted. She had relatives sprawled all over the borders of the greater Sachuru territory and as far as across Mupfure River.

Upon arrival, we found some people that were introduced to me as my mom's relatives, these were already to some extent experts in gold panning and fishing. We were also welcomed by the wonders of Mupfure River! An incredible waterway teeming with fish of many shapes and sizes, making it a true paradise for any angler. But that's not all - the river and it's ecosystem are also home to a wide variety of fascinating animals that coexist with humans in perfect harmony.

As I journeyed through the area, I couldn't help but be struck by the sheer beauty of the forests and landscapes that surrounded me. I was blown away by a double dose of natural splendour that left me feeling curious and invigorated.

To the locals who call this place home, it was all perfectly normal. They went about their daily lives with a quiet calmness that only comes from living in harmony with nature. And it was from these very people that I learned the art of gold panning.

After the formalities were out of the way and we were ready to begin our adventure. We quickly found a spot that had been deserted by other treasure hunters and, with a surge of energy and excitement, we began to dig, allowing optimism to carry us through, hoping this was going to be the change I had been waiting for.

As we worked, I couldn't help but notice that the majority of the people around us were elderly. But then, to my relief, I saw a few other young guys - albeit a little older than me - who I could relate to. It was comforting to know that I wasn't alone in my quest. However, I couldn't help but feel a little disheartened that there weren't more people my age out there with us. One such guy I became closer to was Edison who seemed to have reached a point of understanding every trick of survival in the Mupfure environment. These guys of my age including Edson did gold panning for pocket money and other things, while my case was different. I was there with my mom to fend for the family. Despite this, we continued to dig with all our might, driven by the thrill of the hunt and the possibility of striking it rich. Praying in our hearts for success to remember us in our endeavours.

It was hard work getting Gold enough to fill the small blue cap of the old ever-sharp pen which was the equivalent of one Gram in weight was no small talk. I remember how we toiled and toiled again for days but still failed to get a gram. Riverbanks usually do not produce much gold, only fine deposits or alluvial as it is known.

During the Mupfure outing, one thing occurred while we went through our day-to-day routine. Life can change in the twinkle of an eye, either for the good or the bad and even near misses that would stay memorable and never forgotten. On that day, the morning was calm and the sun shining its brightest and the feeling around me was as normal as normal could be, and there we were, myself and Mom down to work, digging at our usual spot on a high river edge rising as high as ten to fifteen meters. Suddenly Mommy felt like we needed to find another place that could produce more Gold than wasting our time and energy. It was a good move that I agreed with, she took off asking me to carry on in case her efforts bring nothing.

Unbeknownst to me as was the case with my mother as she left me digging, doom was lurking around us and waiting to happen, something that would have changed a whole lot of things, especially for my mom. I only worked for at least two minutes, and immediately felt a need to rest, but not from any exhaustion, I wasn't tired at all as it was still early morning, so exhaustion was still a long way to catch up with me, nonetheless, with that feeling I withdrew myself from the steep edge of the river and went on to sit on a heap of sand just opposite the spot I had been working at. While I sat there, anticipating how long I was to remain seated knowing mom would show up at any minute, and I did not want to be that kid who would be found on the wrong side of my mom's liking. I hated explaining myself for any reason, nevertheless, I remained seated, but deep inside I knew I was risking an explanation, a tricky one knowing I did not have any reason why I was not working as everyone else was.

From childhood, creativity of thinking on my feet in making up a believable story that sounded satisfying had always been my weakness, hence I played safe and stuck to always telling the truth or no answer. However, there were times I wished I had such creativity. I have seen other people, kids for that matter who can think and make up an instant story, not me, and for that reason I learned to behave, making sure my house was always in order.

While I sat there, I continued to linger in my rationale without making up my mind, just felt sluggish. Suddenly and unexpectedly, the river's edge crumbled before my very eyes! I had been working there a mere five minutes prior, digging without any particular intention, when I chose to take a break and ponder the prospect of returning to my task. If the riverbank had collapsed just two minutes later, I would have undoubtedly been crashed upon my return. Alternatively, had I remained working for a mere sixty seconds longer, the vibrations would have hastened the collapse and I would have met my demise?

It was at that moment that the realization hit me: I had been guided by an invisible hand. If that heap of soil had fallen upon me, there would have been no possibility of survival. Soon a crowd gathered to witness the spectacle of what had just taken place.

While everyone was still gathered and talking, my Mom also appeared. She obviously upon realizing what had just happened feared for the worst. I observed how she remained collected while putting up a brave face, but she could not ask anyone, her eyes were scanning for me but could not locate me among the many adults towering above me, I was just a boy, so short among dozens of adults.

There are moments in life when it can be difficult to discern whether an event is a product of reality or a mere figment of one's dreams. As I observed the anxiety etched onto my Mother's visage, I approached her cautiously from amidst the crowd, tenderly calling out to her and clasping her hand. As she gazed upon me in disbelief, her emotions seesawed between extremes. However, upon realizing that I was unharmed and alive, the intense surge of emotions that had been kindling within her was swiftly extinguished. For a brief moment, my mother was utterly confounded, having left me working just a few minutes prior at the same location that had now been reduced to rubble. Despite the lack of any visible evidence that I had been extricated from beneath the heap of earth, my Mother's perplexity was entirely understandable, as any parent in such circumstances would be.

The incident that occurred that morning is one that I contemplate often, for it instils within me a sensation that there was an intangible force that guided our actions and thoughts. Indeed, there are moments in life when we are confronted with unsavoury circumstances that are beyond our control, devouring everything that makes us feel human. As perplexing as it may be, there exists an enigmatic force that operates beyond the limits of our comprehension, with invisible titans that vie both for and against us, directing and influencing our movements in ways that surpass our feeble intellect.

What else could have directed my mother and me to depart from the area for a brief moment, only to have it collapse mere minutes later? Although I would relish in the sight of God's glorious presence to validate my belief, I sensed - and still sense - that He was present with us that day. How God communicates with individuals may be difficult to discern, yet He does so, nonetheless. Often, we listen to His voice and either obey or disobey. What a near miss it turned out to be.

I watched Mom staying agitated to the point of deciding to leave for home in a few days, having been this much shaken we quickly looked for buyers to sell the little Gold we had, more than two grams if I recall well. With the shock from the near-crush incident still gripping Mom, we returned home to the delight of sisters and everyone. I understood how Mom felt, having known how my father possessed a talent for verbal manipulation, I empathized with my mother's emotional state. My father had a way with words that could either break bones or provoke a response, depending on his intentions. The thought of the potential burden of his words left me contemplating the consequences of being crushed by the riverbank.

On another occasion, I had fallen gravely ill and found myself teetering on the brink of life and death. I was admitted to the hospital in Kadoma, where I remained for a month under high care. It was an anxious and uncertain time for my mother, who struggled to afford the cost of my prolonged hospital stay and treatment, Enias footed all the bills while Mom lived at his house. The same man came from Guruve and grew up closer to my father, so he helped and paid for my hospital bills out of compassion. So ironic when my dad heard what uncle Enias had done to save my life from a sickness that saw my life treading on the line, Dad became bitter and Mom was told how my father said ill things towards the very same man who helped save my life. Would he prefer to see me die? I can never certainly know why he became bitter.

Chapter 7

Fading hope

Our days in Nyaunde were increasingly drawing to a close, and with each passing day, signs were increasingly portraying a faded picture of a better life, one after the other, any hinge on which our hopes hanged on were failing us. We arrived with hype for life and a burning desire to succeed, but life's clouds seemed not to fall short of raindrops to shower down on us, watering down our enthusiasm and threating to extinguish any flame of desire for success.

Despite the myriad of challenges we faced, we learned invaluable lessons that have stayed with me to this day. Growing up without a father figure around meant that my mother had to take on the role of both parents, exhibiting tough love, and pushing and nudging me to acquire skills that were beyond my years. She instilled in me a sense of resilience and determination that has helped me weather life's storms.

It felt like life was hardening me for a reason, like I was being tempered in the furnace of hardship to become stronger and more resilient. My mother's tough love ensured that I was not coddled and sheltered like other boys my age. Instead, I was taught to face life head-on, to tackle challenges with a menacing grit and determination.

Life at home and in the community was tough, but it taught me the value of hard work, perseverance, and resilience. School life was an enjoyable experience for me, as I effortlessly made friends with several guys and quickly won over the hearts of my teachers with my unintentional charming demeanour. In fact, my conduct was so graceful that some teachers even dubbed me "Mandela" - not as a nickname, but because they had learned that I had a younger brother with the same name. This sparked a wave of curiosity among my peers and educators alike, who were eager to learn the story behind the naming of my brother.

When my brother was born, the name Nelson Mandela was reverberating all over Africa. The struggle icon was still languishing in prison at Robben Island in Cape Town South Africa, and people like President Robert Mugabe stayed at the forefront making a lot of noise with the Free Mandela campaign. My father portrayed to me a perception that he poured emotions into African liberation and seemed to be following all that was happening, judging by how he reacted to the passing of President Samora Machel of Mozambique.

After hearing that Samora was killed or died, my father shaded some tears. So, at a very tender age I began to understand how he was attached to the events that were happening around Africa, but he was never an activist.

As a child, I was also fascinated by the insatiable appetite of the men of my father's generation for news and information. Regardless of their social status or background, every man in an urban neighbourhood seemed to share a deep hunger for knowledge and understanding of the world around them. And upon visiting the rural areas, they would bring a copy of mainly the Herald to share with their rural connections who also stayed thirst for updates in politics and development. For many of these men, the daily ritual of reading the Herald and Sunday Mail newspapers was not just a pastime, but a basic necessity that could not be missed.

Every weekend, fathers would send their children out to buy bread, milk, and of course, the latest issues of these two revered publications. Many times, I also noticed how on a weekend they sometimes bought four different publications and drink from every page. And once they had the paper in hand, they would sit down in a sunny spot and devour every page, pouring over the latest news in politics, business, sports, and beyond. It was a truly inspiring sight to behold these men. Their hunger for knowledge and their commitment to staying informed were evidence of the power of education and the importance of being engaged citizens.

Looking back on those days, I realize just how lucky I was to grow up in a community where information was valued and sought after. And I can only hope that future generations will continue to share that same passion for learning and staying informed about the world around them. They had an addiction equivalent to the generation of today on a cell phone. So, it was during that period when my brother was born, and my Dad named him Mandela.

My recollections of Nyaunde are filled with fond memories, particularly of the friendship that was fostered through sports. As a talented runner and soccer player for my school team, I was held in high regard by my peers amongst other athletes, showering us with affection and respect. Sports played an integral role in bringing us together, and I recall with great vividness the annual school soccer tournament, where schools from the surrounding areas would gather for two days of intense competition. Despite playing barefoot, we managed to avoid injury throughout the entire season, never once kicking the ground – we were smart.

Playing barefoot and without team kits was a common occurrence during my early years of playing soccer for my school in Nyaunde. Opposing teams were often forced to skin, and play shirtless. However, as time passed, our school purchased proper green T-shirts for us to wear during games. I remember feeling an immense sense of pride and elation when I donned that T- shirt. It was the best feeling ever, and I wore it with pride both on and off the field. On weekends after the tournament, I made sure to wear my new soccer shirt at every opportunity, basking in the admiring glances of other children who recognized me as a part of the school soccer team.

Competitive sports were a thrilling affair in our school, as we faced off against a bunch of gifted athletes from neighbouring schools, including Chehamba, Rusvingo, Munyati, Hwakwa, and Madzivaenzou. Each of these schools brought their A-game to the competition, making for a fierce battle on the playing field.

In football, Rusvingo was the talk of the town, as they boasted a talented player with an unusual skin condition called Vitiligo. This condition left the player with two distinct skin colours, making him stand out from the crowd. The other schools referred to him by the nickname "Mabandomu," which cleverly referenced his unique appearance and served as a reminder of his impressive skills on the field. What a talent he was, he also like my uncle Lawrence sends shivers to his opponents. I remember one soccer tournament where we met his team in the final and we lost because we were all jittery around this guy.

As for a school like Chehamba, the kids that made it well-known were mostly kids from my mom's relatives, brothers, and sisters. They produced a bunch of extremely gifted kids of my age, and some older than myself, some were at Nyaunde, while others were scattered in other schools.

My Mom comes from a family that's so big, it's hard to keep track of everyone. You see, her father had three or four wives, and that's not even counting all the cousins who were practically siblings. And with so many people, there was always something exciting going on. One thing this big family was known for was their incredible talent in sports. They were a force to be reckoned with! Some of the names that stood out the most were Uncle Lawrence and Israel - these guys were legends on the field. Every time they stepped onto the court, pitch or track, you knew you were in for a show.

When it came to athleticism, my Mom's family produced some of the most incredible athletes I've ever seen. Take Uncle Lawrence, for example – he was a physical specimen. A man of exceptional physique with an appearance that left many in awe. Even in silence, his looks spoke eloquence on his behalf, radiating an aura of pure athleticism. Above athleticism, Lawrence transcended mere physical abilities, watching him play was like watching poetry in motion, a rare combination of skill and grace.

I remember staring at him in wonder, envisioning the moment the Creator designed his joints, tendons, and ligaments. It was as if God designed him specifically for sports, with a body so well-balanced from head to toe that he looked like he could conquer any challenge. His chest, in particular, was a sight to marvel at. It stood out prominently, like a devoted chest expander or a consistent bench presser, showcasing his natural well-built physique. But it wasn't just his chest that caught your eye - but as well his sharp-pointed nose and outstanding facial features also replicated among his siblings, making them all look like they were hewed from the same block of granite.

Uncle Lawrence truly was a guy of imposing athletic abilities and appearance. He inspired us all to push ourselves to be the best we could be, both on and off the field. And all kids from my school could not help but make sure at some point they drew closer to study Uncle Lawrence, just to have a glance, and I am sure he took notice that kids from schools around find themselves talking about him at one point or the other, looking at how quiet and calm he remained, he probably knew it was him other schools have been forward-thinking of.

Even the support for Lawrence was deafening to the point of drawing a cult when his turn to compete came. Lawrence was a student at Chehamba, other kids from his school preferred to shorten his name, calling him Rori. His impact could send shivers, jitters and adrenaline pumping before he even took to the starting line. This usually happened after a long-distance event that his brother Israel dominated. So, Uncle Israel's win would have stirred the support. So, from there the support simply intensified, that adrenalin, escalating the euphoria from the long-distance races after a win by Uncle Israel and another guy from that same school called Mago.

With that liveliness being carried forward and intensified, noises of all sorts and jumping and punching of the air became the order. That indeed sent shock waves to whoever was to race against Rori. Once the whistle blew to race, Rori would jolt forward, sending supporters into a frenzy yelling hard to outdo one another, but the wild calls for Rori, Rori, and Rori grew way above any other school that could be yelling in support of their athletes. Then Lawrence would win the race, meaning it would take a moment for teachers and organizers to clear and calm the environment for the next race to begin.

This kind of support made Chehamba a more prominent school among others. For me and other kids that represented our school, especially those of his age group, we knew that whenever we faced schools like Chehamba, Lawrence and his brothers and sisters were our headache, they gave everyone a run for their money, making them the guys to beat. As we trained for inter-school competitions, our thoughts were consumed by the formidable athletes from my Mother's family. They were the benchmark against which we measured ourselves, and we knew that to compete at their level, we had to push ourselves to the limit.

It was a well-known fact that I was a thorn in the side of athletes in my age group, and my appearance only added to the sense of intimidation that surrounded me. Alongside my peers Rashai, Brian Mabwe, and a select few others, we were regarded as a real threat to the established order.

Representing my school was a point of pride for me, and I was determined to excel both on the field and in the classroom. However, many of my rivals were solely focused on their sporting achievements, neglecting their academic obligations in the process. I also had a close friend who could not perform so well intellectually, nevertheless, he was a good soccer player, playing well as a defender. Alphas Madhora, I remember him so well. But he was a little bullish though, probably because he was a year older than me. It's a pity that back then and probably even now, kids get forced to pursue academic pathways despite their dismal routine year after year.

At home, we carried on daily trying to cope each day with challenges as they came our way. Life carried on and naturally, our minds were no longer thinking much about Daddy. Nonetheless, we felt like we did not belong in this place, I felt like I wanted to be somewhere, my spirit was always agitated for one reason or the other, and for sure the clock was ticking, but, what for? We did not know. Despite my feelings of wanting to be out of my situation, we had all surrendered from the idea that our father was going to play a role to see us out of our circumstances.

Chapter 8

Daddy out of the blue

While we least expected or suspected it, my father and his brother visited us. A visit out of the blue, arriving at midnight, which was a surprise to my delight. In those days, it certainly had to be a surprise. Nobody carried a cell phone around because they were still a long way to be invented, and nobody owned a telephone, especially in primitive areas like Sachuru. So, the best thing a person could do was to feature on the scene unannounced.

To find us, my Father went to Uncle Benji, dragging him out in the dead of the night. Together, they arrived at our doorstep and we were called to wake up. My Father looked as dark and handsome as I had remembered him from my childhood - but that night, he seemed even more striking. In contrast, my Uncle Fletcher was the opposite of my Father in complexion. He had a very light skin tone, and the contrast between him and my father was striking. So, they came together with Uncle Benjamin.

My uncle Benji is a very cool and level-headed guy with a steady demeanour that conveys stillness and assurance in any room, making you feel like everything was fine and there was no reason to rush in whatever you do. Benjamin is one of my mom's many brothers.

In life, you encounter certain people with natural capabilities to transfer their energy to everyone around them. These energies vary from person to person. Others are jovial and can easily lighten up a room, a workplace, you name it. Still others may enter a room and with their presence turn a place into a graveyard. My uncle Benji carried his natural ability, the type that feeds calmness into his surroundings.

Now we sat there in our round hut under the dim light illuminating from a homemade paraffin lamp and Mommy pushed together the logs on the fireplace that were slowly dying while we were asleep, soon the fire was alive again and the glow furthered the dim light of the paraffin lamp. For a moment there was silence you could hear the pin drop as we all waited in silence to hear why Daddy appeared out of the blue.

What a night that turned out to be, of course, we never rose to dance, but my heart, in particular, was bubbling inside. I longed for a day when we could catch a bus and drift away from all the things surrounding us. However, that night presented a mixture of delight and sadness for me.

Imagine Daddy coming into the picture when we were almost beginning to forget him, when we were beginning to feel like we were all on our own, when the longing for his presence was dying down. We had at that point stopped imagining a day we would see him. However, he brought us a surprise to our delight. I had not seen him that handsome and smart, his looks exuded sentiments that he was looking after himself really well. I could not take my eyes off him while he sat there.

I kept observing him, hoping to make eye contact with me, but in the end, I made a conclusion that daddy was angry, sitting quietly and tight, giving very brief answers, nonetheless, that did not stop my mind to be at work trying to imagine what change our lives could see.

Despite his tight, tense appearance he called my young brother and sat him on his Lap kissing him repeatedly. Then the first disappointment, so strikingly outstanding was how my father failed to bring even a packet of sweets for the same boy he sat on his lap. I have never seen that much kissing. It seemed like he had made that whole journey with one thing in mind, to kiss my young brother as if he had been rescued from the earthquake. It would have been great after those kisses to give the boy a little chocolate or something small. This turned somewhat contrary to what any kid would expect from a father who appeared on the scene after a long time. Besides kissing my brother, he never spoke to any of us or asked if we were well, let alone calling our names to at least show us he still remembers us and did care.

I felt like he wasn't paying attention to the rest of us, how lucky my brother was that night showering in kisses. What about us? He never cared to ask us about life at home or school or how we were surviving. Nevertheless, his coldness did not entirely quench our delight. We somehow managed to retain the excitement brought by his arrival. Soon that delight was going to be extinguished, it turned out to be a vapour, lasting two hours only.

In my imagination I had jumped the gun; my mind running wild picturing the possibilities of walking alongside the tall, athletic-built gentleman looking sharp in his pristine long-sleeved blue shirt and navy ironed trousers whose herm perched atop his glossy black polished leather shoe. In my mind's eye, I could already see the envy on the faces of the other kids as we strode down the school grounds together. His brother, always impeccably dressed in his signature grey suits, was equally impressive. The two of them were a sight to marvel at, outshining all the other dads in Nyaunde with their effortless style and sophistication.

As I sat there lost in my thoughts, I envisioned a world of freedom where my father could stroll into my school and demand our transfer letters, turning the heads of everyone who had ever doubted me. I longed for the chance to walk alongside my father for other kids to see.

Indeed, it isn't an exaggeration that in appearance he looked great together with his brother, the only difference setting those other dads from him was how they showered their kids with love. So, I hoped his appearance on the scene was going to be a game-changer.

Well, I was wrong, and one thing my imagination never took me to, was to picture him leaving as startling to me as his appearance had been. I am sure he never figured out how I missed him. My imagination only got cut short and so was my delight, he surely knew how to disappoint.

They lasted only 2 hours, leaving a $50 bill for my mother to use for travelling. They agreed in our presence and Uncle Benji was a witness, saying he wanted Mom and the rest of us to follow in a few days.

I looked up to that with an expectation beyond words, but, for some reason, Mom did not do as agreed and my father never came back, this obviously to my heartbreak. I then picked up some courage, and asked Mom why we had not followed, and she said the money was not enough. But my mind told me there could be more to it. I am sure my Dad came to take us with him, judging by how he appeared empty-handed, but I will forever guess what the two had in mind.

Did Dad come with the intention to take us with him? Was there something that made him change his mind? I can only guess, did Mom say something to upset him? Maybe my father saw something, maybe I assumed wrong that he intended to fetch us. Only Dad could tell what the original plan was, only if he could share, but Dad was a sensitive person, and I would not dare pursue my quest. Whatever was going on, I was just too minor to comprehend. So, I left it alone.

Time lapsed and at that juncture, my thinking and understanding of life had shifted a lot and my heart so much longed to see us living as a family. Mainly for this reason, and of course my love for Daddy, I longed for that day we could catch the morning bus and leave, but it seemed the problems between my parents were deeper and required more than catching the first-morning bus for a reunion. There was now a wide rift between the two, the years spent apart only helped widen it.

During that time it was clear they had given up on any possibilities of a reunion. If there was going to be any, they should have doubled their efforts, not just that, but he should have acted earlier. Another thing became clear to us before my father and his brother left, we understood the union between Dad and the fat lady did not last. That lady, we were told only lasted as long as two months, the reason being she was not the only one whom my father had set sights on. Ultimately, Dad married someone else and at the time of this visit, they had one child. So ironic of the people that surrounded and influenced my father that the appearance of the fat lady was only celebrated briefly because it appears to me, they never cared who was in the picture as long as that person would cause my mom and her five kids to leave. Now that my Mom was out of the picture and the fat lady was gone, it happened once again that they disliked exceedingly Daddy's new wife and wished for the return of my Mom. Goodness me, let me leave this one here.

So, we tarried in Nyaunde a little longer. Though we had a field and worked so hard also in it expecting to earn a better living from our toil, the soil always failed to return any favour to our sweat, and rain scarcely fell year after year. If the region would receive good rains, definitely people living there would have good harvests time and time because it is one of those areas where one could farm without fertilizer year after year and still see crops growing.

Chapter 9

Finally, out of Nyaunde

With no other plan to change life in Nyaunde, Mom thought it was time to leave and go to Kenzamba where her mom lived, this probably to the fulfilment of my ever-agitated spirit, which always made me feel like I did not belong.

When Mom mentioned the word departing, to go and live closer to her mom, this to me was a grand surprise, because, for as much as my remembrance served me, this was the first time she had ever mentioned having a mom or her existence for that matter. Any talk about a parent I heard from the past was always about her father. Out of curiosity we enquired more from Mom about granny, and Mom told us in brief how their mother left them while very young, for reasons that were special to granny and only understood by her, leaving my mom, four other sisters and a brother to be looked after by their dad, my grandpa with the help of a stepmom who happened to be the mother to uncle Benji.

Grandma was a little different from what I had in my imagination. In my mind, I was picturing a calm old lady with a walking stick in hand in all smiles and dishing out bubbles of love and laughter.

Our granny was not like that, she was energetic despite her tendency to immerse in strong drinks; drinking anything that had a capacity to intoxicate. After drinking she would vomit trash and call us names. To send the message home, grandma did one more thing, a thing so common in our society, she had dogs that would soon fall pregnant, and all the puppies were given various names. Each name was a message to us and if all the names got combined, they formed a meaningful sentence.

I personally felt like we had encroached into the wrong territory. We had to be patient with her, but most importantly we were not to let her get away with murder. My younger sister Sheba and I were a little withdrawn, while the rest gave her a challenge and strong lessons, more than those she ran away from when her own kids were young. My brother Mandela was at the forefront and always gave her a reason to talk or shout even when she wasn't drunk. Granny's complaints varied, among things like eating her mangoes to eating too much.

As if that was not enough on her plate, Uncle Biggie also remembered her and relocated, bringing his kids, and dumping them at the feet of Grandma while he settled in his new home. The presence of my uncle's kids became one more reason for my little brothers to be around her home more often.

I am sure the lessons began to hit home that she was a granny to these souls, a thing she could not change despite what she did or did not do. Little by little a friendship began between the two parties. I preferred to keep a little distance, reserving myself as always, preferring to watch from a distance, especially on days when she was drunk seeing how I seemed to have a phobia around drunken people. Then there were useful days when she sobered up, on such days it was always me that she would drag to teach all sorts because she was a moving encyclopaedia of indigenous knowledge. There were many days she was a good person, and, on such days, she poured without measure her vast knowledge of traditional medicine.

Each time she got time to go to the woods, she had a trick or two to show me. If it wasn't for her showing us things that could be turned into food from the bushes, we would have probably starved at some point, but she knew how to cook and prepare certain things that had the potential to kill if not properly prepared, she knew how to turn a corner and make food out of such. Such things Mom did not attempt to prepare because of her limited knowledge. Every time we found such, we knew we could only go to her place and give her to prepare or do under her instruction. Her survival tactics rescued us on many occasions. However, in a rugged place like Kenzamba her knowledge and tactics had limits, because Kenzamba is a dry area so inhospitable to agriculture. There were other times when things would turn bad at home, such as those days we could not even find a single grain of corn to roast and eat, and trees in areas we had access to had nothing to offer. To survive in such an environment, granny saved the day through her knowledge

One other astonishing ability about Granny Sirai was her physical abilities, despite the impact of age and years and years of consuming strong drinks, Granny in her seventies had an amazing physique that many people in the prime of their youths only wish for. That is one thing I admired about her and wished it could be passed on. I surely would have loved to inherit it. The distances she would walk were staggering, not forgetting how she used to go hunting with men and outrun them in the jungle. I mean, why would I not envy such capabilities? Imagine if I could have such and practice good healthy living. I don't know, probably there were many contributions from the kinds of things she ate, and I hope those years of difficulties that saw us partaking much in her kinds of foods did us a world of goodness.

I am reminded of the toils of those days. One day, my brother Mandela called me and reminded me of a particularly challenging incident. We had nothing to eat at home except for salt and water, and we had scoured the bush to find anything to fill our bellies. Despite our best efforts, we returned empty-handed and exhausted, having found nothing sour or even insects to feast on. We knew of one last place to search, so we made our way to the corn storage shed. It was that time of year when the storehouses were empty, devoid of a single grain. The only indicator of corn's presence was the brown powdery residue, a mealie meal-like substance left behind by weevils that bore into and consume dry maize. Undeterred, we encouraged each other to sift through the waste and attempt to make Sadza.

We cooked Sadza from such with much interest and curiosity. The end result was embarrassingly disappointing. I have never tasted anything like it all my life. This is when we realized no matter how hungry one can be, there are certain things that our system will never take in, and even the throat itself simply refuses to let it through. I mean the Sadza tasted like poison. It was effort wasted and there was a need for plan B, ooh, maybe C.

Kenzamba was a tough and unforgiving place. Life here was just as harsh as in Nyaunde. The rugged landscape offered little respite and the rivers were scarce, leaving the ecosystem parched and thirsty. Farming was a challenge, with the unfriendly terrain making it difficult to grow enough maize for sustenance. But despite these difficulties, there were still advantages to living in Kenzamba beyond just food security. The people of Kenzamba, though living in a subsistence set up had an insatiable hunger for progress and weren't content with just being laid back.

As soon as we arrived, we caught the attention of those with a similar mentality to the opportunistic bunch we had encountered in Nyaunde. They saw us as vulnerable and exploited us at every opportunity, especially those lucky enough to have fields that grew cotton well. And it seemed that we were marked with the curse of Cain, as whoever saw us sought to use us. It was as if we had "cheap labour" written on our foreheads, inviting others to take advantage of us. Unfortunately, it was only a matter of time before this curse came to fruition.

Exploitation can come from any direction, even from those whom we least expect it. In our case, we found ourselves in the Baptist church, which was closely linked to the Salvation Army where my mom had been a member during her youth. We became close to the leader of the Baptist branch, a man in a wheelchair who had children our age. He drew us in, and soon we were working on his cotton fields without any promise or reward. But we took things one day at a time, just trying to get by. Despite the challenges, we found comfort in living in the present and making the most of every moment.

While Kenzamba had some advantages over Nyaunde, such as the availability of transportation, the travelling experience was often unpleasant. I can still vividly recall the many times I travelled those dusty roads with their rib-like surfaces, causing intense vibrations that felt like a jackhammer. This was especially true on the journey from Kenzamba all the way past Donzamfana, making for an uncomfortable and bumpy ride. Donzamfana was a name given to one well-known brutal incline with much fine dust that could burry your leg up to knee height during the dry season. Not overlooking how it was hard to know if windows should be kept open or stay closed because of much dust getting into the bus. It was always everyone's prayer that the bus doesn't have to get stuck at Donzamfana because nobody wanted the experience of jumping off the bus to swim in dust.

In these bumpy rides, there was no way to avoid dust entering inside, for that reason, people made sure to always wear a second pair of clothes on top of the good ones and a wet towel to use when the bus entered tarred road. Towards Alaska Dolomite, the bus would stop, allowing people to get out and dust off or wipe with wet towels from all the exposed flesh and hair. After that, everyone would look and feel comfortable stepping into Chinhoyi which then looked clean and promising. But upon entering the town, anybody would easily identify you as someone from Kenzamba. Environments have a certain way of laying on you a covering tint. No matter how much one tries, there is sometimes always that tinted layer that only gets lifted when you change the environment. Signs like a change in complexion once one moves from a certain area.

Despite what Kenzamba was or wasn't, we soldiered on, because soldiering on was a requirement in our daily toil and struggle for survival, toiling under the unforgiving heat in Makonde area and surroundings. Gold panning was commonplace as a source of income. Without any other means to earn, gold seemed like the only thing that could level the playing field, the only avenue we could make a bit of cash. We started joining others to go to an area called Zumba to pan gold in Piriviri riverbanks. Life was brutal and punishing in Kenzamba, nevertheless, we carried on like that, even without seeing any significant change in our efforts. If anything, gold panning along the riverbanks was just a waste of our energies. Thanks to this way of earning, I suspect it is from it that I picked back problems that would hit me from young age to adulthood. Without any other way to earn, we kept pressing on.

Thank God, amidst our toil and grinding and soldiering on, things became a little improved when Mom went to court to claim maintenance money, hence the end of the month or sometimes after two months she found herself on the CABS queue in Chinhoyi with her book bank in hand, queuing to withdraw money. This money took us a long way, what a relief, from school fees to shoes and food. But something disheartening happened, and it was repeated more than once. Because my father had to be dragged to court and get forced to pay maintenance, he quickly developed a tendency of quitting jobs at will, knowing many companies were after him, causing him never to struggle to land a job, he could simply pick up a phone and be on another job tomorrow. Mom found a way, of chasing him like a cat after mouse after discovering daddy had left his job as a way to run away from paying maintenance. She knew how to do some research and find where he landed his next job. For some time, it went like that until Mom gave it up, meaning our struggle carried on.

Despite these hardships, we were growing up as a bunch of happy, energetic, and hopeful kids. Growing up meant our needs became more, my two elder sisters were fast becoming big girls, and I was following up too. Our father seemed not to care at all. Despite his lack of responsibility and the pain and toil due to his absence, for some reason, or no reason, I continually loved my father a lot, at times it felt as if there was something wrong with me, trying to force myself into a father who pretended we never existed. I had no idea what had gotten into my dad, we were probably better off away from him. He definitely needed an overhaul to his entire life view. It looked as if his conscience had been sneered by a hot iron, but there was no way we could see him change. My father was not the type that learn or unlearn something no matter how many people tried to convince him. He was a very rigid man, I had seen many times some of his uncles trying to help him change a view, and my dad wouldn't have any of such.

I understand people are different and there are more like him out there and even worse, but I can't think of any qualifying reason why a father can let go of five kids and live day after day not knowing what they eat, wear, or where they sleep.

Chapter 10

Kenzamba, a better school

Kenzamba Primary which became my new school after our relocation was 7km from our home. So, it meant treading barefooted 14 km of gravel road every day.

Treading on gravel barefooted turns out to be one memorable experience, so brutal to the feet, mostly in winter. Going to school without shoes was never considered an embarrassing thing, in these areas, many kids never cared or worry about shoes, even those that had shoes would not wear them every day, and for this reason, we fitted in so well. However, this comes with a challenge when one considers how messed up the pit latrine toilets at school could be. It was one area that we always thought twice before entering, and with no choice we entered every day, stepping carefully to avoid trampling whatever mess on the floor.

We spent all day and hardly took any food to school even from the days at Nyaunde. The few times we did, it was mainly boiled maize called Mangai. In a thick plastic sugar bag where everyone could see the contents. Pocket money was a word that sounded like a taboo, only hearing it from others at school. I never had pocket money in my school days. On the positive, Kenzamba was a different school with proper structures like Mucherengi in Guruve where I attended grade one, they had three classes per grade. Above everything, this school had no shortage of bright students. For the first time I found myself facing a real intellectual test and my first term results came as a wake-up call to me.

In Nyaunde I had become accustomed to finding myself in the top 3. I found myself sitting at 16, meaning in Nyaunde I was probably the best amongst the worst. This triggered a willingness towards doing more. Thank God we moved to this place than carrying on in intellectual mediocrity. What a different school, with a little rigorous exams and upped standards. Most of the teachers at this school had passed through teaching colleges and looked a little more advanced than those at Nyaunde. I realized how much I was supposed to up my work to fit into my new environment with so many bright kids.

Pulling up to try and match the standards was definitely the thing to do, I have to admit it was not easy. For a moment it seemed like the bar was lifted much higher than I could attempt but I told myself to keep trying my best, and it paid off. In the last term of Gr 5 I found myself in the top ten and would linger around top ten for my class while combined I found myself among top 20, I was not content in this because there was still more work to be done.

I wondered if back in Nyaunde Fadzi ever came to realize that we gloried in mediocrity believing we were doing the best. It was now from within, from inside I felt the urge to do a little more. Through my efforts, I began to also feel like I belonged, but never a top-five student, bear in mind we were never taught to study or encouraged to read, nor were we given notes to carry home.

In sporting activities, there was nowhere I could go unnoticed no matter how many good athletes they were. And as soon as I got a chance to take part in athletics, I began to represent the school. My anticipation of the competition, the vibe even on inter-school games was that it would be five times than the small schools that competed with Nyaunde. My perception was proven wrong, everything sporting here was nowhere near the Chehamba Nyaunde rival, but I found a lot of good athletes and team sport players.

It is always given that whenever one goes to a new place, they make friends, and I made a few friends there too. In my class I had two brothers that lived in the same area as me, we clicked easily and automatically became closer, the brothers were Samuel and Dzingai Murindagomo. Another guy that became outstanding above all the friends I had while at Kenzamba Primary was none other than one figure in the person of Wycliffe Tawadzana, what a friend indeed and need. Will probably have to call him a heaven-sent Angel. Sadly, he passed away in an accident years after we parted ways, but he came into my space and became some sort of saviour when I needed a saviour the most and I have no idea why out of all the people he singled me out. He always had pockets full of money every day. And during lunchtime when I had no food or drink, Wycliffe would call me and buy coke and bread for the two of us. I never asked why he chose me: it could be because other kids teased him saying he was born prematurely, a wit that I never found amusing.

To be honest, at first, I was a little sceptical assuming the guy would ask for my turn to buy in one of these days, that guess caused me to ponder, and I even thought of retreating. I did not want to be an embarrassment in case my turn to buy comes. However, he was not like that. This guy was not even from the same area as me. We were only friends at school and never get to walk home together because we each took a very opposite direction. We never saw each other during holidays or weekends, and neither did we care for what each one did with their lives during weekends or holidays. The only thing that brought us together was, that he identified me as someone he could share a meal with. So, we became buddies hinged on that factor.

Wycliffe was also an excellent athlete, and although I was a fast runner like him and other gifted kids, we always found ourselves representing different houses. This separation made the competition exciting, especially on the day of the inter-house competition. Wycliffe's house consisted of other well-known athletes, and he teamed up with top performers like Pension Hofisi. On my side, I had strong competitors like Robson Gore. Robson lived close to my home, and we had countless encounters outside of school. Sometimes, he even came to our house, but most of our meetings took place during the rainy season in a small stream near our home. We would regularly meet there to bathe and discuss any topic that was on our minds that day. Wycliffe only ran as far as the school house competition, after that, his parents would not allow him to take part in inter-school because they belonged to the Jehovah's Witness. One cannot tell why their kids were not allowed into sport unless you dig into finding why, but we never bothered to ask beyond what we were told. All teachers wished Wycliffe could compete in inter-schools, but everyone respected their values.

While we took part in the school's local competition, at first very few people knew or talked about me since I was still new and quiet. They looked up to Pension and Wycliffe in our age group, only to be shocked when they saw me losing these guys from the start of the whistle, some never knew the physical me, so after the run, they talked about me while I was standing right there with them.

One thing for sure was the competition at Kenzamba was good, but I considered my competitors in Nyaunde at the inter-school level superior. One element about me from those early years was, that I never participated in sports for fame or girls, yes, some guys my age had already involved themselves in dating. It was all far from my mind even when I was not extremely ignorant of these; I had some kind of understanding of love and all around it. I remember as early as Guruve, one guy called Lloyd only a year older than me, with a strong desire for sex tried to introduce me to sex, at that early age, as early as six, but honestly speaking I had no idea what was going on or why a man and woman have to have intercourse. It's astonishing that people get such a desire for sex while they are still infants.

Life in Kenzamba continued on its usual course, and as we approached grade six, my mother became increasingly aware of the challenges that awaited us in grade seven. In particular, there were final exams to consider, as well as registration requirements that necessitated having a birth certificate. Unfortunately, I did not have a birth certificate, which was a cause for concern. To address this issue, my mother decided to take swift action and took me, my sister Sheba, and my brother Mandela to Chitungwiza to see our father.

Chapter 11

How daddy watered my spirit

The prospect of going to see my father stirred a dormant energy within me, filling my mind with endless possibilities and a sense of anticipation. My thoughts turned inward, consumed by the possibilities of what lay ahead. While my imagination had initially ran wild, building on my childhood recollections, hoping and praying for a resumption of those childhood experiences, my current preoccupation was with the potential for change.

As I lay in bed each night, I found myself asking whether this trip would be a turning point in our lives. I refused to entertain any negative thoughts, allowing only positive and glamorous visions of a new era to fill my mind. It felt as though, with my father back in the picture, we were finally on the path to regain our dignity and move forward.

The excitement of the impending journey filled me with a renewed sense of purpose, and I felt a surge of energy that had lain dormant for far too long. I was eager to see my father and discover what the future held in store for us. Despite any reservations or doubts that lingered in the back of my mind, I was determined to embrace this opportunity with open arms and an unwavering sense of optimism.

I have childhood memories of my father taking me to the Borrowdale race course to witness the magnificent horses in action. The excitement of those days at Lona Park still lingers in my mind. I was eagerly anticipating a similar thrill and hoping for a change in our fortunes.

However, as it turned out, the reality was far more complex than we had ever imagined, and it was clear that resolving our situation would necessitate multiple trips and a significant expenditure of our hard-earned funds, earned through tireless toil.

Despite putting in three concerted efforts, our endeavours yielded nothing but disheartening words. My father's bitter attitude towards both my Mother and me was evident, despite our intentions of merely visiting him to obtain crucial life documents that required his facilitation as our parent. Whenever he got drunk, he had a tendency for rambling, and his words were often hurtful. Sadly, his anger was not limited to my Mother alone but extended to me as well.

My father had a way with words, he knew how to mingle them and dampen any excitement or enthusiasm we might have felt. This was especially disheartening since we had not seen him in many years, not since his unexpected night visit to Nyaunde. This trip was more than just a simple visit to the registrar general; we saw it as a step towards reuniting with our father. However, he seemed to have no qualms about ruining all that we had hoped for.

As a result, the energy and eagerness that we had initially felt were quickly extinguished. I was moved to tears on several occasions, as every word he spoke seemed to sink into my already broken spirit. The entire adventure became an emotional rollercoaster, leaving us feeling drained and disheartened.

Looking back on all those years since my parent's divorce, I never realized just how much emotional turmoil I had endured. Like a sponge, I soaked up every emotional blow that came my way, never realizing the damage it was doing to me from within.

It wasn't until I found myself sobbing uncontrollably for an entire day, tears flowing like a river, that I truly understood the depth of my emotional pain. I struggled to regain control of my emotions, but it seemed like the more I tried to hold back my tears, the more they poured forth.

I spent countless hours hiding my tears from others, secluding myself in the bathroom to sob in private. I hoped that my eyes would eventually run dry, but the tears just kept coming. It was as if I had a stomach bug, taking endless trips to the bathroom to hide my pain.

A fruitless trip it turned in the end. Leaving Chitungwiza with heaps of words to digest, all the efforts proved vain and we would return to Kenzamba without stepping into the office of the registrar general, regretting why we ever wasted our hard-earned money.

Several times Mom tried to convince me, pressing me hard to go for the idea of taking her maiden surname, but she realised I wouldn't go for her idea, I was prepared to wait until we found a way.

So, with a watered spirit, I returned to carry on with school feeling unsure where life was heading. Returning to school to face a new teacher being unveiled at the school's assembly as our class teacher. This was something our class least expected. The school decided to give us a very well- known strict teacher who at some point left the school to go teach elsewhere, now that he returned for a second bite, nobody ever wanted to imagine him as their teacher.

To mark his return an announcement was made at the school's assembly. The whole school waited in total silence. Then the announcement was read, so surprising how the rest of the school except for my class exploded in jubilation.

A roar of jubilation as if it was planned, rejoicing because John Mabika was not going to teach their classes.

While others roared in jubilation, we all looked down and considered ourselves doomed, that day there was total silence in our class as we began with Mr Mabika.

A dedicated teacher, a rigid man with lots of compassion, it was my first time to meet a no- nonsense person whose rigidity was enveloped in compassion, always putting over 100% into the things that he did, while expecting from his students a response matching his efforts.

When he walked, he looked motivated, always pushing to get the best out of every student. One thing we never knew when he took our class in grade 6 was John intended to take us through to grade 7. It turned out he wanted a method where he can take a class from the 6th grade through to the 7th and mould them in the way he preferred.

It was hard at first to imagine going along well with John but ultimately, we became used to our John Mabika to the point of personalising him, and he was now our John, our teacher. We felt like a unique bunch because of his way of handling things.

Going along with him meant striving to remain disciplined and meeting his every demand, his demands called for excellence and punctuality on time. While school starts at 07:30 our class daily commenced at 06:00 sharp, mind you this was a school 7km from where we lived, but we learned how to manage our time and make things work.

Fridays were usually days for mental math, making sure every student shouts an instant answer in five seconds flat. This was not a day we looked up to because it brought up bad news many times as he kept pushing us to our limits. Most of the times the class would go silence as everybody fails to give an answer. Just then, would our saviour raise his hand, none other than Webster Muchenje, Webster joined us in the middle of our first term in grade six. From day one he exhibited a wealth of knowledge and confidence than none among us had, so whenever we felt dry like the Kalahari, Webster became our Oasis of knowledge and confidence from which we could all gather a lick every drip.

As if the extra 30 minutes a day in class was not enough, we had Saturday classes too, those Saturday classes were very relaxed and he would smile a lot and make us freely talk and express ourselves, sometimes calling me and two other boys to go with him to his house and make tea for everyone in a 20L container. We became used to it and looked forward to such days.

Everyone would arrive on time during weekdays except for valid reasons a few kids that came from a faraway place called Naison Dip, their arrival time was always a few minutes before 09:00 because they stayed a very long way from School.

No matter how they tried, they never made it early and for that reason, their performance was, by all means, dismal. It still feels insane to me to think kids can travel that long to go to school. For them to arrive at 09:00 they jogged and trotted the greater part of the distance.

Because of the impact of the distance, they performed poorly at school save for one girl, Letwin who used to win long-distance running.

Their lack of confidence was palpable, and my heart went out to these individuals. Their challenges may have seemed insurmountable, but they persevered nonetheless, treating school as a mere routine in their rat race existence. Without passing judgment on either people or places, I firmly believe that it takes something extraordinary for children from such challenging environments to find their purpose and fulfil it.

Whenever I encounter individuals from such places who have managed to succeed in life, contributing positively to both the economy and society at large, I am filled with admiration and respect. No one from these forgotten corners of society has had an easy life, regardless of which angle you choose to view things from.

It was through working with these children that I discovered John's true character. Despite his no-nonsense demeanour, he exhibited compassion towards these disadvantaged individuals, understanding the immense effort it took for them to attend school.

On first impression, it would be easy to dismiss these individuals as being unserious. However, upon taking the time to understand their circumstances, any preconceived notions would undoubtedly change.

I am grateful to John for demonstrating a compassionate heart towards these underprivileged children. His commitment to helping them catch up with the rest of the class was commendable. He went above and beyond, even allowing them to leave a little earlier than the rest of us so that they could have sufficient time to rest before waking up early the next day. Mr Mabika took us to Gr 7 and taught us many valuable lessons, I wouldn't have known punctuality, and I wouldn't have internalized it to have it as an attribute within me forever, if it wasn't for my teacher, he is the reason why I don't miss time or appointments.

Chapter 12

My first experience in high school

In primary school, in a greater sense kids looked like a flock of birds with matching feathers, I mean, it was really difficult to distinguish between the haves and the have less or nothing for that matter. As we entered Secondary level, there appeared a very clear mark of distinction. Besides proper school wear, it is also that stage where both girls and boys begin to feel that urge to add a little swag and dress up. For me, it felt like a taboo to think of any swag, the only thing my heart longed to have was the basics for a form one student. My two sisters were already in form three at the same school, Kenzamba Secondary, with them, things never looked so bad, Mommy had pushed and bought the sisters uniform the previous year.

When it came to my entrance into high school, I didn't expect to make a grand entrance. I had no clear picture of what was in store for me, so I was prepared to handle whatever challenges came my way. But what I experienced on the first day of high school was beyond anything I could have imagined. I was immediately swallowed up by a sea of sky-blue shirts, scanning the crowd desperately for anyone who looked like me. I hoped to find at least a few kids in the same boat as me, to spare me the embarrassment of standing out like a sore thumb.

As I began my first day of school, I still held onto the hope that there would be others like me, still wearing their primary school uniforms and carrying their books in plastic bags, with no shoes on their feet. But I quickly realized that I was wrong. I was the only one who looked like a lost puppy, and the thought of being the odd one out made me feel even more self-conscious. Despite all of this, I knew I had to be strong and face any obstacles head-on.

Scanning around, I couldn't help but wonder if my Mom and I had missed a caucus gathering that conspired to make sure every kid had proper school attire, including shoes. It turned out that I was the only kid in the entire school without shoes! It was a huge risk, and I felt like my sanity was being thrown on the balance scale. The embarrassment was overwhelming, and I could sense that the other guys didn't want to associate with me, fearing that my presence would diminish their status. Anyone who stuck with me needed a ton of guts, and it was to the detriment of their swag.

This was the stage where boys would do anything to impress girls and dressing up was a prerequisite. Both boys and girls started to separate themselves into groups based on common interests, drawing together like-minded individuals. It was a clear sign that the journey through high school was going to be a bumpy ride, but what else could I do other than mind my own business and return the next day?

For a little while, it felt like the honourable thing was to group alone and do my own business, but I have learned that in life one will never be entirely alienated. In one way or the other, there's always going to be someone that stands with you and believes in you no matter the circumstances. Despite this factor, I kept it in my mind to always exercise caution. The last thing I wanted was to annoy someone, even when it came to approaching my sisters, I made sure to always make good timing or wait for them to approach me, and I tried not to make them feel embarrassed among friends. Mom made sure to cover the girls first and at times everyone else while I came last in most cases. So whatever burdens our small family had, I became the face of it, yet I tried always to put up a face and remained positive among other kids.

It became clear to me that high school wasn't all sunshine and rainbows. I remember one incident in particular that left me feeling embarrassed and singled out. It happened during a woodwork class in my first year. The teacher, for reasons unknown to me, decided to call me out in front of the entire class, saying, "*Sifelani, never attempt to walk into the workshop without shoes.*" I was mortified. We weren't even in the workshop at the time, so his comments felt completely misplaced. I could sense that he was hoping for the whole class to laugh, but to my surprise, there was total silence. You could hear a pin drop. That was the first time someone had singled me out, and it hurt even more that it came from a teacher. After that incident, I didn't know who else might try to embarrass or push me away. But little did I know my answer would come from the most unexpected source.

To find out the next in line to embarrass me, I only needed to draw closer to two of my long-time friends. From the time I arrived in Kenzamba, there had not been anyone closer to me than the two Murindagomo brothers Dzingai my closest friend and his brother Samuel. Having fooled myself into thinking it was going to be business as usual. To me business as usual meant sticking together, and doing what kids always do, however, things were about to change, and our friendship was just about to end abruptly.

Seeing my two friends from afar, decked in everything new, with the backpack, the black shining shoes, and long grey socks matching the grey shorts to the sky blue ironed and tucked shirt.

The guys were looking spiv, beyond smart. Then Dzingai noticed me approaching, they all stopped walking and scanned me from toe to head and Dzingai delivered the verdict. Telling me not to linger around them. *"Stay away from us, don't try to spread your poverty to us"* Those were the words that ended our friendship. That was a bone too hard for me to swallow, maybe Dzingai simply echoed what a lot felt when I was around them. If anyone felt the same, they probably never had a chance to tell it to me because I had tried at all costs to avoid hanging around many people.

After Dzingai delivered this message, it really hit home, I know one would be interested to know what my reaction was to that. To be honest, I did not at all react, I became tongue-tied, and neither did I feel angry. The message had come home, all I could do was to listen and do what the brother had asked me. "Stay away from us" was a clear message.

I had always known things were bad but had never looked at my situation from an angle where my presence would contaminate my friends and bring them untold suffering. I went home and felt embarrassed to even tell my mother how other kids were looking at me and what they felt when I was around. The only thing I asked Mom after about two days was *"Mommy, do you think I will ever wear shoes in my life"?* The question probably sounded redundant to someone who had no knowledge of what drove me to ask such a question.

Those were the cutting words that ended our friendship. So, I walked away, I couldn't help but feel a mix of emotions - hurt, and sadness. But I knew that I couldn't let this get the best of me. I had to keep moving forward and continue doing what was expected of me - attending school and striving for success.

Despite my impoverished state, I refused to let anyone pity me or give me handouts. I didn't want anything from anyone who saw me as a charity case. I never saw material possessions as something that defines my worth. So, from that time I took notice of what people felt around me, I minded just attending school without failure. I felt embarrassed to even draw closer to Wycliffe who had been good during primary years.

Wycliffe looked extremely presentable in brand-new everything. "What if my presence gets to make him uncomfortable like others? What if he felt the same way?" I felt like I would not want more hurting words. Besides, I also saw how a few beautiful girls orbited around him like a spaceship circling the Moon. The best thing for me was to withdraw myself from him. I was probably right, this time we simply said "Hi" "Hi" to each other without him inviting me like in my days in Primary. I also felt comfortable doing my things.

All these things played negatively on me, but never caused me to drag my feet around, neither did my head feel heavy above me, and I continually assured myself that I am capable of doing better and I behaved normal while drawing my lines to minimize negative energy. Before long I picked a new company, a bunch of other kids that appreciated me and saw value in me. Ruchiva Bvunzawabaya was one such. Despite the challenges that came with my impoverished upbringing, I was just like any other kid at school. Sure, my circumstances were different, but at the end of the day, we were all facing our own unique challenges.

As I grew older, I began to realize that our circumstances - whether good or bad - were not of our own making. We were born into them, and it will take our commitment to change or improve. And as time went on, I began to realize that we all had our own struggles and challenges to overcome. While mine may have been more visible than others, it didn't mean all was rosy to all other kids. Secondly, those circumstances were not a guarantee of failure or success, we were just teens and looking ahead to a real taste of life where each would be tested on their merit. Because life started challenging me while young, I looked cool during the day but developed a habit of sleeping very late. Thinking and picturing a future away from the problems we had then.

These things around me left one dent that became a Mammoth to overcome. It seems like the habit of withdrawing myself became natural in me, and again, public speaking is not one of my strengths. I also became an ever-anxious and restless person, ever agitated in anticipation of a change in fortune, always feeling and looking up to something good happening, but days would pass and nothing significant happening. I wanted something good to happen, other times I felt like walking away to another place for a good change. I also developed a tendency of avoiding a subject to do with my father because I never looked like someone with a living working father. It was hard telling anyone that, out there was a man who fathered me. But deep inside I longed for a reunion with him, preferring to keep my feelings concealed, wishing above all that differences between him and my mother could change and usher us into a new season. Daddy punished us by turning his back on us. Whatever the case was, we soldiered on, humbly focusing on those things we could do or change, personally making sure hope was never lost, keeping alive that willingness to do well.

During those early days in high school, it became clear that I was doing better than most of the kids in uniform in subjects like

History and English, I liked woodwork too because of its practicality. One English teacher singled me and two other students and brought us into a combined English class of the form three and four. I realized he had an agenda to shame the form four students. That was the reason he came to fetch me and two other guys to go and sit in that combined class. So, whatever he knew they could not answer, he deliberately asked, and those big brothers and sisters repeatedly failed to answer, then he would turn to us for answers. After that, it seemed I was the most recognized form one student by guys in the upper grades, recognized obviously for two things; one as that guy without shoes and secondly as the same guy who got regular calls for English class attendance with them. At least I wasn't getting noticed for the wrong reasons.

Despite all these struggles, my mother remained strong and resilient. She never gave up on trying to find a way to see us reunited with our father, recognizing that it was their mutual responsibility to care for their children. One of her strategies was to send us on holiday to Chitungwiza, but unfortunately, my father's behaviour left me feeling confused and upset. His temper flared up often, and I couldn't understand why he seemed to resent our presence. Despite this, my mother never stopped trying, and her unwavering love and dedication became our only point of strength to keep going.

My father's insensitivity blinded his ability to read my heart and see how troubled I was, and whatever potential I possessed inside, he had no time to identify or nurture. Whatever happened between them, how much anger each of them felt was by no means any reason to make me into a punching bag? Dad became bitter when Mom had other kids with another man.

Despite all this, I hoped to see things improving, but for some reason they never did, and it came to a point during our holiday stay when Dad would go and buy clothes for everyone and leave me out. Same fate for me from both parents, but with mom, her reasons were valid, and I understood. At times, it felt like my father harboured a deep hatred for me. When I finally worked up the courage to ask him why, he revealed that it was because I was his son and was not supposed to live away from him. It was a punishment that I had to endure, and it left me feeling hurt and confused. Looking back, it feels like his irrational chastisement inflicted a wound that would never fully heal.

Despite the pain and trauma, I endured, I refused to let it break me. I learned the value of patience and perseverance, qualities that have served me well in all aspects of my life. No matter what I set my sights on, I approach it with unwavering patience and determination, knowing that success is possible with hard work and a positive attitude.

Sadly, my father's hurtful behaviour didn't stop there. When he would drink, he would say things that cut me to the core, watering down my spirit and leaving me feeling emotionally battered. I'll never forget the day my father said something that cut me to the core. Auntie Chipo, the sister to my late auntie Perisa was there to witness it all. Despite my father's flaws, Tete Chipo loved him deeply, and she sat quietly as he spoke. But as I listened to his hurtful words, my mood plummeted and my heart ached. I excused myself to the bathroom, where I couldn't hold back my tears any longer. This wasn't the first time my dad's words had overwhelmed me, but this time it felt like a new low. The pain was almost unbearable, and I couldn't help but wonder how much longer I could endure it. After a while, Auntie followed me to the bathroom and found me crying uncontrollably. She tried to comfort me, but I couldn't bring myself to talk to her. Instead, I left the house and sought solace in the company of my friend, Lucky. Lucky was my auntie's son, and we had a bond starting when we were younger.

When I arrived at Auntie's house, I tried to distract myself by watching TV, but my mind was elsewhere, lost in a world of wishes and dreams. The black and white Phillips TV seemed to flicker in and out of focus as I struggled to make sense of all the emotions swirling inside me. I felt like I was in a daze, disconnected from reality and lost in my own thoughts. But Lucky was there for me, and his presence brought me some much-needed comfort and peace. As we talked and laughed together, I felt my spirits lifting a little.

Never had I imagined that the man I loved most, my father, would be the source of my pain. Despite this, I loved him deeply and fiercely protected him from my mother's fury. I made it clear to my father that his belittling comments about my mother were excruciatingly painful and that I refused to be a football in their toxic dynamic. However, it seemed that my message never truly resonated with him. Perhaps this was because my mother spent more time with me during my formative years, allowing her to better understand my passions and sensitivities.

When I left Auntie Chipo at our house, she found it hard to continually carry on with my father, hence she followed me to her house and found me among her kids, at that point all the tears had vanished, but upon seeing her, giving me that sympathetic look, I knew she wanted to comfort me, I was immediately on my feet ready to leave, trying not to give her a chance to revisit the topic. I didn't want to be drawn back into the subject even when I knew she meant good. Above all people she was working hard to see a reunion between my father and us. She never hid her joy and delight in seeing us around.

So, when Auntie came in, I left and went back home. I wasn't comfortable going home, if I had another place to go, I could have gone. When I got there my Dad said nothing further that day, but as time went on, I began to realize it was a problem within him and he did not know how to handle things that troubled him.

One more incident happened when my cousin Swisdai was around. We were making our way to Rusununguko beerhall where my dad went to drink as his custom was, although we came back home with the things he meant to buy, he started with me out of the blue. Daddy knew how to water my spirit. He had mastered the art of how to upset using words. Later that day he tried to cheer me up, but the damage was already done. I began to learn that in general, he had a problem in handling matters, I saw him freaking at many people, especially his young brother who seemed to have been used to it and never cared to answer back but only smiled.

There's one thing if not two, that I would thank my father for; it is the role he played in discouraging me to drink beer, I mean, if it wasn't for him, I wouldn't have hated beer and kept a distance from it as I do. Many thanks to him for that. Looking at him in his drunken state helped to further authenticate my decision. Funny enough he tried to convince me into drinking, thinking it would encourage me to liven up and speak more, but I had a decision sealed already in my heart and nothing would move me from it. Naturally, I am a person who strives to settle for decisions and stick to them unwavering. Once I set my mind on things that I perceive to be right, I do not shift so easily, but beer to me was a non-starter.

After spending an emotional holiday with my father, my siblings and I delayed our return to Kenzamba and ended up missing two months of school. We all hoped that he would find us a school in one of the Seke schools scattered around Chitungwiza, but it never happened. I couldn't understand what his strategy was, and I felt lost and adrift without any clear direction or plan for the future. As the weeks went by, it became clear that my father had no intention of helping us find a school. We were left to our own demises, forced to spend our days loitering around and watching other kids make their way to school in their smart, beautiful uniforms. It was a painful reminder of all that we were missing out on, and I couldn't help but feel a deep sense of longing and despair.

But then, one day, my mother learned from someone that we were not attending school. She was furious and demanded that we return to Kenzamba immediately. Upon hearing that, Mommy's heart got pricked and she made efforts to come and fetch us without negotiating with Daddy who at that point had gone back to Kadoma for work.

At last, after a long holiday, we were back at school and it was time to catch up with what other students had been doing in my absence, I had no time to waste or listen to negativity. Not only was my problem to do with handling emotional things happening around me, but I also faced a lot of disruptions as well from school due to non-payment of fees. Not necessarily saying all the things that transpired around me did not erode my confidence, they, in a greater way, had a bearing. But looking back now I try to imagine and say life could have been better if I had the things that other kids had, and if only I was given a chance to focus on school and other things that my heart desired.

Returning to Kenzamba was a harsh reality check. Life in this area was challenging, and the people here were focused solely on subsistence living. It seemed like commercial pursuits were a foreign concept, and the thinking was limited to just getting by day-to-day. Most of the kids in this area went up to O level without any clear sense of purpose or direction, unsure of why they were even going to school in the first place. And for some, the lure of quick cash was too tempting to resist. They dropped out of school and turned to poaching, selling game meat to make a few bucks and buy trendy items.

Life in Kenzamba was simple and uneventful. For most kids, the future was a vague and distant concept that they never bothered to contemplate. But for a select few of us, football was more than just a game - it was our passion, our driving force. We lived and breathed football, constantly seeking out new sources of inspiration and knowledge. Our walls were adorned with posters of our favourite players, and we devoured every issue of football magazines like Complete Football and Kick Off. But our thirst for football news could not be quenched by magazines alone. We had our methods to source for copies of the Monday Herald newspaper, knowing that the soccer section on the back pages held the key to the latest football news. We were obsessed with the beautiful game, and nothing could distract us from our pursuit of football glory. Whether we were reading football magazines, pouring over the latest scores in the back pages of the Monday

Herald, or practicing our skills on the dusty grounds, we were always striving to improve ourselves and become the best footballers we could be.

Luke, Mao, and I shared the burning desire and envisioned ourselves playing in the premier league and beyond. Yet, we lived far away from Harare where things happened, worse for others, they did not have relatives in the big city that could accommodate them, but whatever our fate was, we kept doing and working according to the knowledge we had. I had that little privilege of training with other kids in Chitungwiza, sometimes going out to watch Darin T juniors playing. That made me feel like the dream can become real, some of the kids were of my age, all wearing football boots and I felt like that could be the best thing ever happening to me.

Each time I went for those extended school holidays in Chitungwiza, my heart burnt seeing other kids smartly dressed going to school while we were still on extended holidays. During those meaningless stays, we had to find a way to burn the energy we possessed in abundance, so we played a lot of money game soccer, and knockouts, and when tired and fed up with football, we engaged in wrestling matches. That was a lot of precious time wasted. I felt like I would do better given a chance in such an environment with a supply of all things a kid requires. It seemed to me like I had a chance to do both football and athletics if there was a chance for me to begin attending school in Chi-town.

It was a mystery what our father wanted from us. He had complained about Kenzamba, but once we arrived, there was no school or explanation of what we were supposed to do. It was a frustrating and confusing time for us. My Mother regretted ever sending us on that ill-fated holiday.

But the worst was yet to come. The last time my mother came to fetch us, I fell dangerously ill as soon as I landed in Kenzamba. It was a nightmare that still haunts me to this day. I was coughing uncontrollably, my head pounding with intense pain. And then came the nosebleeds, spilling out in a crimson stream. I remember being at home with my eldest sister Vaidah, who looked on helplessly as I suffered. She was in tears, and I could see the fear in her eyes. It was a moment of pure terror, and I thought I might not make it out alive. All day long she stayed agitated and could not eat as I went out to bleed more after every short while. The next day Mom took me to Chinhoyi hospital for treatment, and they gave me cough medication among other things including sleeping pills. When we returned from Chinhoi, I remember disembarking the bus at Gondia 2 which was a distance of 5km, I started coughing as soon as I jumped of the bus, coughing so alarming we had to sit down until coughing subsided.

That was a good 30 minutes of sitting down for everything to calm down, ooh boy I had never coughed that much. My head felt as if it were splitting in the middle, my ribcage ached also because of persistently pushing my lungs during coughing.

This went on and wouldn't relent until Mom was left with only one choice, to take me to a prophet Called Chauruka Bosha leading an apostolic church we used to attend. We went there as a family during the Easter gathering. Then he prayed for me and caused me to vomit, sticking his two fingers down my throat to bring out a small black charcoal like substance without saying anything or explaining anything. That marked the end of coughing, followed by the subsiding of pain everywhere. Whatever he did worked, I was healed.

Chapter 13

Trying to discover myself, alone

With no promise of good fortune or glimpses of change on the horizon in Kenzamba. Life continually showed no mercy, and without proper means to earn a decent life, Mom decided to try life in Gokwe in the Chireya area. I was doing form 2, still hoping to make a breakthrough with education and be a bearer of light to my family. Now Mom in her never-ending research bumped into information that reconnected her with one of her nephews who lived in Chehamba. Once they started talking, he managed to lure Mom to his new home down in Gokwe. I perceived his intention was that we can take a second bite and be his labour force as we did in Chehamba. His name was Uncle Hoi-Hoi. He was one person who seemed closer to Mom. Though I never got to ask Uncle Hoi why he lured Mom to Chireya, my gut feeling tells me he wanted to use us as cheap labour. When we were kids, we spent a lot of time at his place, in turn, he never cared much about how much food we ate, I later realized he saw in us a team of strong workers. I mean we did put in a lot of work in his fields of cotton and maize, and he did not have to pay a cent or buy us anything, only made sure to cook food. I am sure when he invited Mom to come to join him, he felt things would work even better for him now that we were grown up.

Upon deciding to leave for Gokwe, Mom thought it was important that I continue with school undisturbed, so she arranged with one of her nephews who is a businessman, Uncle Foni, an elder brother to Uncle Lawrence the fast runner and brilliant centre-forward at Chehamba primary back in Sachuru. When Uncle Lawrence finished his primary at Chehamba, he was brought to Kenzamba to begin high school there. However, Lawrence did not spend a lot of time at Kenzamba, by the time I went to live with Uncle Foni, Lawrence and his look-alike sister Mavis transferred to another school. Lawrence's sister was beautiful, a look-alike of her brothers especially with that prominent sharp nose replicated in all of them, only different features came with her feminine looks that set her distinct from her brothers, and she too was a fast runner. After leaving Kenzamba they only came during some school holidays.

Ultimately Mom put her plan into action and went down with the rest of the family except for my eldest sister who was now living in Harare. So Mom descended to Gokwe while I began to live with Uncle Foni attending Kenzamba secondary. My uncle owned a shop in the Kenzamba shopping area which stood only five hundred meters from the school, what a blessing and relief from walking the seven kilometres journey back and forth. By this time, I had some sort of independence, my uncle never lived at his shop, only came, and spend a few days each time. My uncle exhibited commitment, a hard worker, a well-disciplined and assertive man with a clear vision. The kind that never shied away from the truth.

Here I was, now with life seemingly letting loose and handing over to me slowly a chance to discover myself and begin to shape destiny. From childhood mommy had always been there and guided me, now I was at this place living with a young lady in her early 20s, her name was Ella and she was my uncle's employee. A young lady she was, older than me, nonetheless a youth, a beautiful one for that matter.

At school I developed a good friendship with some girls in the fourth form, our friendship started and grew slowly that time when I was still new in high school and being called to attend English classes with the O levels, that time when I was without shoes, using my feet to type the ground. Typing was a derogatory term used to describe someone walking without shoes.

Shoes or no shoes a fact remained, undeniably so, that I tried to maintain good looks even in cheap old rags, making sure they stayed clean, walking around with a daring arrogance as if to say, "I don't have shoes so what"?

Despite my ragged appearance, I had a heart of gold that shone through when I was with my friends. Moline Dhakwa and Susan Chimora were two girls who saw beyond my tattered clothes and into the depths of my soul. They didn't care about the negatives that made others shy away from me. Instead, they focused on the positives that made me shine like a star. Moline, in particular, was my closest friend. She never judged me or made me feel uncomfortable. Instead, she embraced me for who I was, flaws and all. It was an empowering feeling to know that my positives outweighed all the negatives, and I had friends who saw the real me. I loved both of them, but Moline grew much closer to me, both were older than me, Susan was more beautiful and lighter in complexion, but she had a boyfriend in the same class. Given a chance, I would have not minded falling for her, but girls were not in my mind then.

When I began living at the Shopping centre with my uncle, it became easier especially for lonely Moline to come looking for me. One thing I never certainly figured out was her position on relationships. I don't remember the two of us ever talking on the subject of relationships, so it was hard to know if she felt ready to be

in love or not. But many times, her comments portrayed she longed for love, sending an impression I had an open cheque before me. So, we kept that subject in the grey, I did not have the courage to engage in that area.

Assuming that she needed to date, then that person wasn't going to be me because I had a lot of factors to undo and many things to put in place before exploring that world. I was not ready for that, and I was younger than her, I realized how tests were beginning to encroach on my territory. Even though I owned nothing, just that mere fact of living with a privileged uncle, running his errands in his absence placed me on the spotlight and other girls thought it wasn't a bad idea to hang around me. But I knew how to stay away from trouble and kept only my all-weather friends.

So, at any time during any free day, Moline would come looking for me, especially on weekends. Whenever she pitched up looking for me, I played hypocritical by trying to ignore her in the presence of Ella. Ella being more mature than me soon noticed a problem and rebuked me, having spotted me with Moline, Susan and Surety, she realized they were all my friends.

On a more honest admission, it was less of hypocrisy than me being me, all my life I had always avoided situations that send people into wrong assumptions, now not knowing how to handle

my friendship with Moline, I thought I could look the other side when she came to the shop but once we stepped out, we became good buddies.

Thanks to Ella for making me realize how I was playing a hypocrite, or let's just say I was a shy person and preferred to keep things to myself. But good old Ella would not have me play hypocrite, she pushed me a step into being a little courageous, and from that day my approach changed, and I started to freely welcome them in front of Ella but only avoided my uncle. I did not want to give him the impression that I was flirting with girls. He was just a strict and straightforward person with a rigid character. This was not the first time I avoided a girl in trying to keep people out of my business.

I recall at one point after bowing to influence or probably being pushed by peers making me feel like I was a coward, and scared of girls, I picked up some courage to show them I can do these things. I singled out a girl that looked better among all that were at my disposal, her name was Tasiana, but she preferred calling herself Betty. Betty was a better name. I think she tried to distance herself from whatever story her real name was trying to address or express. It's true in the African culture and beyond, names aren't just names, but mostly an expression maybe of anger, gratitude, or

jealousy. When I convinced myself, I also wanted to prove to my friends that I could go for a girl and win her, I knew exactly how to go about it.

In the countryside, my approach was simple: I would hang around the borehole or well point, where girls would come to fetch water. This setup was reminiscent of the Serengeti or Kruger national parks during times of water scarcity when the lions would wait patiently at the only remaining water hole, conserving their energy for the inevitable arrival of their prey.

One day, I summoned the courage to walk with Betty halfway towards her home, engaging her in conversation and appealing to her reason. In those days, simplicity was key: one only had to state their intentions plainly and proceed from there. However, the routine was well scripted: it was customary for any girl to decline even if she was interested, and it was expected that the boy would persist. Some of my more mischievous friends would resort to other tactics to infringe upon the girl's personal space. Unlike them, I was a well- mannered boy who intended to reason with Betty, rather than take advantage of her while she carried a bucket of water on her head. Individuals like Tendekai and his crew were known for such behaviour.

As I walked away with Betty, one of my sisters caught sight of us. I was oblivious to what she might have perceived until we arrived home and sat around the warmth of the fire. It seemed that she had assumed I was dating Betty when in reality, I was simply trying to make a move. However, that was enough to put me off pursuing anything further with Betty. I decided to drop the matter entirely

Now coming back to Moline. Because she stayed at school, there were teachers, probably experienced in the business of pouncing on students. Two of them were trying to take advantage and find their way under her skirt, but she came forward a few times narrating to me the attempts. I later understood the school head too had tried one of the O-level students. On one occasion, for reasons I failed to comprehend, the school head, a tall slim guy saw me walking with one shirt button out, he called me, when I stood in front of him with my hands on my hips. The man hammered me with his fist on the chest. I later figured out he considered me a distraction to the girls he was after. These were the kinds of people that bothered Moline, trying to set traps and bait around her.

One black night when dark clouds hung above us threatening to send a storm, I was in the back room at my uncle's shop, wrapping up the day, thinking of nothing but sleeping. Then Ella called out to inform me Moline wanted to see me. Moline had been tricked and baited using another girl who pretended to seek Moline's company at the shops that night.

On that pitch-black evening, Moline realized she had been tricked into a trap and quickly sought a way out wanting to have none of it. That's how she ran away with only me in mind. I was about to sleep and going out into the thick night was the last thing beyond my imagination. Penetrating pitch-black nights was never my thing! That was unlike me. On a night covered by thick clouds threatening to let raindrops, that was a night too black for my liking. I grew up that scared, I had always imagined while penetrating the pitch-black night, being swallowed whole by some gigantic invisible monster. This was a fear that took residency in me after believing the strange stories in which people disappeared after being taken by unknown things.

Moline never knew the level of guts I needed, she had no clue how terrified I was by the night, she never knew that many times we went to Jitis or Church night services as a group, I always made sure to walk in the middle being shielded by others. I had fears of a dreadful monster sweeping through the night to come and steal one of us, and per-chance something like that happened, I tried to position myself that the person didn't have to be me, so to be safe I played safe. Moline without any knowledge of my fears came all the way to cast a challenge at my feet, and silently I was going to find a heart to face my phobia.

When Ella called me, I reluctantly dragged myself into the shop where she was just doing a few things to wrap up her day. Then my eyes landed on a package of surprise wrapped in a figure so familiar to me.

"Moline"! Was my only expression. "Sife, can you go with me home, I will explain along the way"

I studied her face and saw worry written over it, then my mind juggled between, my phobia. Then my mind whispered to me saying.

"If you're this scared Sife, it must be worse for the lady, please go".

After a quick processing in my mind, I turned my gaze to Ella standing there trying to understand what was going on, but there was never going to be an explanation for her because I was already darting my way out through the open double door. Off we dived into the night, daringly arresting my fear, feeling agitated to wrestle any nameless monster. Moline was indeed a special person to me, a rare one who managed to break into my inner circle. And now without objection, I was bracing myself to wrestle any night giant. On our way, Moline drew herself closer to me as a sign of her vulnerability and surprise, surprise, I never felt scared.

For the first time, I felt like "Oh boy I can be brave." I had never considered myself to be that guy on which a girl could base security. I had always felt I was still far from such, but here I was, playing hero, risking for a friend. With all the feelings of short falling gone, we carried on talking on our walk until we reached her place. Just a room at one of the houses on the school premises, she stayed alone, being far from her parents in Alaska Dolomite, a place just outside Chinhoyi, only a stone's throw from the paranormal spot at Chinhoyi Caves. I never got to ask her why they chose Kenzamba when there was a school in Alaska, Chinhoi and Murereka also not too far from the Dolomite.

Before we knew it, we were entering her dark quiet room; imagine if the outside was that pitch dark, what more of the inner room? As we entered she whispered to me the two golden rules to adhere to as long as I was still in the room.

Rule 1, we could only whisper as we anticipated the teacher could return and try to find out if Moline was back. We also did not want anybody to know that I was in Moline's room in the dark on a dark night. Also, for the fear of being caught on the wrong end of things, I could not object to Moline's idea of staying in the dark while keeping voices only to a whisper.

We sat closer one to another on her small bed. My mind strongly told me it was time I take advantage of the given opportunity; I knew Moline liked me too much for a friend, how I knew that? I could tell by the looks, by her never-ending comments that made me feel like I was the most handsome and cool-headed guy on earth, if anything, it felt like she flattered me on many occasions. My only problem, at that point, was not only feeling timid but I wasn't planning to have a girl yet and had not had one before, I could never be certain if Moline really wanted sex with me. But the signs were betraying her willingness to explore.

That evening felt like everything was being presented to me on a silver platter, but a lot of things were racing in my mind.

Having sex was just something that happened in my imagination, at that point in life I wasn't even planning to have it. I tormented myself with many questions that for answers I only afforded a "maybe, maybe not" type of answer. As we sat side by side whispering in the dark, knowing how I had gone past the challenge of protecting a girl in the dark, I now faced a double challenge wrapped in temptations. I felt divided into two halves, and I had to decide faster. One half fighting the other within me, each side trying to convince me to do the right thing. The other side said doing the right thing was to take advantage of the opportunity, the same side also condemned me for being slow and timid, failing to grab the opportunity. That side felt like a new voice within me, and I was highly unsure if I should obey. "Did she run away from another man to me because she was not ready for any men, or she felt ready for me"?

Then the opposing side, another side taking to the podium of my heart, a voice so familiar and natural to me, a side so scared and willing to plead guilty in admission to the timid allegation, and the same respected Moline as a friend, saying, "she came to me for asylum and the right thing would be to leave her alone." Such were the thoughts that competed within me, while this competition raced in my mind, my blood as well was racing and boiling, adrenalin pumping hot.

"What if Moline is thinking the same and waiting for me to take the initiative"? "What if I don't do anything and she walks away disappointed by my lack of action?"

One thing for real was each of us had something racing in our minds, I would never guess exactly. But my imagination wasn't too alien to think she wanted to wrap her arms around me at one point or the other. Other kids of our age were already way ahead in exploring the love world. But I was too innocent, Moline of course never figured out how innocent, how scared, and fair play guy I was.

I had some kind of idea through talking to friends as they time and time came forward bragging in excitement, sharing their experiences while also encouraging me to explore, not forgetting those times I witnessed my friends getting naughty and fondling breasts without consent while the girl carried a water bucket above her with both hands stretched up high to keep the bucket balanced making it look like a perfect surrender position. Those days' phrases like sexual harassment were not so common, in fact, I had never heard it.

I felt like I should hang on until the time ripens when I could do things my way. As for Moline, I don't know what was racing through her mind, but she was thinking something, if not the same. Maybe silently boiling and blaming me for being a coward during those silent moments when it felt like none of us did not have the next discussion to throw into the fray. Without a doubt, the girl admired me that much, having been without a boyfriend.

It's not embarrassing at all to admit I found Moline attractive to my liking, the only wall that stood between us from the look of things was my unreadiness' to enter into the love world. Standing out more for me about Moline were her strong two boobs that stood out dominant like Bozez and Seneh, the two prominent mountains of 1 Samuel 14:4. Each time I looked at them under that tucked white shirt, they provoked me, the message being "dare try us." Moline was undeniably attractive, with a figure that spoke volumes without her even saying a word. Every guy who laid eyes on her couldn't help but feel a stirring in their heart. She had a way of captivating people's attention with her beauty, overshadowing any minor imperfections like the occasional appearance of acne. Although she mentioned her insecurities to me occasionally, I knew that they were just superficial issues that didn't detract from her stunning appearance. As a teenager, she was probably eager to explore the world of love, just like me. But I knew that I wasn't ready for a relationship yet.

Despite my attraction to her, I had other priorities that had to be taken care of first. And so, I kept my feelings to myself and focused on building a strong foundation for my future.

Finally, I felt like I had stayed enough after I had sealed a decision not to touch a friend. I left her house feeling she was safe. My mind was thinking of making a rush ahead of a storm that was threatening to fall at any time. As I left her house that night, walking in the dark, feeling a little terrified by the thickness of the black night.

With that kind of darkness, I could not run as I knew any rushed step could send me tumbling in the rugged pathway, so I took each step with all carefulness while being tormented by mixed feelings. Feelings of losing a prospect of a lifetime. I was just 15-16, this is the time you have these Red-hot feelings that had the ability to control you to the point of going wild. For days I felt like that night needed to repeat. I convinced myself this time I would have the courage to do what I failed to do that night. Nonetheless, Moline and I kept growing much stronger and closer. I would not go a day without seeing her, but a friend she remained. So, our friendship carried on with Susan also in the mix now and then, but time was fast approaching when Moline would finish up writing exams and catch the first early KK bus to leave for Alaska Dolomite.

When she was leaving, we couldn't help embracing each other. It felt like a funeral to me for a few days, I was down. She also shed a tear and gave me the address of her parents' place asking me not to forget her. It felt like she was my first love, but I never knew we were in love. After a month I tried writing to her, but never got a reply, only God knows if she did receive the letter. Susan went on to marry Fungai just after completing their O level.

As to what happened to Moline in life, I never got to know. Even Facebook doesn't seem to know where she is.

During my stay with Uncle Foni, I endeavoured to prove myself as a productive and valuable asset to him. I took it upon myself to handle most of his errands at Chinhoyi Jaggers, much to his satisfaction and approval. I found great joy in assisting him and learning from him in the process. My trustworthiness was well-established, and I executed every task with precision and an astounding degree of innocence. Our living arrangements were pleasant, and my eagerness to help only increased with time. I lent a hand with everything that was required at his grocery shop, eager to be of service. Occasionally, I would venture to Uncle Foni's other shop in St. Cecilia. The journey itself was quite unforgettable--to get there, one had to take a bus as far as Hombwe and then embark on a long, arduous walk in the sweltering heat while carrying large sums of money. The experience of travelling from Kenzamba to St. Cecilia was etched into my memory and remains difficult to forget.

When I stayed with Uncle Foni, I understood the arrangement was temporary and a day would arrive when I would find my way forward. Every passing day meant drawing closer to the expiry of my days. When that day arrived, it came while I was still wondering what my tomorrow would be like, nonetheless, I had to go, leaving with good memories, special memories of my experience, the things I learned. When my time to leave came, I left to join the rest of the family in Gokwe Chireya.

Chapter 14

My brief stay in Gokwe

Before embarking on any new adventure, our minds often race with vivid images of what lies ahead. As I prepared to journey to Gokwe, I couldn't help but feel a sense of unease. The idea of descending into an unknown place was daunting, and I struggled to muster up any excitement. Despite my reservations, my mother's plans left me with few alternatives.

As the journey approached, my nerves only intensified. What would I find in this unfamiliar land? The fear of the unknown loomed large and kept me on edge. I couldn't shake the feeling that something unexpected was in store for me.

Moving to a new place can be an exciting adventure, but my journey to Gokwe was different. I felt broken and unprepared for what lay ahead. As we arrived, my fears were confirmed, and I found myself struggling to adjust to the unfamiliar surroundings. Gokwe was a jungle of the unknown, a place that challenged me in ways I never thought possible. The vast and flat terrains covered in sand made travel difficult and often required long, arduous walks to access basic services. As I looked around, I felt humbled by the resilience of the people who lived there, who braved the harsh conditions every day.

Despite the challenges, I couldn't help but feel a sense of wonder and curiosity about this new world. Gokwe may have been a short episode in my nomadic life, but its impact has stayed with me. Even though I've tried to move on from those experiences, they still linger in my memories, reminding me of the strength and determination of the people living there. I still remember the feeling of dread that washed over me as we arrived in Gokwe. It was like being thrown into a bottomless pit, one where sickness and discomfort were the norm. Malaria was rampant, and the itching that came with the disease was almost unbearable. I'll never forget the side effects of the chloroquine tablets we took to treat it. But it wasn't just the malaria that made Gokwe a challenging place to be. The sheer volume of mosquitoes was mind-boggling. I remember spending a night sheltered on the veranda of a shop, waiting for the bus to arrive the next morning. Even with a light blanket covering me from head to toe, sleep was impossible. The buzzing and whistling of the insects were like a dozen violins playing in unison, drowning out any chance of silence.

The mosquitoes in Gokwe were unlike anything I had ever seen before. It was as if they had evolved to be the ultimate bloodsuckers, with their needle-sharp proboscis that could penetrate through even the tiniest gaps in clothing and blankets. If you made the slightest mistake and left a gap, they were quick to sneak in and feast on your blood. The thought of being surrounded by so many of these insects was terrifying. It was almost like they were waiting to drain every last drop of blood from my veins and risk a cardiac arrest. I'll never forget the feeling of dread that came with each passing night, as we struggled to keep the mosquitoes at bay. It was a constant battle, one that left us feeling drained and wearied.

Life can be a ruthless teacher, and I found myself at the bottom of the pit with no hope of escape. But just when I thought things couldn't get any worse, fate dealt me another blow. I was forced to care for someone else's livestock with no chance of ever pursuing my dreams of going back to school or pursuing sports. It felt like the universe was conspiring against me, trying to rob me of any potential or opportunity that lay within. Dreams, ambitions, and achievements became taboo words, forbidden to even ponder or speak aloud. If I had a chance to write a letter to my father before I was born, it would be short and sweet.

Dear Dad,

As you have decided to bring me to your world. As I enter your universe and prepare to face the world on my own, I have one simple request. Please surround me with other dreamers, kids who share my ambitious mentality and drive to succeed.

I know that as a loving father, it's not too much to ask. You have been blessed with the privilege to work and pave the way for our family's future. And I know that you want nothing but the best for me. So, I ask that you do everything in your power to create an environment where I can thrive and grow into the best version of myself. A place where I can spread my wings and soar to new heights, with like-minded individuals by my side.

I know that the road ahead won't be easy, but with you as my guide and mentor, I'm ready to face any challenge that comes my way.

Together, we can make my dreams a reality.

With love and gratitude,
Your future child.

For me, being surrounded by ambitious kids wasn't about attending a fancy school like Prince Edward High. It was about having the chance to explore different career paths and discover my true passion. I had a dream of becoming a soccer star, among other possibilities, and I was ready to do whatever it took to make it a reality. But instead of living out my dreams, I found myself trapped in a job where I wasn't even paid for my hard work. Each day felt like I was sinking deeper and deeper into quicksand, with no hope of escape.

Nyaunde and Kenzamba were bleak, but Chireya was something else entirely. It was a place where people had settled for less, resigned to a life of despair and hopelessness. Even when presented with an opportunity to better themselves, many turned it down, their minds too trapped in a cycle of poverty to see any other way of life. It's no surprise, really. When you grow up in an environment that teaches you there's no life beyond growing cotton, it's hard to imagine anything else. Growing cotton is never a less important part of the mainstream economy, but it is good to also dream of other things. I knew that there was more to life than what I had been taught, and I was determined to find it. I was always pondering the constant thought of breaking free from the chains of poverty and creating a better life for myself and those around me. Because sometimes, the biggest opportunities are the ones we create for ourselves.

Growing up in an environment that limits your potential can be a real blow to your self-esteem. It's easy to feel intimidated by the mere thought of change. But I knew that if I wanted to break free from the cycle of poverty, I needed to summon a courage greater than anything I'd ever known. I longed to be inspired, to hear from someone who understood what it was like to be a dreamer. But instead, I found myself in a place where nothing challenged me, nothing inspired me. It was as if my spirit had been crushed under the weight of my surroundings. Still, I refused to give up on my ambitions, even though I kept them hidden deep within my heart. But as I looked around at the bleakness of Gokwe, I knew that something had to change. It was then that I realized that the relationship between my mother and Uncle Hoi had reached rock bottom. I felt agitated and disconcerted, unsure of what to do. But deep down, I knew that I couldn't let their problems hold me back from pursuing my dreams.

With the passing of time, we began pressurizing Mom that we at least go back to Kenzamba, and Mom had no choice but to listen. There are many bitter things about Gokwe that I would have loved to say, such as the kind that leaves a bitter taste, and the taste lingers longer. But to cap it all it was a bottomless pit, at least for us, because some residents there had things all put together.

As we lingered in Gokwe, I couldn't help but feel a sense of unease. It seemed that if we stayed there any longer, I would end up like the countless young men in the area - either dead or married early and stuck farming cotton for the rest of my days. As

I looked around, I saw guys my age already settling down with wives and carving out their little pieces of land. While I respected their choices, that was not the life I had envisioned for myself. I had always dreamed of something different, something more.

Don't get me wrong, I admire the resilience and tenacity of many people I see in these communities. I love farming and the rural lifestyle and if I could get a chance to do both, I would. But I have always hoped for a more systematic approach to agriculture and a more modern approach to marriage. I wanted to chart my own path, to make my own choices. And yet, despite these desires, circumstances were pushing me in the opposite direction. It was frustrating and disheartening, to say the least.

But at the end of the day, I recognized that everyone's path in life is unique. Whether it's farming or marriage, there is no one "right" way to do things. What matters most is that we make our choices out of love and free will, not out of obligation or circumstance. So while I may not have ended up farming cotton or marrying young, I still value those choices as important - as long as they are made from a place of genuine desire and passion.

Growing cotton and getting married are wonderful things in their own right, but for me, they represented a path that I simply wasn't ready to take. My difficult childhood had left me with a burning desire to carve out my destiny, to follow my own dreams on my own terms. As a result, I remained steadfast in my stance I wasn't ready to date, let alone get married. Leaving Gokwe and returning to Kenzamba became the only logical choice for me and my family. It was time to go back to the drawing board and figure out where we could go from here.

Despite her best efforts, however, my mother was simply unable to withstand the pressure. In the end, we returned to Kenzamba, unsure of what the future held.

But that uncertainty was also exhilarating. It meant that anything was possible, that we were free to chart our own course and make our own destiny. And while the road ahead was sure to be bumpy and filled with challenges, I knew that our journey would be all the more thrilling for it.

Chapter 15

Resettling in Kenzamba

As we resettled back in Kenzamba, it quickly became clear that life was not going to be easy for our family. Our mother was struggling with health issues, and the weight of responsibility fell on all of our shoulders. We were not kids anymore, life had taught us enough, I was constantly picturing the future and contemplating how to end up there. My sisters were growing up fast, and their thoughts turned to marriage and starting families of their own. Meanwhile, I remained focused on carving out my path in life, determined to make something of myself.

As our family struggles to make ends meet carried on despite waking up and toiling daily, my sister Vaidah decided to take matters into her own hands. She stayed with our dad but would often venture to Harare to work as a housekeeper. It was a tough decision, but one that ultimately paid off. After some time, one of our relatives - Uncle Brian - offered Vaidah a position as a housekeeper in his own home. It was a lifeline for her, a chance I guess to finally breathe a little easier. And so, as Vaidah set off on her new adventure, the rest of us remained in Kenzamba, determined to do whatever it took to make a better life for ourselves and our loved ones.

As the days turned into weeks and the weeks turned into months, my hope of returning to school began to dwindle. It was becoming increasingly clear that I needed to figure out a new path for myself, one that would allow me to learn and grow on my own terms. But with nothing to look forward to and the few belongings we had dwindling, it was hard to know where to start. The few cows that my mother had tried to raise had all vanished in Gokwe.

The one thing that I was able to hold onto was my love for football. I resumed my training with Luke Kachenga, whom I had always looked up to. But beyond that, there was a palpable sense of uncertainty and confusion. Ultimately, I decided to try going back to school - even without fees - that I did hoping to rekindle any glimmer of hope there was. But even that method was fraught with interruptions, leaving me to learn only a few times a term.

Still, I refused to let the hope die, I knew that if I could just find a way to stay in school and continue learning, anything was possible. And so, with grit and determination, I woke up each day to weather the storm.

Then a thought, one that called for courage hit my mind. I scraped hard and raised a bit of money feeling the urge to go and face my father, I can't remember how long it had been since the last time I saw him. I was going to look for my dad and ask for school fees or give him the floor to tell me what he thought our lives should be. Then information came to me that Daddy was no longer living in Chitungwiza Unit M.

My father had sold his house in Chitungwiza, going on to buy a stand in Norton. The reason behind the sale of the house in Chitungwiza was to shame Mom after she mentioned at some point that it was better that house be sold to fund our education, then dad could not wait a moment, sold the house, buy a small residential stand which he did not occupy right away. Dad went on to rent, living in a rented backyard somewhere in Katanga Norton. I had not any slightest idea about where Norton was, and neither did I have all the information on how to find him. I had no proper plan, but seeing my father remained the only thing making sense in my mind, doing this even though I knew it would be an uphill task, I had to try than sink, it was better for me to try than watch my hope drift to the horizon.

Time as always did justice and the day for me to put thought into action arrived. I left for Harare with no excitement, going to Harare alone for the first time, this was a sign of how time had lapsed, and I was not a kid anymore. That excitement and goose bumps I had as a child were no longer happening; it was simply taking a journey while my mind wrestled heavily with the issues at heart.

Back in those days, cell phones were nothing more than a futuristic gadget seen only in science fiction movies. Even telephones were a luxury that most people in Kenzamba and beyond couldn't afford. If you needed to communicate quickly, your best bet was to use the police radio system. But that was reserved for police use only, and civilians didn't have access to two-way radios in their homes. The only way to stay connected was to keep an address book with the contact information of relatives living in the city.

I also had an address book, and it was my lifeline to the outside world. In it, I had my Uncle Brian's home address in the Belvedere neighbourhood, just a stone's throw away from the bustling Harare CBD, overlooking the majestic Warren hills. I convinced myself that finding my father was the key to unlocking a better future for myself.

If I could locate Uncle Brian, I thought. I would also reunite with my uncle Fletcher and, most importantly, my eldest sister who worked as Uncle Brian's maid. I knew that if I failed to find my father, they would still find a way to help me return to Kenzamba.

With these thoughts in mind, I set out on a risky journey. It may sound strange to call a journey to see my dad a risk, but the possibility of a volatile environment loomed large in my mind. Nevertheless, I had no choice but to close my eyes and take a chance.

As I journeyed, I said countless prayers in my heart, hoping for a change of heart and attitude from my father towards me. I knew that school was my gateway to a better future. There were few opportunities for me outside of education, and even my chances of making it in the world of sports were slim away from schools.

Finally, I was in Harare navigating my way in the buzz of the mid- day hype, finding my way to Belvedere for the first time. Remaining calm while feeling a little assured that I would eventually find the place, but it was after much struggle that I found my uncle's house in Belvedere.

I knocked on the back door, which I later learned led to their kitchen. After a few seconds, the door opened, and there I stood, a heap of surprise in front of my astonished sister. She was the one who answered the door, and for a moment, she was speechless. No one in their wildest dreams was expecting me to show up at their door like that, but I did it anyway.

As I sat at the table, struggling to drink the hot tea my sister had given me, I explained my reason for coming – "I needed to find Dad and ask him for school fees." My sister agreed that it was the right thing to do, but we both knew that things could turn sour with my dad. We never knew what he valued or what his reaction would be, but he was still my father. If push came to shove, I had no choice but to gather my courage and face his avalanche of words.

Then my sister gave me important advice, her opinion of Dad was always going to be better than mine because she had mastered how to stand Dad.

"Whatever Dad says, you just do, I don't think he will give you money to go and pay your own school fees."

My sister was under the impression that Daddy might suggest that I come live with him and attend school in Norton, it was something that I also preferred, but only time would tell if my Dad would listen to anything that comes out of my mouth.

In the evening I presented my story to the two gentlemen who listened to it with utmost thoughtfulness. Although they could have helped me, they probably deemed my case tricky, having known my father's approach to issues, they deliberated and reached a consensus to give me money the next day to go look for my dad in Norton with all directions given.

My heart pounded with anticipation as I counted down each passing minute, getting closer to seeing my dad. It was like waiting for the results of a high-stakes test. I knew I needed to summon all my courage and humility to make this meeting a success. Daddy's heart was never agitated even though my life seemed to be falling apart and the future looked bleak.

Despite all the negative factors and the high likelihood of returning in shame, I chose to be optimistic. I clung to the one positive possibility out of a hundred and gave my father the benefit of the doubt. With more than a thousand compelling reasons to turn back, I pressed on pinning my hope on one.

As I set out on my journey, I hoped to find my destination easily, but the address turned out to be incorrect. So, I called Uncle Brian from a pay phone to his house phone, to give him feedback that I did not find the place, he tried to give me new directions, but it was already late, so he bade me return and carry on tomorrow.

The following day I braved myself and took the same courageous journey back to Norton, with new directions. This time I found the house and it was around mid-morning, and the sun was shining.

I eventually found the house with a spike in my heart rate. Approaching the house I knew it was going to be a shock to my unsuspecting stepmom. My appearance unannounced, I prayed in my heart that it not be seen as a disrupter of peace, but even when it looked more like a disrupter of peace, who else would I approach for help? That left me with courage as the only spear left in my arsenal.

Upon arrival, my stepmom welcomed me, and we spoke a little but spent the greater part of the day in much silence, probably because I was naturally a very reserved person and very few people had an idea what kind of stories would agitate me to talk. So, we waited like that until late when my father appeared on the scene.

Before his arrival, I was bracing myself all the while as I sat in silence. Taking inventory of how my Dad was living, at this stage, nothing had changed much as far as living conditions were concerned, truth being said, things looked a bit worse.

I sat there trying to picture possibilities for myself. At the same time giving him the benefit of the doubt, I didn't want to dismiss the possibility of a delightful surprise, if anything, it was that hope for a joyous surprise I had anchored my journey on.

I thought, "Maybe daddy will be glad to see me, perhaps my father misses me and longs to see me like I do. Maybe he will give me the fees or arrange for me to attend St Eric's in Norton. " All these possibilities I had in my mind, understanding that my mother was more than willing to let me go live with my dad seeing that things were becoming heavier and heavier for her. I was also more than willing to transfer and live with my father, I longed for an opportunity for proper and good education, and I longed for an opportunity like such. A change of circumstances was all I wanted; my heart was yearning for one uninterrupted year of school in a peaceful environment. I knew such conditions would help me unleash my potential and begin to dream and be ambitious in setting my goals higher in academics and sport. I considered myself to be a person with potential and a willingness to work a little harder.

I wished, my father with whatever little income he earned, could emulate other people that lived in harmony with their kids. When I arrived at Uncle Brian's, his family looked like an example one could follow, looking at how he was raising his boys, they were in good schools and lived in a good neighbourhood. I knew my father could not afford expensive neighbourhoods, but I was sure loving us was one thing any parent could afford despite what status they have. If someone can't show love towards their own children, it could be an illusion to think the next person can Love and respect your kids on your behalf.

While I sat there waiting for sunset and Daddy's return from work, all I kept praying for was that I find favour before him. But judging from the past, my observation painted a picture where he had no space for us in his new life, I mean over and over his conduct simply spoke volumes. From the days when he pitched up at midnight empty-handed, to the extended holidays among many other things.

As I sat waiting for the clock to tick, my mind was cooking a simple request for my dad - just enough money to pay for one year or at least one term of fees. It was a basic need that most people take for granted, but for me, it was a make-or-break moment. I needed his help to buy some time and figure out a plan for the future.

As the clock ticked down, I felt my nerves wear out. I was glued to my chair, fingers crossed and clenched, hoping against hope that my father would come through for me. I needed him more than ever, but I was also afraid of what he might say.

Finally, after what seemed like an eternity, my father returned from work. At first, he looked surprised to see me, and a little frown creased his forehead. I had hoped he would be glad to see his eldest son, but his expression told a different story. At that moment, I realized that my expectations had been misplaced. He wasn't willing to fake a smile or pretend that everything was okay. I had to face reality - and it wasn't going to be easy.

As my father looked at me with his furrowed brow, I felt a surge of courage welling up inside me. I had taken a huge risk by embarking on this journey alone, without telling anyone. It had been an act of sheer determination, fuelled by my love for my Dad and my desperate need for help. I had braved the elements and overcame countless obstacles to get to this point. I had raised the money through sheer grit and determination, and I was proud of what I had accomplished. I had no other place to turn to and no other Dad to look up to - he was my only hope.

As I looked into my father's eyes, I knew that this was the moment of truth. I had to find the courage and strength to ask him for help, to lay my heart bare and tell him how much I needed him. It was a daunting task, but I was ready to face it head-on.

For a parent, under a normal setting, the pain of seeing a child at the bottom of the class, constantly ridiculed, and derided by other kids, is almost unbearable. Thinking about it brings back all the memories of my own struggles and embarrassments at school - the taunts, the bullying, and the feeling of being an outcast.

I had always longed for my father to be there for me, to offer comfort and support, to be my main source of inspiration and assurance, to be that little voice whispering courage and encouragement. *"Things will get better child"* But time and time, he had let me down. I had fooled myself into thinking that he was the only one who could help me, I was wrong.

It was painful to admit that I had to turn to other people for help and comfort, at least they could offer me a kind word or a whisper of hope. Their encouragement carried me through the tough times, even when my father had mastered the art of breaking my spirit.

But despite all the hurt and disappointment, I was not giving up hope. I kept it burning, hoping that someday, somehow, things would get better. And even if my father couldn't be there for me, I felt in my bones a voice never relenting, and as a result, I would find the strength to carry on.

As I sat there in tense silence, my stepmom briefed my dad on the purpose of my journey. Nervously, I confirmed her words, bracing myself for his reaction. Suddenly, my dad's demeanour changed. He instantly went livid, mounted the podium of doom, unleashing a torrent of rage that left me speechless. Every word and phrase were delivered with a precision that made my blood run cold.

It was clear that he had been drinking, as he often did. In fact, drinking had become his second nature, and to me, I considered him a drunken master in his own right. He had even been known to drink on the job!

Despite his alcohol-fuelled anger, I couldn't help but be captivated by his eloquence. Every word was so well-crafted, so perfectly delivered, that I couldn't look away. It was like watching a master at work, even if that work was fuelled by booze.

If I were to try to enumerate the number of times I saw my father sober, I'd only need the fingers on my right hand. He was rarely without a drink in his hand, and when he was sober, he looked like a completely different person - more like me, quiet and reserved.

The few times I did see him sober, he would sit for hours without uttering a word. And when he did speak, it was always a single word. I almost preferred him drunk, as confusing as that was. At work, he wouldn't lift a finger without taking a drink first. But when he was in his cups, he was a completely different man - jovial, funny, and full of life. It's the only side of him that most people remember. But when dealing with me, he would portray a fierce countenance, like a fierce king on his throne. It was as if he was trying to be someone he wasn't, trying to be tough and intimidating.

In the end, I was left with mixed feelings about my father. He was a man of many contradictions - a jovial drunken master at work, a quiet and reserved man when sober, and a fierce and intimidating father towards me. It was hard to know which version of him was real, but one thing was for sure: he was in one way or the other unforgettable.

If they were any days he and I had a good conversation, all smiling, those days were few and probably overshadowed by the dark days that I hardly remember them. It is this more dominant side, that of anger and bitterness.

That evening in Norton, my father had a lot to say to me. I wished I had somewhere else to turn to for help, but I was stuck listening to his relentless hammering of words. At times, I felt an urge to tell him that I didn't ask to be born, but the thought of saying it out loud to my father made me feel like the earth would swallow me whole, like Datan and Khora in Numbers 16.

My father began by belittling my mother, saying cruel things that made me cringe. He never once acknowledged the hard work and burden she carried in raising us. Instead, he continued his onslaught of words, sounding like an eloquent preacher on the pulpit of doom.

I was trapped, forced to endure his words for what felt like an eternity. At that moment, I felt small and insignificant, like nothing I could say or do would ever make a difference. It was a night I would never forget. I felt completely overwhelmed by my father's words. I couldn't bear it any longer.

After more than an hour of his relentless preaching, my father finally gave some money to my younger sister and brother, Caroline and Khumbulani, and sent them off to buy more beer from the pump. "Go get me more beer," he said, "I want to talk to this person."

Those words - "this person" - stuck with me more than anything else he had said that night. It was as if he didn't even see me as his own flesh and blood, but as some sort of outsider he was forced to deal with.

At that moment, I felt like I was drowning in a sea of emotions. I was angry, hurt, and confused all at once. But most of all, I felt like I didn't matter to my own father. It was a feeling that would stay with me for a long time, a reminder of the painful reality of my relationship with my father.

My father was making efforts to get himself more intoxicated for him to talk to me, and he called me "this person" my father. It made him so angry that I had come to him for help when all the things in my life were crushing, I failed to understand how he would prefer that I suffer than come to him. I was not quite sure what my father's plan was, but to me, it looked clear he did not want to help me, I am still surprised by a certain level of hypocrisy that my dad exhibited, how he would welcome my cousins and help and accommodate them, if you ask any of them, they only have these nice things to say and remember about him.

That evening, when it became clearer that all my dad was going to do, was venting his anger. I finally decided, braved the night, and went back to Harare. When I returned to Harare, I saw expressions of displeasure on the faces of all the people in the house. I mean, it probably defied all logic that my Dad had shouted at me and I had failed to withstand the relentless hammering from him, it's an ugly part of history, and nevertheless, it happened.

The thought of making another journey to Norton made my stomach churn. I knew it would be a fruitless endeavour - my father had made it clear that he didn't care about my education or my future. I remembered how he would deliberately skip me when buying clothes for my siblings and cousins, and how he would keep us out of school for weeks on end without a second thought.

Despite their suggestions, I refused to make the journey the following morning. I knew it would only lead to disappointment and frustration. I had learned from past experiences that my father didn't value my education or my well-being, and I wasn't about to subject myself to his callous treatment again.

As much as it hurt to accept, I knew that I was on my own. I was left at the crossroads of opinion, to either give up any pursuit of a better life or forge my own path and close my eyes to the difficulties I would encounter.

I had made up my mind I was going back to Kenzamba, even if it meant returning empty- handed. I had no money for the bus fare, but I was determined to make it happen. That's just the way I was raised. Whenever I felt a burning desire in my heart, I knew I had to find a solution, no matter how tough it might be.

With a steely resolve, I left Belvedere without telling anyone where I was going. My sister might have guessed since she knew me better than most. But everyone else tried to push me to go back to my father, and I said nothing. I walked all the way from Belvedere to town, knowing exactly what to do to find my way back to Kenzamba. Thanks to my Mom, who had taught me about government institutions that could help in times of need, I made my way to the social welfare office in Harare. They didn't hesitate to offer me a form, I used to board the bus from Mbare Musika, which is the biggest bus terminus in the country, from there I took my gloomy journey home.

As I arrived home, my stomach growled with hunger. I had no money for pink creamed candy or even a freezit to cool my throat from the scorching sun that beat down on me with unrelenting force. It was a rude awakening after my journey of shame.

But it wasn't just the hunger that gnawed at me. It was the realization that no one was willing to stand up for me, not even those who saw the way my father treated us. I had hoped that someone, anyone, would be willing to sacrifice even a single term of payment to buy us some time to figure out what to do next. But it seemed like I was on my own. I understood it also when I lived with Uncle Foni, knowing that he was indeed helping me with accommodation, and in turn, I did for him tons of errands that he would have hired other people to do. I tried my best to be a good kid, withstanding any peer influence. I felt a little useless many times, failing to see what my life would amount to. It was now only a matter of letting time do justice and reveal if indeed I was useless. I felt so ashamed having taken that long trip in confidence only to get humiliation in return, it felt like nobody understood my tribulations.

Mom decided to say nothing and neither did she push me to tell her how things transpired when, but I told her in not so many words and I avoided looking her in the eye because I didn't want her to read me and get hurt, however, she knew I was hurt judging by how she chose not to press me for information. She waited for me to normalize and come forward with information in bits and pieces.

Okay, I was back empty-handed. What was I to do? If anything, how about gambling back my way to school without fees? Now we had reached a point we knew Mom had fought a good fight and we now had our lives before us, that was true mainly for me and the two big sisters. At this juncture, Mom needed our help more than her doing anything.

Mom's health was at this point not up to scratch anymore. I remember one night while Granny was still alive, we all woke up in the middle of the night to go and call Granny, because Mom had gotten so sick complaining of pain in the chest. It's a night we all remember, it was my first time to see such a thing, none of us knew what to do but only stand helpless and terrified while she agonized. This incident happened after she returned from Mhangura where her sister and brother-in-law lived, that brother-in-law being a traditional healer gave her some herbs to drink, but everything went wrong the night she took some of those herbs before going to sleep, that was the same night we awoke to pandemonium, it was painful to watch her in so much agony. Thank God she recovered from a near heart failure, but from that time her health was never up to scratch.

My eldest sister couldn't take the heat of living with our Mom's no-nonsense way of life, so she made the bold decision to move in with our dad. But it wasn't long before my second sister followed suit and left us too. She headed back to Guruve, where she started living with our grandma. It wasn't that she didn't want to go to our Dad - he had actually disowned her for reasons beyond our understanding. Perhaps it was a clash of attitudes or maybe it was due to my Dad's own emotional issues.

My sister had always been a wild child with an untameable spirit. She was always at odds with someone, often getting into running battles with boys. My sister had always been a force to be reckoned with. When she was younger, she got into fistfights with boys for various reasons, and as she grew older, her issues only got more complicated. But no matter the situation, she always managed to pull off a surprise move that left everyone stunned. She was a true wild card, and you never knew what she was going to do next.

My father, who was driven by a similar spirit, often took things to the extreme. But it was all good he had a younger brother who had learned how to endure his shouting fits. Despite the threats of manhandling, my uncle remained calm and always returned a smile. There were times when he felt like his brother was doing too much, but he knew better than to answer back. Instead, he would quietly slip out and wind down while sipping on a cold Coke at any place people could hang out. Even when my uncle was staying away, he never stopped visiting my father. The bond between the two of them was unbreakable. My father made it a requirement for him to visit, and if he stayed away for too long, my Dad would wait for him to come back and rebuke him for not visiting sooner. My uncle, however, never bothered to explain himself. Instead, he simply smiled and found a way to move away from the subject. But my father foreseeing his brother's intent to change the subject would remind him.

"When you take off your shoes, give them to your son," my father would say, pointing at me. "He'll polish them for you."

My father complained that my uncle never polished his shoes - the same crime he accused me of. He always made a comparison between my Uncle and me whenever he talked about my shoes. And one thing about my father is at times he seemed to glory in embarrassing people. He was never diplomatic in the way he spoke, under normal circumstances one would expect that he calls someone privately and settle matters, Daddy wasn't like that, and he was always ready to take you on any time. There were times when my father took things too far, it was this brother who used to step in and neutralise things, and when my daddy announced he wanted nothing to do with my second sister, he cast the responsibility on the shoulder of his brother.

But one thing remained, it was hard to understand what my father wanted and why he reached that point. So at home, my sisters were now all away while I still carried on in Kenzamba. At this point, my interest towards school had diminished after a failed attempt to go back without paying any fees. Then my second sister Zodwa who at the point was living with granny returned from Guruve with the news that she was getting married, so it was important that Mom and I be there. I also received the news with gladness and could not wait to step on my feet again in the land of Guruve after many years away.

The word from my father was a continual reaffirming of his position, he wanted nothing to do with it, hence his young brother oversaw the formalities.

After more than a decade, I finally set foot back in Guruve - a land I hadn't visited in over 10 years. I wondered if any debts were still owed from my past, but I hoped that time had erased any mistakes I made in my kindergarten. As I walked through the plain, I couldn't help but wonder if the memories of the incident where I charged at my friends with a stone before leaving were still fresh in their minds. But alas, it was now a laughable incident, time had done justice and erased any bitter memories, and we were all grown now. The memories of that incident still lingered in my mind, but each time I thought of it, I couldn't help but laugh at my own arrogance. "What was I thinking that day?" I often asked myself. But now, I was ready to make amends and reconnect with the people of Guruve.

My arrival turned out to be a delight for my granny. Without the front teeth, she spread her lips as wide and gave a generous smile, from time to time spreading the impression that this was the day she had waited all her life, I was back, a grown eighteen-year-old boy with a calm demeanour.

For me, the encounter was a little emotional, if I was to be a little honest, I had mixed feelings and perceived it was worse for my mother. It seemed a delight to every relative to see me after many years of being away. I took notice of many grinning faces, nonetheless, I returned those smiles with a heavy heart especially when I could read my mom's mood. At this point my grandma wasn't very old, only had a back problem. One other thing I took notice of was how upon seeing me, every other grandchild seemed not to matter in the eyes of my grandma, nonetheless, no matter how much all our relatives would smile, the truth was, our lives were in a mess and needed more than smiles to get back on track.

The following day all the marriage arrangements for my sister went accordingly and without delay, Mom had to take a journey back alone while I stayed behind with the hope of resuming school. This was my mom, at any time she was willing to let us go and get united with our people, so when my father harboured bitterness that we were living with Mom, it failed to hold. Mommy was not selfish; she was willing to let us be away from her in order to pursue a life hoping for a better tomorrow for us.

When Mom returned to Kenzamba, I stayed behind for a reason, so that I could try to find a way back to school, because in Kenzamba, I had completely stopped attending and my mind was beginning to get tired and distancing myself from things to do with education.

After my mother left for Kenzamba, I felt lost and alone. My heart kept telling me to pay a visit to the place we once called home, to track my footsteps back and try to re-route. It had been the site of my most vivid childhood memories, the place where all our troubles began.

One day, I decided to listen to my inner voice. Making sure I was alone, I took a walk to the place we used to call home. Of course, it wasn't home anymore - just a desolate place with two heaps of dirt where our two houses once stood. Everything was destroyed, and the only thing that remained was a prominent feature: the grave of my aunt, Augustine's mother. His brothers called her Perisa, short for Priscila. As I stood there looking at her grave, I couldn't help but feel a sense of sadness wash over me. It was a reminder of all that we had lost, and all that we had been through. But it was also a sign that life goes on and that we must find a way to move forward despite our past.

Returning to that place was a crucial step for me. The last time I had been there, the houses were still standing, etched into my mind's eye with vivid clarity. But with each passing day, those images had become increasingly fragmented and faded. So, it was essential for me to return and update my memories of the place.

And I'm so glad I did, because now my mind holds two distinct pictures of that special spot.

As I stood there alone, surrounded by the ghosts of my past, I couldn't help but feel a sense of melancholy. But even in the midst of those bittersweet memories, I knew that I was at peace with my soul. Recalling the moments of my childhood spent in those now-destroyed two structures, I tried to resurrect their images in my mind's eye.

I conjured up the memory of my Mom's standalone bedroom, a place that held great significance for me. Behind it was a spot where I used to play alone, a place where I could be free and imaginative. I fondly remembered how I used to heap soil while talking to my imaginary friends, Foniken and Randken. Looking back on those moments, I couldn't help but smile. With each passing moment, I felt as though I was reconnecting with a part of myself that had been lost. And even though the houses were gone. While standing there my mind was quickened to the days, I would sneak into the bedroom looking for the hidden cane of condensed milk.

Lastly, I found myself smiling when I turned my focus to the mount where the round hut once stood, it was from inside that same hurt that one-day Mom returned from gathering fired wood to a surprise, shockingly so when she saw her beloved son sitting with a pan-full of sugar dissolved in water after a failed attempt at making sweets. Then I burst into laughter alone when I remembered another incident when Mom was away and I was home alone, then passed by one uncle called Rinzwell, Uncle Rinzwell loved smoking home-grown, letting smoke sink in before letting it come out in puffs while talking, once he got high, he loved eating, so on that day he said to me; "Sifelani, take a pan and start roasting maize corn, make sure you fill that plastic dish, I am coming back soon okay" he instructed me pointing to a small dish sitting there. So as a loyal child, I started doing that until the small dish was almost full, that's a lot of maize for one person, in fact, more than enough for 10 people. Then Mom returned and could not believe it when I told her, and worse when the uncle never returned, Mother was very upset.

Standing there for what seemed like an eternity, I caught the attention of my granny, who was watching me from a distance. It had been twenty long minutes, and I was still lost in thought, lost in this place that held so many memories of my father's love. It was here that I hoped to start a new chapter in my life, to mend the broken pieces of my heart, to win back my father's affection, and to rekindle love and luck. But returning to this place didn't mean everything would be fixed overnight. My father's bitterness towards me still lingered, fuelled by his belief that I preferred to live with my mother. I was determined to prove him wrong, to show him that I was willing to make amends. However, being back here did not guarantee that I would be reunited with my father or receive his support immediately.

For the first year, I stayed with his brother, but it wasn't a long-term solution. Eventually, I moved in with my grandma, who was overjoyed to have me with her. It was a fulfilling experience, and I cherished the memories of spending time with her. Though my father's love remained elusive, I had found a new source of warmth and affection in my grandma's embrace.

Chapter 16

School again

Soon I joined Actor, my cousin who was 2 years older than me, he was the eldest son of Uncle Fletcher. Actor was a clever cousin of mine, and together we began to attend school at Nyamhondoro secondary in Guruve, Actor having written his O level at St Phillip's Magwenya, decided to go back and redo, after failing the exams.

It's difficult to articulate my experience in Guruve without simply recounting it in full. It is in Guruve where I spent two memorable years attending Nyamhondoro Secondary School, and if I'm honest, the experiences left a bitter taste in my mouth.

Coming from a tight-knit community, I had always longed to be reunited with my father and be among my people. I had hoped that the people in Guruve would be my kindred, but I soon realized that I was mistaken. The reality was that many of the people I call relatives only added to my pain and struggles.

Despite the hardships, there was a silver lining. I did not become an alien, in the end I found solace in the one person that my Mom had always warned me about, my grandma. She provided the comfort and support that I so desperately needed, and I will always be grateful to her for that.

Looking back on my time in Guruve, I know that it was a challenging period in my life. But I also know that it taught me valuable lessons about perseverance, resilience, and the importance of family. And while the memories may still be bitter at times, I'm grateful for the experiences.

My Mom considered grandma as one of the people at the forefront of the influence that led to her ultimate divorce from daddy, so when mom left me in Guruve, she was not for the idea that I live with grandma. Despite their differences, the two had love towards me. For the first time in a while, I felt loved and valued I felt loved by someone who wasn't my mother. I also became a person Granny found easier to live with, I became a darling to her heart and she could not help but express her joy.

It's not an unusual thing to find comfort in a grandma, in my case I have to count myself fortunate that I got a chance to see and experience the love of my grandma, but I had to go through a torrid period before granny took me into her arms.

Initially, I resided with other relatives who harboured animosity towards me without any apparent reason. Despite my best efforts to please them, I seemed to have fallen out of their favour. To my dismay, they had no accusations against me. Upon reflection, I realized that I had become a victim of past controversies. The remnants of events that transpired before my birth had craftily infiltrated the family, leading to an irreparable strain in our family relationships. Because of these things, I lived through a memorable time, how can I forget Living on one small meal every day, eating only in the evening after school? These things happened during the time I opted to live with other relatives instead of grandma.

I never knew people would dislike me when I had done nothing wrong, even without any bad report, I realized some people can highly dislike you beyond what you can ever imagine. Unbeknownst to me, there existed established boundaries that had been put in place long before my arrival. These boundaries were not meant to be transgressed, but unfortunately, no one had informed me of their existence. Consequently, upon my return, I inadvertently crossed those invisible barriers without even realizing it. In contrast, my cousin Actor had a keen understanding of these boundaries and had developed an astute sense of caution when navigating familial relationships. It is likely that he had learned to navigate these invisible lines with great care and precision.

Here is the long story short. Actor was the son of uncle fletcher, meaning his Dad and mine were brothers, not half-brothers as in certain cultures, that means Actor and I were more like brothers in our culture than cousins according to foreign cultures.

Actor and I had two grannies because his father and mine were born to two different women but shared the same father. To bring it much closer, Actor's granny and my grandma were siblings, both ladies had children with our grandpa. It was because of the friction and controversies around two siblings clashing for one man that led to eternal tensions. I had no good knowledge of all this, and when I returned back among them, I loved everyone and felt free to visit all relatives or be with them, but in doing this I walked through barricades that were being extended to new generations.

My grandfather died while my father and Aunts were still young. But he failed to close that rift before he died. When he was gone, the two sisters each went away and marry the man of their choice, but the rift was never closed, time failed to heal the pain and it also failed to quench hatred.

In my context, I consider these to be subliminal issues of the inner room, and I usually don't willingly open cans because they house worms. Nonetheless, upon observing the whole drama, I concluded whatever drama went around was not great for my father and his young brother. However, despite the drama or lack of it, I commend one beautiful thing between the two brothers, it was a thing of beauty how they maintained a strong bond when their mothers would have loved to keep them separated like the way I was being pushed away by other relatives that identified with Actor's grandma. The two brothers share one father, and different Moms and those Moms were siblings, it was as simple as that and not alien to our society. I think they felt like there was nothing to divide them, most probably because their Moms were sisters and for that reason, they became inseparable growing much closer than any factor could separate them, not even the freaking of my father.

My father and his two sisters, Auntie Priscila/Perisa and Chipo all grew up under the care of a stepdad. The stepdad was a good man, Edmond Kamutseta, he was one rare figure who raised my dad like his own and went on to briefly live with me that time I lived with grandma. You do not meet people like him daily.

Now to understand my fate well, when I started school together with Actor, at that time I was living with his father while Actor preferred staying with his granny so that he could attend a school closer to his grandma.

Growing up I considered my uncle more than an uncle, this understanding is not unique to our family but it's prevalent even among my mother's family, so while I spent my childhood away from my father's side, I was groomed under the same values. I could have lived with Grandma from the beginning but I couldn't do that because Mom before going back had expressed unhappiness over the prospect of me staying with Grandma, so I did as per my Mom's wish, a wish that came out of her emotions, Mom had it in her bitter memories that my grandma had a hand in the collapse of her marriage with my dad, for that reason Mom felt everyone else was a lesser evil compared to my grandma. Also, I later realized that mom's enemies according to her would automatically be her children's enemies, but little did I know that I was entering into old controversy.

When school commenced, Actor and I lived with her grandma nearer the school while returning back to my uncle during weekends and school holidays. I liked the arrangement, after all, we were brothers, and the people we lived with were not strangers but relatives, I innocently went there, and it was all well with me first term. Our stay at that place proved an advantage because grandma was very limited in mobility, so in the morning, first thing before we leave for school we would go into her field and do some work, me, Actor and Addie, her other grandson from her daughter. Before taking the weekend's journey back to see my grandma, we would also work in the field early morning.

Over time I realized each time I went for weekends I would proceed to go and see grandma, Actor would stay behind at his father's place, but it never bothered me. Then, whenever I would visit my grandma, she expressed her displeasure and asked several times if all was well and I told her I was happy, she would go into deep thought, I thought she only wanted me closer, nothing wrong with that, but I felt it was too much of a burden for me to walk that long stretch when there was an option to live closer to school, after all, we were one people. I never heard grandma comment negatively, only once in a while she emphasized how it was the right thing to live with her.

One other reason it did not dawn well to live with her was how it seemed to me like a burden to his husband who raised my father, now it did not feel alright to come and live with him also seeing my dad did not send any support or assistance during my stay. When the school term ended and we were about to go on holiday, I was called and told not to return when school resumes, only me! And the given reason sounded like a joke. I could not believe being told: please don't come back because we don't have relish.

What would I do besides abide by the verdict, I only listened and simply said, "Alright" Of course I was troubled, and got to think about it a little deeper, I did not ask Actor a thing, but for some reason, he decided to open up as we went our way, and what he told me discouraged me further, I was troubled.

Now I had some answers to certain little things. I was affected yes, but, just like every other thing I faced before, I simply brushed it aside and refused to be broken down, I focused on what was coming ahead. I knew worry or bitterness would not be of any positive help, but to some extent, I blamed myself for not thinking things through, nonetheless, life went on. I was going back to live full-time within the original living arrangement. In this arrangement I only agreed to please Mom, but deep within I did not feel great about it.

When Mom spoke to my uncle's wife I was there, she said all was well, but I am not entirely astonished by people who say yes to something they do not like. I should have probably had a voice and said my opinion, but I held back so that mom would allow me to stay behind and attend school.

My uncle's personality besides being such a cool person, a calm gentleman in good-looking suits, is one person I never heard shouting or freaking out for any reason. Even though I commend his character, I find him also to be very passive, preferring autopilot, keeping quiet to the point of not correcting certain wrongs and not pushing and edging kids or shaping them for the future. His passion was for game meet, nobody could beat him when it came to looking for game. Making a trip every Friday after work from Harare to Guruve.

After the school holiday, I knew I was going to be living far from the school. Grandma was still displeased that I had not made up my mind to stay with her. For a moment I carried on going to school, now walking that long 7km distance which in itself was not a problem but a norm, not only to me but to other kids from the same area. It wasn't so long before I realized again, that I was at the wrong place, my struggle at this juncture escalated to another level, taking another ugly face that I did not picture coming. It is not an exaggeration to say for a long time I would only have a small evening meal, and life was tough.

It's a frustrating feeling when people are inhospitable towards you for no apparent reason. I've experienced this before, and it's truly baffling when no one can give a reason for their dislike towards you. It's even more frustrating when you've done nothing to provoke anyone. In my case, I found myself in the wrong place at the wrong time. It was a situation that I had no control over, but

I ended up being the target of unwarranted hostility. Despite my best efforts to understand the situation, no one could provide a valid explanation for their behaviour towards me. It was not an easy situation to be in, but it's important to remember that their behaviour is not a reflection of who I was.

At this juncture, food became an important thing to me than at any time. There was food in the food storage and containers of people I lived with, but they settled for allowing me to eat properly, so all my school days I would eat only a small evening meal. This forced me to go to my sister's place at weekends. If I couldn't go to her place, I would linger around the home of any relative until they cook and I would eat, while sometimes I would go to grandma who repeatedly noticed how I was getting thin. Some Saturdays I visited my sister at Disi farm, and life went on for a while like that. I wasn't lazy to get up early morning and do a quick meal for myself before leaving, the fact of the matter was, I was denied that opportunity.

I remember those first days when I would wake up around 04:00 and prepare porridge without sugar, only salt, just to give me that energy to carry through the day, I did that because I had only mealie meal, salt and water at my disposal. But that was soon going to change because soon all the salt and the maize meal was being taken to the bedroom every evening, so when I awoke the other day thinking its business as usual, things had changed, and I had only access to water. It was at that moment that I realized things were very bad beyond my imagination, I had no idea what I was doing was so displeasing to such a point. I was probably considered a parasite. What a way to deliver a message home, and the message did reach home.

I had no option but to carry on attending school every day on an empty stomach. I remember there were days, especially hot days when I would feel hungry and powerless. Under such circumstances, you don't even feel the energy to hang around and make friends. Any food that I could find on the ground became tempting.

Chapter 17

Living with grandma

Finally, the point came where I decided to do what was good for me, which was to leave and go to Grandma.

That move solved my hunger problem instantly, starving became a thing of the past. Soon I became nourished and in a short time there was a noticeable difference in appearance. Sad to say while I was going through all this, my father never cared to check on me. With him, it was all well as long as I still had breath within me. What I wore or ate did not bother him in any slight way. From the time I arrived to the time I went on to live with Grandma, my father never bothered to buy me clothes or shoes, nor did he pay for my school fees while I was there. Sad to mention that the only fees he paid for me at this school were only the initial school fees just after the marriage of my sister. I had the worst shoe at school, falling short of going without.

One morning while Actor and I were preparing to go to school, I was trying to put together my broken shoe, stitching it using a sharp strong wire with a hook. Something went wrong in my rush to catch up with time, so the sharp wire slipped and dug deep into my left thumb. Actor saw it and wanted to violently pull the thing out but I protested knowing what damage that could cause, I only managed to pull it out after two hours. Then I finished my shoe before following him to school.

I had so much hope in my dad, nonetheless, he never cared to think of my needs. So, I continually visited my sister at Disi where she stayed with her husband, she was always good to me back then, apart from her and Grandma, there were other people I could share a joke with and talk and engage at different levels. In a world where partiality seemed to be the norm, there were a few people who stood out for their fairness and generosity. One such person was my Uncle Leonard. I remember going hunting with him and a group of elders at night, using a borrowed rifle. Despite being the only young man among them, I was unfairly allocated a smaller portion of the spoils. Uncle Leonard noticed this and said nothing, but he didn't forget. Eventually, he bought a rifle and took charge of distributing the spoils. This time, he made sure that I received an equal portion. It was a small gesture, but it made a big impression on me. It showed me that there were people in this world who valued fairness and were willing to stand up for what was right.

Uncle Leonard was also one of those people who showed me kindness and hospitality. Whenever he came back from Harare, he would invite me to his place for a meal. It was a welcome respite from the challenges of everyday life. In a world where partiality can seem like the norm, it's important to remember that there are people who value fairness and kindness. Their actions inspire us to be better and to strive for a more just and compassionate world. As for my father, this time I wondered why he would not care to help me. Despite all these things, I continually sought to get closer to him, but things remained the same.

I was just a school kid without any income to buy things for myself and there were no opportunities to talk about. I carried on silently not knowing what the future held, but despite everything trying to put me down, something within me gave me the energy to carry on every day, even though things were that bad, something from within me kept my hopes alive, every passing day I felt like I had the potential to do well. Then a surprise came when I was doing form four, after I had failed to register for final exams because I had no birth certificate, Dad sent a message calling me to come and see him in Norton. Surprisingly he gave me money to go and fetch Mom, my sister Sheba, and my young Brother Mandela. That came to us all as a surprise and we wondered what brought that, maybe it was my staying in Guruve that did the undoing.

So, I travelled to Kenzamba and brought the three to Guruve where my father also came and together we all went to the registrar general for birth certificates. For the first in many years, Daddy was calm, and sober in the presence of Mom, there was truly a tide of change. My brother and sister got theirs at once while mine because of my age, had to delay as I had to follow a process and fill out some forms to be sent to Harare for clearance before coming back in a month. It was all well with me. It felt like at long last I had managed to tread on the soft side of my father, what a victory it felt for me. To have him acting in our favour, asking Mom to come, having to go and meet without incident.

I have learned to wait in life, many times I have become impatient a let go of opportunities, and it took me almost a lifetime to realize that most of the things I thought were not for me only needed patience. With me everything gets delayed, even the simplest things that others get on a click of a button, somehow, I find glitches along the way, it took the Bible to help me learn that at times even when things have been given, granted, obstacles still come your way to try and offset your course.

When we finished O level at Nyamhondoro, I was still without a clear plan, only a willingness to change things, causing me to feel like everything in my life was not moving at all.

Chapter 18

Living with daddy

Then I thought of imposing myself into my father's life. One day I took a bus to Norton with the hope of seeking opportunities. I understood from what I witnessed the time Daddy called me, I knew it was not going to be any glamorous, I knew there was no room for me at my father's place, and things looked tough for him for one reason or another. Dad was living in a very small cottage and everything was crammed in there with kids and our big sister. I wondered why things were like that for my dad, he had always been working before we were all born. Was it possible that his addiction to beer played a lot in the way things became? If the answer is yes, then beer is a great evil than I imagined.

Daddy was not dumb, he was intelligent with a razor sharp mind, I will always remember him as that man with some outstanding natural abilities that many of us will always wish for. My father had natural intelligence, I don't know if there was any math he could not work out, any kind of math at every level, taking very little time to figure the math out and work a solution. Intellectually, he would do in minutes without practice, the things that many of us need time to study and probably fail. In a few words, he encouraged me to read anything that I lay my eyes on, a short lesson I took seriously and from the day he spoke those words I tried increasing how I read. Each time I remember his intellectual abilities, I wonder how many aspiring academics would cross the ocean to acquire the kind of brain retention he possessed.

But in life application, I failed to understand why things failed to reflect what he possessed inside. Dad was one of the first lucky people to get a house in Unit M in Seke while my Mom was still around. I still have very faint memories of my childhood days there. I know during those days before Mom decided to take that one-way ticket to go and settle in Guruve and venture into farming, my parents had bought stones, sand, etc. with the intention to build.

When I came back years later during those long school holidays, the sand and the stones were still there and the house which stood by the conner only 2 streets from St Aidens Primary, stood out prominently as the only house not extended, and it stood like that until my father sold it. I failed to figure out why life kept pushing Daddy to the peripheries, I wasn't sure if it was spiritual or his drinking habits or both. I wondered if it was possible for spiritual darkness to influence or drag someone into destructive behaviour. Those days I remember when we went to visit him and spent time with him even unto extended holidays, how we longed to also have at least a black and white TV, many other houses were already upgrading from black and white TVs to colour ones, with some already installing satellite TV. My father could not get one for us, hence we used to travel to my auntie Chipo to watch Wrestling. I honestly think there are certain demons that torment people for reasons that only God knows.

Now he was in Norton, I went there to try and stay with Dad, but there was no room for me to sleep. I was fortunate to find Uncle Charles. Charles is one of the sons of my grannie's brother, he was renting a one-roomed cabin. My father arranged for me to sleep at Charles's place, it was all good, I had to stick to the arrangement while figuring out what to do next with life. I remained ambitious, but I needed a way to begin. I had not surrendered my dream to be a footballer, at all times I was in constant preparation, even in Guruve I maintained my fitness and work with what I had at my disposal.

I tried to speak with Daddy several times, and during those discussions, he seemed to like the idea and he would express it: "You know son, white people are good at supporting any career their children chose." Despite having that understanding it was very clear that my father was not willing to support me in buying soccer kits, I was not asking for continual support, only a once-off thing to do.

From those conversations I could tell the man was not ignorant to how things work, he knew what was expected of a parent for his child to succeed. Away from sports, I looked forward to him for some guidance thinking he could be having other ideas, maybe to go and study at night school or some private college. My father's suggestion was one that I never saw coming, the only thing he had in mind was that I go and be a security guard. I realized he had no intention to spend a cent on me. I felt diminishing in value, "was my push worth the trouble"? I passively protested my father's suggestion, a suggestion that gave an impression he had wanted to see me earning any amount anyhow as a way to shake off responsibility.

My dad was not willing to do anything for the lost years, I was still willing to study, or at the least a little support in my quest to become a sportsperson. I kept on trying my chances in spot because it seemed like a field that could uplift me in a short while.

A few months down the line, only two from the time I came to Daddy if I recall well, I became sick and lost much weight that a lot of people expressed their astonishment. While I was still unwell my father began to also complain of stomach pain, then the leg. I never guessed how far that same sickness was going to push him. When my father fell ill, we were all hopeful for a quick recovery, but unfortunately, it turned out to be something more serious - a hernia. As the days passed, his condition remained unchanged, and we began to feel concerned. In the midst of this uncertainty, I decided to move to Harare and live with my uncle Fletcher and Actor, as I believed it would provide me with more opportunities. Nonetheless, I made it a point to visit my father every weekend, despite the long and tiring journey. As time went on, my father's health continued to deteriorate, and he was eventually forced to stop working. This was a significant alarm for my auntie Chipo, who loved her brother dearly. She suggested taking him to a traditional doctor for alternative treatment. Due to my stepmom and auntie not getting along, I was the one who accompanied my father to my auntie's place, playing caretaker along the way. We faced numerous challenges during the journey, due to using public transportation and helping my father get in and out of each bus was challenging.

It's heart-breaking to say that my father's hernia surgery was scheduled, but due to the ongoing doctors' strike in our country, it was postponed indefinitely. This left us feeling helpless, and we began to explore alternative options, including seeking spiritual intervention, which I knew very little about. My father was in excruciating pain, and it was evident in every step he took. As his caretaker, I was the only one who could assist him, despite still recovering from my own illness. On a personal level, this was a challenging time for me because my father, who had pushed me away during childhood, was now opening up his heart and allowing me to be by his side.

During this difficult time, I felt a renewed sense of hope that I could finally build a deeper connection with my father. I yearned for more meaningful conversations with him and felt a strong desire to do everything in my power to help him. Unfortunately, I felt helpless as I lacked the means to provide the level of care that my father needed. However, I did what I could, and I remained determined to be by his side every step of the way.

It was during these trying times that my father revealed a side of him that I hadn't seen since I was six years old. He drew me closer, and we had meaningful conversations that left me feeling grateful for what seemed like a renewed connection. His discussions had in them a substantial element of respect making me wonder if he had forgotten it was only me he was talking to, many times he expressed a great concern about how reserved I remained at all times. He wanted to see me talk more and open up, breaking myself free from my self-incarcerated cocoon.

He relayed to me a lot of family history, not much about his dad, but much about how he grew up, his brothers and sisters and all the names of the many cousins, his information was too much that I would lose some of the relevant family connections he tried to tell me. This side he began to exhibit days leading to his illness. Any free time my father got he preferred going to the beer hall, dragging me many times to sit with him and his friends while he bragged to them about his beloved son' trying without success to urge me to stay longer and test beer. A few times he tried politely, encouraging me to drink and when I waved drinking away, he asked his friends to ask if I could join in drinking, I said no.

I couldn't help but ask myself how my father could encourage me to drink when my life was already in such disarray. All I wanted was a better, more fulfilling future, and I wondered if this was the inheritance my father wanted to leave for me. Drunkenness was not an inheritance I could cherish, and I refused to end up like those who became subservient to the command of alcohol. Despite my father's insistence and the pressure from his friends, I remained steadfast in my decision not to drink.

I knew what I wanted in life, and no amount of peer pressure or persuasion could sway me. I refused to let alcohol ruin my life like it had for so many others. And in the end, my father saw how resolute I was and gave up trying to convince me to drink. As my father's sickness progressed, we watched helplessly as he wasted away before our eyes. Despite my willingness to help him in any way I could, I couldn't ignore the fact that he had failed to groom me or provide any sense of purpose to my existence.

Watching him suffer was heart-wrenching, and I was willing to do whatever it took to ease his pain. But as much as I wanted to help, it seemed like our willingness wasn't enough. I couldn't help but feel a sense of sadness and confusion. Why was my father only getting closer to me now, in his time of need? Was this his way of saying goodbye or perhaps his way of apologizing for everything that had happened between us?

As I watched my father slipping away, I couldn't help but reflect on the missed opportunities to connect with him. But even in his final moments, I held onto the hope that we could find some peace and closure before it was too late.

Chapter 19

Losing my father

In just a matter of weeks, the crisp November air of 1999 heralded a stark reality for me and my siblings, our fear of the worst turned into reality when we were suddenly thrust into the unknown, forced to navigate life's treacherous waters on our own.

When our father passed away, he left us with nothing but chaos and confusion, leaving us feeling powerless and vulnerable. In the aftermath of his departure, the daunting question loomed large: what were we to do next? And, more pressingly, what was I to do next?

Amidst the wreckage that our father's death left behind, we found ourselves on equal footing and without any clear advantages. Besides age, nothing separated us, we stood level as if on the ground before the cross of Calvary. Yet, even in the midst of that dire circumstance, we were grateful for the precious gift of life that he had given us. Despite his failure to provide us with any material inheritance or formal education, I took solace in the fact that I possessed an unwavering determination and willingness to carve out my path and write my own story. I was determined to climb out of the abyss.

One peculiar aspect of my experience was that, while naturally I was drowned in a myriad of emotions, I couldn't help but feel a sense of sadness at the loss of a parent - albeit one I was still in the process of attempting to forge a relationship with. However, in terms of his support, his passing left no void, as I had not experienced a father's love and support since I was six years old, nor did I find myself yearning for his affection.

The memory of experiencing fatherly love was a distant one - the last time I truly felt it was when I was merely six years old. Since that painful day, the day my parents went their separate ways, my father had never shown any form of interest in our lives or well-being. I have realized that love, is not just a feeling or mere rhetoric but an action that required effort and commitment. Despite my attempts to reconnect with him over the years, he had always seemed indifferent to my presence, even resentful many times.

Now, with his passing, it was time to turn the page on that painful chapter of my life and start anew. But where to begin? The blank page before me was both exciting and daunting, as it offered endless possibilities but also required me to act and chart my own course forward. What would my starting point be? What story would I write on this fresh page of my life? The answers were yet to be discovered, but I was determined to create something meaningful and positive out of the ashes of the past. It quickly became apparent that we were all on our own now. I was perhaps better situated than my siblings, having reached the age of 19 with a well-maintained, athletic physique I was ready to take on the world - whether it be through work, sports, or cultivating a plot of land to grow vegetables. Despite my relative advantages, my heart ached for my stepmother and my younger siblings, who were still in the formative stages of their lives. I couldn't help but think of my older sister, too, who had lived with our father up until his passing. Adding insult to injury, our extended family members had descended upon our father's possessions in Norton, snatching up the few items of little worth that he had left behind. It was an embarrassing and regrettable experience, one that I wished I could undo if only I could turn back time.

With all that had transpired - from our father's sickness to his eventual passing - my mother was in a state of total darkness, she had no knowledge of everything that had unfolded.

After two long months of grappling with my grief and trying to chart a new course for my life, I made the decision to return to

Kenzamba and break the news of our father's passing to my mother. I managed to scrape together enough money for the trip, and after a dusty and exhausting journey on the afternoon bus, I finally arrived in the familiar surroundings of my youth hood home. As I made my way down the well-known paths, I couldn't help but feel the weight of my weariness, which went far beyond the physical strain of the four-kilometre walk under the scorching sun. My emotional burden was palpable, as I carried with me the knowledge of our father's passing and the heavy responsibility of being the bearer of that news to my unsuspecting mother. As I walked, it was hard for anyone not to notice the toll that this experience had taken on me. I was empty-handed, without any groceries or material possessions to offer my mother, only the raw emotions that I carried within me, waiting to be unpacked at her feet. As I made my way home, a wave of emotions washed over me. It had been quite some time since I last laid eyes on my dear mother, and the thought of seeing her again made my heart race with mixed emotions. As I walked along the roadside, anyone could spot me from a distance, but my mother was sitting outside, facing the opposite direction.

Finally, I arrived at our doorstep, and it was only when our dog alerted her that my mother turned around and saw me. She was overjoyed to see me, and her warm embrace enveloped me in a sense of comfort and security. She asked eagerly about my life and hoped that things were looking up for me. Despite her love and concern, I knew that I had to break the sad news to her about my father's passing. It was a struggle to find the right words to deliver the heart-breaking news and not dampen her spirits. After all, my father was the first man she ever loved, and I knew that this news would hit her hard. Still her face never once betrayed even a hint of suspicion about the news I had to share.

Even in the face of their tumultuous relationship, my mother still cared for my father, and she immediately asked how he was doing, as well as how I was faring in my new environment. I couldn't hide my troubles from her; she was the woman who taught me how to communicate and raised me. She knew me better than anyone else on the planet.

As I revealed the news to her, my voice dropped, and my mood became sombre. "Dad passed away," I whispered. There was a moment of silence, during which I could feel her heart breaking for my father. But true to her resilient spirit, she soon began to talk to him as if he were there with us. I sat there, listening as she poured her heart out to my father, her emotions raw and palpable. Her tears flowed freely, and my heart felt heavy too. The memory of that moment still evokes to this day a wellspring of emotions in me.

When Mom met my father, she had hoped to spend the rest of her life with him, but life happened, and things fell apart, after that she hoped for a better life for her kids, she toiled and laboured in vain and now things were looking bleak, in Shambles and shackles, her kids were now wondering like sheep without a shepherd.

"It's alright" She finally said as she wiped her tears.

My father, Willie Masamba was gone, departed, leaving without teaching us any purpose in life. But it wasn't the end of the world, and it didn't mean we were doomed. Life is filled with many success stories of people coming from circumstances much worse than ours. So whatever way we were going to use to see ourselves out of the abyss, we knew we didn't have to re-invent the wheel.

Do we miss him? Oh yeah, why not, if it wasn't him, we would not have been born. The good and the bad cannot take away who he was to me and my siblings. I am sure if he had been afforded a chance to live, he would have made up for his mistakes and lost years and I am sure we would have helped him in any way possible. Now that he is absent, the vacuum is there, and memories will definitely linger forever.

The question hung heavy in the air like a thick fog: What were we going to do? We couldn't just sit around feeling sorry for ourselves; that wasn't going to get the job done. My father loved to express these same sentiment as "wishes don't wash dishes" We needed to act, to find a way forward despite the challenges that lay ahead. My stepmother and her three children, along with our sister Vaidah, faced the daunting task of cramming all of their belongings into a small wooden cabin that now occupied the once-empty plot of land that belonged to my late father. Every day was a struggle, and they had to work hard to make ends meet. They sold vegetables and became experts in the art of informal trading, grinding away day after day to put food on the table and send the kids to school. Just like our childhood, they had to be strong.

Meanwhile, in Kenzamba my mom also did not stop grinding in poverty, nobody dared to give us a hand as long as we were alive it was well. Life went on like that. On every side I tried to turn to, I saw poverty staring at me with a wide grin. I carried on trying a break into football while leaving in Tynwald with Uncle Fletcher and Actor. Actor was now working at ZESA in Belvedere where his dad worked, things were beginning to look better for him.

As the next soccer season approached, I found myself facing a daunting challenge. My trusty Adidas goal soccer boot, which had seen me through countless matches, was in a sorry state. The once-sturdy studs had worn down to nubs, leaving the boot almost resembling an iron. Undeterred, I set about reviving my beloved boot. I fashioned new studs out of the soles of women's shoes, using my expert welding skills to secure them in place with a red-hot knife. Despite my best efforts, however, the studs kept falling off during training sessions. To make matters worse, the boot was also too small and caused my feet to overheat, making it almost impossible to play. But it was my only faithful companion. I had to find a way to make it work, or work with it no matter. It was at the start of the season when I summoned all of my courage and faced every obstacle head-on. I knew I had to prove myself to Dynamos FC, the team to beat at the time. They were soaring high in the CAF Champions League, and everything about them was glamorous. But with a steadfast belief in myself, I set out for the national sports stadium B arena, the very place where they trained. As I arrived, I gathered my guts and confidently approached the coach, David George. I informed him that I was there for trials, and without hesitation, he directed me to change and join the hundreds of other hopefuls. Though I knew no one and wasn't a product of Churchill high school, Alan Wilson, or Prince Edward, nor was I a member of any of the prestigious academies scattered around Harare, my bravery carried me there.

When I failed trials at Dynamos, I kept on putting effort thinking I could break in one day and play. My obstacles remained great, and I also had no income to fund my movements. I was getting encouragement from Augustine. He seemed like a person whose life was taking shape. Now married with a child whom they named after his mom. He was the first person to give me such encouragement and expressed his joy, talking out of his imagination about how he foresaw my life taking shape, he spoke like he truly saw value in me. He is one person I would freely visit and felt welcome, urging me to visit more often, and these visits I would do without notice.

Augustine and his wife, Mai P, had a remarkable ability to keep a positive vibe around their home. I was drawn to their infectious attitude and how they always seemed to radiate happiness. I was particularly impressed by Augustine's playful antics - he would stand up and dance while holding the tummy of his pregnant wife, who was expecting their second child. It was a beautiful sight to behold and left a lasting impression on me.

Witnessing their joy-filled interactions, I couldn't help but aspire to be Augustine. I had never seen a couple that happy and proud of each other, and I felt inspired. I looked up to them as role models, and in many ways, I hoped to emulate their love and happiness when I got married. My Auntie Chipo also expressed a great desire to see me often, and for that reason, I would often make the journey from Tynwald to DZ on weekends just to spend time with her. She had a genuine concern for my well-being, and it brought her immense joy to see that I was doing alright. Her unwavering support and love were a constant source of strength for me.

Uncle Leonard has always been one other source of compassion and support for me, even from our days in Guruve. Though he never expressed his feelings in words, his actions spoke volumes, and I have no doubt that he prayed for my prosperity. When Uncle Leonard acquired a house in Hathcliff, just after Borrow-dale, out of the goodness of his heart, he began to invite me to his home to spend as much time as I could. Despite his rigorous questioning and hard-to-please nature, I have come to see him as a compassionate and generous man. His willingness to open his home to me and offer me a safe haven speaks volumes about his character. I am truly grateful for his kindness and generosity. Countless times, he showered me with kindness, never once expecting anything in return.

Each act of benevolence was a bright beam of positivity that radiated through me, easing any stress and anxiety that plagued my mind. In those moments when I doubted my own abilities, he made me feel at home, like a welcomed guest in his world. One day, he entrusted me with a hefty sum of money to pay the people working on his home while his wife was away. It was a testament to the level of trust and faith he had in me, and it sparked a newfound sense of responsibility within me.

As fate would have it, he had a young son named Talent, and it was through our interactions that we became bonded for life. Like two peas in a pod, we shared similar values and perspectives, and our friendship grew stronger with each passing day. Even the vast distances that now stand between us have not weakened the unbreakable bond we forged.

From Uncle Leonard and a handful of other mentors, I gleaned invaluable life lessons that I began to implement into my daily routine. Their wisdom and guidance helped me navigate through the trials and tribulations of life. Uncle Leonard's difference from other people was his boldness to go a mile extra when it felt unpopular to house someone that seemed useless. He probably had that extra eye to see potential and an ability to find a way to unearth smiles hidden in agony. At first, he did not have a job or something specific to help me with but simply called me to come and be with him for as long as I liked. Along the way I learned some valuable lessons from his conduct, I began to look beyond his prominent hard and fast rule approach when dealing with children and even young adults.

When I was still in Guruve, I found it hard to get used to him, and a few times I would find excuses to be away from him. Eventually, I found a soft spot in him and discovered he was not that hard but only needed to be understood. He was not the only person I struggled to get used to. I also struggled with Uncle Brian, he was, and I still believe to be a strict man who could not tolerate disrespect, but with time I found out he is the man to go to.

While I was at Uncle Leonard's place, trouble was stalking me, and I never knew. Trouble was encroaching in all glitz and smiles wrapped in the form of a girl named Arbigirl, a sister-in-law to my uncle's friend - a man who was more than just a friend to my uncle. He was a boss and a confidant all rolled into one, occupying the role of a transport department manager at their workplace.

Arbigirl, who was my age, exuded an air of affluence and sophistication that belied her lack of employment. She seemed to be well taken care of, whether by herself or by someone else, I could not say. Her daily routines were filled with trips to town, changing outfits more than once a day, and carrying a cell phone in her purse at a time when owning one was considered a symbol of high social status in our society.

In my society, certain things were deemed to be markers of status and wealth, such as owning a cell phone or being able to change outfits multiple times a day. These were things that were associated with individuals from affluent families or those who were still climbing the socioeconomic ladder. However, my circumstances were far from enviable. I was jobless and penniless, not enrolled in any educational pursuit and with little hope of anything great coming my way anytime soon. My struggles were visible for all to see, and I am sure Arbigirl could tell that I was not doing well.

Despite the obvious disparities between us, Arbigirl seemed to be drawn to me, making her intentions clear and expressing a desire to pursue a romantic relationship with me, including the prospect of sleeping together without delay. For a moment, I felt like the luckiest man alive, as if fate had finally smiled upon me and brought me the good fortune I had been waiting for.

Looking at her, I couldn't help but wonder if a girl as privileged and sophisticated as her could ever be interested in someone like me. As a young man, I had always envisioned finding a love that was pure and virtuous, a woman who held herself in high regard and didn't succumb to the whims of others. But Arbi was different. She was persistent, pushing the boundaries of my comfort zone and testing the limits of my self-control. Her advances were tempting, but I couldn't shake the feeling that something was off. Was she truly interested in me, or was there another motive at play? The thought of impregnating a woman was daunting, and it wasn't a decision I was willing to make lightly. I had other priorities in my life, and finding a partner wasn't at the top of my list. I wasn't going to rush into a relationship, especially not with someone who seemed to be imposing herself on me. Despite the allure that Arbi presented, I knew it was important to exercise caution and buy myself time to assess her true intentions. I refused to let my guard down, determined to protect my heart from any potential harm. My biggest challenge at that point was convincing myself to overcome the temptation of entering into an unplanned relationship, it can be a little tricky when you meet someone who is trying to   self-impose time and again, self-restraining has never been small talk in these issues. Even though my heart desired to have a relationship, I restrained myself for the reasons that were so obvious to me.

How could I steer up Love and possibly make someone pregnant without figuring out where life was taking me? I was still trying to find myself; I was telling myself "Things have to change." The kind of change that turns tables and affords us the good things in this life. I knew that kind of change was not going to just fall on my lap, neither was there any chance I could just bump into a deserted fortune. It needed discipline and a lot of work.

Arbi tried to take advantage when I was alone at the house. She developed a tendency of coming to spend afternoons with me, and many times I felt like taking advantage of the situation and simply following where life leads if she became pregnant. After all, she seemed to have money, yet she was never bothered that I had nothing. At one point she called me to accompany her to town, and I gave excuses. Furthermore, she came up with a good idea that appealed to me, yet in all these, she was furthering her intentions, she wanted me in bed for a reason and she could not understand why I was not forthcoming.

What she did not know was, I had my concerns, and I had questions, and above everything, there was an order of things that I wanted to see happening in my life. I was poor, yes, but I desired to see myself rising from the dust. I understood that for me to do that I had to be disciplined, and deprive myself of certain pleasures, love being one of them. It didn't take long for the truth to come out. Arbigirl was pregnant, and the father was none other than her brother-in-law. They had both conspired to use me as their scapegoat. However, by the grace of God, I survived their wicked plot. It was a miracle that I had escaped such a dangerous trap.

Arbigirl went on to become a second wife, and the incident seemed to fade away into the past. But over time, I had lost touch with her and her family. It wasn't until I heard rumours that I learned the shocking truth. The husband and his first wife had both passed away from AIDS. When I heard the news, I couldn't help but feel an overwhelming sense of relief. I knew that I had dodged a bullet. It was a simple escape from a black hole of deceit and danger.

The incident with Arbigirl and her deceitful brother-in-law was a dark chapter in my life. But I emerged from it unscathed.

Chapter 20

Earning my first income

For a while, I found myself caught between two uncles, Leonard, and Fletcher, making a seesaw as I carried on the pursuit to make ends meet. But just when I least expected it, Uncle Leonard surprised me with a phone call. He told me to prepare for a new opportunity: a job in Mhondoro Ngezi.

My heart leapt with joy upon hearing the news. It was the chance I had been waiting for, a glimmer of hope amid my struggles. Despite the short-term nature of the contract, it was an important opportunity that had the potential to change my life. It was like an oasis in the desert, reawakening my dormant sense of hope. Without hesitation, I climbed into the bed of a haulage truck driven by a man named Kizito. The vehicle roared to life, and off we went on a journey to Mhondoro Ngezi.

As we made our way to this new destination, I couldn't help but feel a sense of excitement and possibility. This was my first time in Mhondoro, and this job offered me the chance to earn a salary and take the first steps towards a brighter future. And I wasn't alone - my Uncle Major, the younger brother of Uncle

Leonard, was also there, armed with letters of recommendation from our wise and respected uncle.

I embarked on this adventure filled with determination and hope. Was this a turning point in my life? A chance to make progress towards my dreams and build a better future. I couldn't wait to see where this journey would take.

Uncle Major was the first to get hired, leaving me waiting for three long weeks until I finally received the good news. I couldn't help but blame myself for not trying harder to secure the job earlier, but at least now I could move forward with renewed hope and excitement. During my waiting period, Uncle Oliver came to also camp. He was also dear to me and went by the nickname "Fox". Uncle Oliver was already working for Tarcon as a tyre fitter, so for him, it was just a matter of transferring from the head office to the worksite. Tarcon was a construction company that was involved in building the highway that connected the Ngezi platinum mine and the old crusher plant in Halfway.

Oliver Fox and my father shared the same mother, making them either brothers or half-brothers, depending on which cultural lens you choose to view it through. Despite any potential differences, Uncle Oliver always showed me an abundance of natural love and affection. I have fond memories during the holidays with my father, Uncle Oliver would come when I was young. At the time, Uncle Oliver was employed by a security company and lived in the bustling town of Chitungwiza, in unit B. He had a passion for sports, particularly football, and was a devoted fan of the Dynamos football club. I vividly remember the day he took me to my first soccer match at Rufaro Stadium to watch Dynamos play. It was an exhilarating experience to see the likes of Henry Chari, Kaitano Tembo, and Tauya Murehwa playing on the field.

Although I can't recall the exact year, I do remember that it was a thrilling game in which Dynamos emerged victorious against Tanganda FC.

Uncle Oliver was a man of many passions, and football was just one of them. He had a deep love for movies and spent countless hours watching films by heroes of the past, studying the greats like Sylvester Stallone and Bruce Lee. But that wasn't all - he was also a fitness fanatic, spending hours in the gym sculpting his body to perfection. He often dressed like a movie star himself, donning long grey overcoats girded at the waist with a stylish belt.

When he was young, Uncle Oliver was closest to Uncle Leonard, growing up as relatives, Olivier's Mom being Leonard's sister. The two of them shared a love for boxing. They would spend hours practicing together, perfecting their jabs and imitating Muhammad Ali. They even competed in real-life boxing matches, thrilling crowds with their skill and agility. Even now, as an adult, Uncle Oliver and Leonard remained dedicated to physical fitness, inspiring those around them to do the same. They both avoided alcohol and maintained a sober way of life, always striving to be their best self. The two of them would often lift weights together in their home gym, passing on their knowledge and passion to the next generation. We all learned to lift at their home gym.

Uncle Leonard's sons - Talent, Bright, and Lawrence - had inherited their father's love for martial arts, particularly karate. Talent, in particular, went an extra mile, seeking out tutors that he called Sensei to train him in the art of combat. His skill was so impressive that I began calling him "Jet Lee" in admiration. As I watched Uncle Oliver and Uncle Leonard work out together, I couldn't help but feel inspired by their dedication and passion.

As I began my new job at Tarcon, I couldn't help but feel a sense of accomplishment and excitement. It was a moment that called for celebration, even that one small step was a reason to be grateful and celebrate. However, that feeling was short-lived as tragedy struck just two days later. The news came that an important person in my life had passed away - my beloved grandmother. The loss felt personal to me, and I struggled to come to terms with it. I wanted to be there for her funeral, to say my final goodbyes and honour her memory, but financial constraints made it impossible. It was a heart-wrenching decision to make, but I had no choice but to stay behind. Thankfully, Bambini Oliver, my uncle, made the journey to bury his mother. I couldn't be there with him, but I felt comforted knowing that someone was representing us and saying goodbye on our behalf. I couldn't recall if Uncle Major, my grandmother's brother, had joined him for the funeral. They had grown up together as a family, despite having different mothers but the same father.

The suddenness of my grandmother's passing caught everyone off guard. She had been healthy and active, and no one had suspected that anything was wrong. It was a painful reminder that life is unpredictable and fragile.

In Mhondoro, my job entailed being a watchman, a role which did not require any formal training and did not leave me exhausted. As part of the internal security team, I was responsible for monitoring the machinery at night. It was a rather relaxed job, which afforded me ample time to rest. It often felt like I was being paid to sleep. I was not alone in this, as a significant number of my colleagues also had similar roles, with some working in the afternoon and engaging in other activities. Despite the simplicity of the job, I found it enjoyable, especially since I made a new friend in Raphael, with whom I shared the night shift.

The construction camps were a hub of activity, and the environment was alluring to people of all ages. It was a place where hard work and sweat were the norms, and the promise of a good pay check at the end of the day was enough to keep anyone coming back for more. Unfortunately, the allure of these camps also made them attractive to women who were looking for opportunities to make money.

While some of these women may have been seeking genuine opportunities through selling merchandise, others were drawn to the prospect of making quick cash by providing services of a more intimate nature. This gave rise to a thriving sex industry around these camps, where women would offer their services to the workers in exchange for money. At the same time, some women saw the construction camps as a potential hunting ground for finding a life partner. These women would have to find a way to distinguish themselves to meet a man who could offer them a stable and secure future. While some of these relationships would turn genuine, others were built on false promises and broken dreams. Overall, the environment around the construction camps was highly tempting, and it attracted people from all walks of life. While some were there for legitimate reasons, others were drawn by the promise of quick money or the hope of finding a life partner. Regardless, the camps remained a place of opportunity, both for those who worked there and those who sought to profit from them.

As I made the journey from Harare, I knew exactly what I wanted to achieve, and I remained disciplined and steadfast in my pursuit. I didn't allow myself to be swayed by the temptations of bad company or indulgences that others found pleasure in. Instead, I kept my focus on my goals and worked hard with the hope of pulling out of the abyss. One of the things that I did to stay motivated was to buy myself a new pair of soccer boots - the first that I ever bought with my own money and the first new soccer boot I ever worn. Joining the company soccer team was a natural choice, given my love for the sport, and it was a great way to connect with the other youths in the company. Despite the pressure to conform to the norms of the environment around me, I refused to give in to temptation and continued living my normal life. However, I felt that I was falling behind in the area of dressing and looking presentable. To remedy this, I began paying more attention to my appearance and started investing in my wardrobe.

Having learned a thing or two about dressing good from friends in Harare like Actor and Harmony, I also looked up to my uncle Kodza as a role model. He had a keen eye for fashion and always looked impeccable. I admired his attention to detail and his ability to dress perfectly for any occasion, and I aimed to emulate his style.

Every day, he diligently tended to his physique by lifting small weights with dumbbells. I often found myself mesmerized by his discipline and demeanour, silently wishing to emulate his composure. He was of a reserved nature and reluctance to engage in small talk, and we considered it an honour to exchange even a brief conversation with him. He emitted an air of importance, hinting at the potential to lead the glamorous life of a television star.

It was individuals like him who taught me the art of dressing well, and I strived to at least, partially match their impeccable style. As I began to don more stylish attire, the people of Mhondoro began to take notice of me. Even younger individuals my age seemed drawn to my presence, though the reasons eluded me. Perhaps, like Kodza, I too was beginning to radiate an aura of importance.

Despite the temptation of having a large social circle, I found no compelling reason to amass many friends. Instead, I selectively added only two individuals to my inner circle, Aaron, and Sign.

Aaron, like all the Aarons I have encountered in my life, was diminutive in stature but exuded an air of charming sophistication.

As I tried to discern the reason for the attention I was receiving, it became apparent that my attire was not the primary factor, rather, it was my comportment that drew people towards me. Many of the younger generation were under the impression that I came from a wealthy background, whereas the elderly often took the time to reach out to me with compliments or to offer words of encouragement. Some even commended me for following the right path. People were willing to help further develop and cultivate the good morals I already poses. It is a biblical principle of talents, taught by Jesus that those who possess more will have more added unto them. In my case, my disciplined conduct and prudent spending seemed to have garnered the admiration of others.

I held myself to a high standard of dignity and respect for all individuals, regardless of their social standing. This mindset garnered the favour of those around me, as I conducted myself with unwavering adherence to these principles. Indeed, as I learned, when one chooses to be disciplined, others are compelled to lend a helping hand in building them up.

I honestly had no idea how many people were looking at me and why, because I just carried on from day to day doing what I considered normal. If there was any change in me, it was nothing more than putting on new clothes. So, the only time I realized certain people were having an opinion over me was when they began to echo sentiments. One afternoon while walking past a group of middle-aged to old men gathered under a thatched gazebo at the shops, gathering there for their drinking routine. I did not know these people much, I also felt I had nothing in common with them and felt they had no interest in me or how I conducted myself, but this notion was proven wrong when two of them called me to draw myself closer, feeling hesitant at first, but they noticed my hesitation and pressed on repeatedly and ultimately cornering me. I did not want to go because I am someone who has always tried to distance myself from people when they are drinking. But, here I had to strike a balance and not appear rude to these happy people, so, I hesitantly drew myself closer. I got relieved when I learned they only wanted to pass good comments on me, one of them who looked much older wished he had a daughter to give to me. "Even if you have no money to pay Lobola" he said, "It does not matter". Unfortunately, he did not have one. From the way he expressed his sentiments that day and many other days after, I thought he was talking sense and if he had a daughter that pleases me, I was going to fall for the deal.

These comments were increasing as more people came to know me, old dads and young guys of my age perceived I was from a rich family, while some wondered why I chose to come and work in an environment like that. Surprising that all these people were talking from their own perception, I had never lied to anyone or portrayed to be what I was not. Whoever elevated me in their mind did so because of reasons known only to them. The elevation of my status beyond what I truly was came across as a sarcastic twist of fate. While I found it amusing, I also felt that correcting people's perceptions was not my responsibility. After all, how could individuals make assumptions and draw conclusions about me when they barely knew me? It seemed to me that the same could be said about negative perceptions and sentiments; people often form opinions without any basis or evidence.

I recall two senior guys on separate occasions calling me to their cabins and showering me with praises, one old man wished to meet my father thinking the man had done excellent work. Again, he assumed my daddy was sitting somewhere and he worked well and raised a good human being, all this without asking me for facts. My father was gone and there would be no meeting. And of course, that old man would never know I did not receive any meaningful teaching from my Dad. I said in my heart: "he probably has to meet my Mom." I couldn't help but wonder how many others had made assumptions about me without seeking the truth. While I appreciated the compliments, I refused to bask in their glory, as doing so would breed complacency. I knew that I had a long and arduous journey ahead of me, one that required humility and focus.

Despite the moral decay that permeated my environment, I remained steadfast in my discipline. In my heart, I knew that if my life were to be played back, many would revise their perceptions of me. I recognized that the accolades I received were based on surface-level observations and assumptions, rather than a deep understanding of who I truly was. And so, I remained grounded and focused on my goals, knowing that true success required more than just fleeting praise. I was determined to forge my own path, regardless of what others perceived of me.

On another day, we found ourselves at the company's headquarters in Masasa, waiting for the bus to take us back to Mhondoro after a regular one-week break. As we stood there, I was clad in a simple pair of high work boots provided by the company, along with a new pair of blue jeans and a black, long-sleeved shirt that I had tucked in. My simple attire caught the eye of Mr Jericho, a workshop manager at the head office. He looked at me as he passed by, and his gaze lingered until it drew the attention of everyone around us. I was taken aback by his scrutiny and found myself staring back in bewilderment. Realizing that he had drawn too much attention to himself, Mr Jericho made a comment before disappearing into the office.

"You are wearing smart new shoes and looking smart," he said.

The gentleman standing beside me nudged me on the shoulder and remarked; "You see, we told you that even the company owners are noticing you."

If they were surprised, I, in turn, was doubly surprised, I had done nothing special. The smart new shoes the gentleman remarked at were the same high cut safety boots provided by the Company to everyone and many people were wearing them. What a stark contrast from the vivid memories of my high school days. Back then, I was viewed through a lens of pessimistic judgment and scrutiny. My poor dressing was one of the first things that drew people's attention to me. It was as if my clothes were a billboard displaying my perceived flaws to the world and it probably was hard for many to imagine my head housing any intelligence. Yet, in the present day, I was commended for positive things. I couldn't help but feel a sense of relief. However, despite this praise, I remained true to myself. I couldn't see in me what others were noticing. But I knew that staying authentic was the only way to live.

I began to feel that it was possible that life could offer me a chance to undo the impact left by negative surroundings in the past. I yearned to break free from the shackles of my past and create a new life for myself. To understand why my behaviour was such a big deal to the people around me, I started to pay closer attention to the environment around me.

The camping life around the construction industry was filled with enticing opportunities for an independent young man like me. It was a place where I could draw people's attention and make a name for myself. They had a reason to marvel at why I remained restrained when all ripened sides seemed to be yearning for my attention. The secret was simple, I grew up that way and I was just being me. I carried on living my normal life which to many appeared extraordinary.

With the passing of days, when my workmate Raphael began to drag me around familiar spots around his uncle's shop. One of the places he dragged me to was a canteen belonging to a young lady my age or probably a year above me. The woman got my attention at once, her name was Rudo. She looked smart in a red jacket and her face was glowing too. I liked her and decided to come back alone to talk to her.

She did not know me, but she remembered me, and I was back to find out more. I decided to ask her out, the dating kind of thing, and it became the third time in my life I consciously made a move for a girl. My first encounter was the brief Tasiana experience which I aborted because my sister found out. My second was an ugly experience in which I made a move toward a girl named Catherin at Nyamhondoro secondary while in form four, having spoken with her twice, I failed to find time to see her again and I decided to write her a letter as a continuation of our discussion. That did not end well, I got humiliated the following day when I discovered the letter was read by her whole class. I never bothered to go find out how it ended that ugly. I simply gave the many girls more time to tease and giggle at me, and my crew too took a dig at me as well, but we simply laughed it out, it was embarrassing though.

My beautiful encounters with many people were very encouraging and created a positive vibe in me and it encouraged me to maintain my way of living the way it was. The other guy came through, and I knew little about him than to greet him in passing, but one day he bought me a plateful of meat which I hesitantly accepted, his reason for buying me the meat was, "because I like you, because of your behaviour". Another guy who happened to be just older than me by a few years, Tinashe I remember him, he was driving a dump truck, and he was someone I considered calm and inspiring. One day he urged me; "Strive to work hard in life young man, because poverty doesn't suit you"! That was a way to motivate me.

Oh, let me tell you more about the girl at the canteen, Rudo, I think she was someone I just crushed on, I wasn't even sure what I wanted to do with her. In the past I had always had a clear view of relationships, I always wanted to go into one for serious reasons. So, long story short, the thing did not work out because she was also in love with another guy who went shivering at my appearance on the scene as a potential competitor. Ultimately, I made it easier by retreating, but had I kept pushing and promising something tangible, she was indeed mine to win. The guy was running scared, and he even came to speak with me, not in a rude way though, his approach was polite and in return, I decided to retreat. I was not ready for competition or in that case to wrestle a girl from someone else, surely not with my first experience. After all, she was a little older and ready to settle, I had not a clear way forward then.

Yes, I was still pursuing football but had recently met Sign Tshuma in Mhondoro who had relatives in South Africa. Sign Tshuma, a dear friend, in Mhondoro, encouraged me to obtain a passport, igniting a desire within me to explore the wonders of South Africa. "If you can raise the funds for your visa, we can embark on this adventure together," he had promised, and I knew he meant every word.

During the December holiday, Sign's grandmother, a South African native with a son working in home affairs, visited Zimbabwe. Sign confided in her about my unwavering ambition to travel to South Africa, and to my delight, she pledged her willingness to assist. South Africa sounded like the real deal, a nation passionate about sports, I sensed South Africa held a wealth of opportunities to be discovered, and I was eager to explore this new horizon.

While I was working in Mhondoro, trying to find my feet and my way, Actor also carried on with his life. At that stage he was madly in Love with Hazvinei, a decent type of girl, the wife material kind, working for one rich old man in the Tynwald area. From the moment he met this Hazvi, she seemed determined, the kind of

258

person who wanted to build something with Actor and she hesitated not and showered Actor with many gifts and delicacies time after time, she knew what she wanted, and the two gelled together so well, that before long they were living together.

Actor was a man with a promising future ahead of him. I looked up to him in many ways and even found myself copying some of his mannerisms. He was an intelligent brother who had a unique way of speaking English that involved imitating white people. I remember back in high school; he was the kind of guy who would turn heads with his confidence and exhibition of knowledge. And let's not forget how funny he looked in his prominent, strong brown leather shoes he wore - the ones called Dakota with a tire sole. Despite my admiration for him, I wasn't compelled to follow in his footsteps when it came to dating. For a while, I focused on other things and didn't bother myself with thoughts of love. It wasn't that I didn't believe in it or that I didn't want it. I just didn't feel the urgency or the need to pursue it at that moment. Instead, I preferred to focus on my own personal goals, knowing that love would come in due time.

My job in Mhondoro provided me with the means to visit my mother every month-end break, and her elation was palpable. She would proudly boast to her peers about raising a son who turned heads wherever he went, in turn I was humbled by her praise. Even strangers couldn't help but envy me, some even expressed a longing to have me as their son-in-law. Others were keen to meet my family, particularly my parents. However, despite the admiration and praise that surrounded me, my mother never openly lauded me or offered compliments in my presence. The only time she spoke highly of me in my presence was when I fell ill, and she took me to Chinhoyi Hospital. Her words of praise were uttered in front of the doctors, and it was a moment that will forever remain etched in my memory. At that point my mother had finally bided farewell to Kenzamba and successfully relocated to Mhangura, which was undoubtedly a better location - one of the best in Zimbabwe for farming. My sister Zodwa had separated from her husband and now resided with Mom, though she sought employment in Chinhoyi. As for our eldest sister, Vaidah, she had given birth to a son named Simbarashe. Despite her best efforts to enter into marriage, her endeavours had faltered from the outset, and tragically, the baby's father passed away not long after the birth. Vaidah was residing in Norton with my stepmother, and my father's small pension from the Council had allowed for the construction of a two-roomed structure, which had been his final gift to his family from beyond the grave.

Visiting Norton had become a customary routine for me, and I would make it a point to pass through whenever I had the chance. My sister Vaidah was more than just a sibling, she was like a brother to all of us. She was living alone, renting a single room in a house located just across the road. Thankfully, both Vaidah and my stepmother were employed by the Norton town council, but they always instilled in the younger ones the value of hard work. They would sell various items, mainly at the vegetable market, and on other occasions, they would prepare ox trotters and set up shop at their established point. My sister possessed a unique quality - whenever she spoke, her words were always imbued with sound advice that resonated with everyone who heard it. Her guidance was not something you would typically hear from a woman. At home, she wielded her authority in a manner that was far from authoritarian. She was strict with the three children, yet they loved her unconditionally. She would also give stern rebukes to our stepmother, but the latter never resented or exhibited any ill will towards her, instead continually speaking highly of her. What surprised me the most was how she approached me - she would seek my opinion and share her plans, treating me as a person on a better reasoning level than hers. Whenever I visited, she would confide in me about her troubles and sorrows. I soon realized that she missed having a father figure in her life, and often spoke of her illness, despite appearing perfectly fine. It got to a point where she called me urgently in the middle of the month, and I rushed to her side. I listened to her with keen interest and sincere concern, and it was evident that she appreciated having someone to confide in. She had stayed closer to my father while so distant from Mom, but soon she found a way back and began mending her relationship with Mom.

When my contract ended in Mhondoro, I left the place with good memories. Not forgetting to mention I had also finally landed my eyes on someone and liked her. I felt like I could be serious and begin a new season and see if love could bring along any good fortune. It turns out we were not compatible, and she acted in pretence. So, the whole thing stalled as soon as I left Mhondoro. Too bad I had told my sister out of excitement, I had begun to cherish high hopes of a future with her, but I never knew she was foolish. I wanted her to come to Norton and meet my sister. Despite my good efforts and honest intentions, she took my efforts for granted. I had given her some money and invited her to Norton, everyone there waited anxiously for her arrival on the said date. My sister was glad to hear that for the first time I openly came forward to talk about a girlfriend, and everyone around me was waiting for that day when they would see my girlfriend. It was a disappointment because she never pitched. So, I decided to waste more money by going back to check on her. That was the last time I saw her, and I allowed any feelings for her to die naturally. My sister never got to see her, only Khumbulani who at one point came with me to Mhondoro.

Chapter 21

Losing Mom

After some soul searching, I decided to temporarily relocate to Mhangura to seek solace with my family. I craved a serene environment to reflect on my next steps.

Upon my arrival, I was warmly welcomed by my mother and family. It was evident that my mother had been singing my praises to her friends in my absence. The thought of the potential gossip and bragging among her circle was not lost on me. It became apparent that some individuals were eagerly anticipating my arrival and recognized me by name. It was a strange feeling, but one that gave me a sense of belonging. I couldn't help but wonder what rumours my mother had shared with her friends.

My suspicion that my mother could have been whispering with others was raised when she sent me to buy tomatoes while my younger brothers were all around doing nothing. To further confuse me, she gave me my youngest brother Para to accompany me to Mrs Nyadzayo's place because I didn't know where she lived. When we arrived, Mrs Nyadzayo asked about my mother, and I couldn't help but wonder, "Who is this woman who seems to have been waiting for me?" I expected my brother to do the introduction since it was the first time meeting each other.

I carried on like that in Mhangura, doing what I could do, mainly things revolving around hot culture. My mother's health at that point was diminishing, slowing down continually to our concern, and the rest of us were there except my elder sister, who had come at some point to see her before mom got sick. Mom went through a moment of stress, in the days leading to her illness. I only knew after a while that she was carrying around a worry after she called me and surprised me by revealing my two sisters that lived with us in Mhangura were both pregnant. The environment became tense between mom and my sister who is the second born. From that time Mom became worse, but her sickness was a continuation of her long time health issues. During her sickness I made means here and there to find money to help buy her food and also travel to Chinhoyi, we informed her young sister for her to come and be of assistance.

Mom was the first among her siblings, followed by this same sister. Mom Regina had only one son and no other child, he is my cousin, Amos. From the time I met Amos, we grew closer and shared dreams, he also loved football, once played for Mhangura, and was still looking for a breakthrough into the topflight seeing

Mhangura FC ceased to play when the mine got closed. He is one tough player or man in general, many agree he was national team material, but in life, I came to learn that talent, passion, and hard work may not be enough.

When we sent our dear mother to the hospital, we held onto hope that she would receive the much-needed treatment and return home with vigour. Alas, fate had other plans in store. The hospital was unable to provide further assistance and we found ourselves stranded at home, grappling with the weight of the situation, and preparing ourselves for the worst. As Mom's condition deteriorated, she yearned to be transported to Nyaunde, the ancestral land of her family, where she could be reunited with her family and find solace in the embrace of her roots. We knew the journey would be a challenge, but we also knew it was her heartfelt wish. With no time to waste, I reached out to Uncle Foni and asked him to act swiftly. The very next day, he arrived with his sturdy pickup, ready to transport our ailing mother. We carefully loaded Mom into the back of the vehicle, her frail body wrapped in a warm blanket, accompanied by her sister Regina, and set them off on the journey to Nyaunde, a pilgrimage of sombre love and devotion.

That was the last time I saw my mother, and she left never to return. We all watched Uncle Foni driving her off, and as he did so, as the car drifted away, my heart felt a tearing away of a part of us, and we were left standing there. The home turned gloomy all day, even the night was quiet, each of us having their thoughts unspoken. We had not imagined a life without Mom, but at that point it felt like that reality had knocked on our doorstep. There was no talking among us, and there was no singing or teasing. We all knew Mom would not be coming back, but none of us knew what to do, whether to cry or mourn or just stay still and wait. That evening upon going to sleep I reminisced how mom grinded through the years to see us growing. My heart was cut upon feeling how life had conspired against her and treated her unfairly, I felt she deserved to see us doing something meaningful during her lifetime, but that was not to be, it seemed like her toil and grinding all ended in vain.

In a few days, Mom succumbed to her sickness. My sister Zodwa followed and was there, arriving on the day of her passing. When mom died, her relatives never bothered to try to let us know, or should I say were overwhelmed. Of all her eight children, only my sister Zodwa was there at the funeral. Amos's mother was still there, but the rest of us waited anxiously together with Amos, waiting to hear how things were going, awaiting in suspense knowing what was before us, nonetheless, we hoped for a miracle. I only came to learn of Mom's passing and burial when I took a journey to Chinhoyi, knowing that Uncle Foni was a regular at Jaggers wholesalers, I took a deliberate decision to try and find him. And as per my expectation I met him, and that's when he told me the sad news, and that was the last time I saw Uncle Foni.

In the days that followed, as I prepared to visit the final resting place of my dear mother, my mind was awash with memories of the past. I wracked my brain, trying to comprehend what we had done wrong, what missteps we had taken that prevented life from favouring us. My thoughts drifted back to my childhood, to the days spent in Unit M in Seke. I remembered the sense of community and belonging, the laughter and playfulness that filled our days. But then, we had to leave Seke and moved to Guruve, where life took an unexpected turn with the divorce of my parents. The memories of those tumultuous times flooded my mind - the struggles we faced, the pain of separation, and the uncertainty of what the future held. Again, my thoughts turned to the days of toil in Nyaunde, the place where my mother longed to return to. Despite the hardships we faced, we persevered with discipline and determination. We eventually left Nyaunde for Kenzamba, but life continued to be a challenge, with more toil and suffering.

As I prepared to visit my mother's final resting place, I realized that the journey would be much more than a physical one. It would be a journey through time, a reckoning with the past and a reflection on the present. And while the memory of my dear mother would always be with me, I knew that her legacy would continue to guide me through the trials and tribulations of life.

A few days later, I embarked upon a journey to Nyaunde, and the bus from Chinhoyi dropped me off at Obva, a place nestled near the banks of the Mupfure River - the very same river where I first learned to pan gold.

The distance between Obva and Nyaunde is no mean feat, requiring over half a day of energetic walking. Unfortunately for me, the bus dropped me off in Obva towards the end of the day, at around 16:00 hours. With less than two hours of daylight remaining, the option of sleeping at Obva shopping centre was not a viable one. So, I set off on my journey, aware of the treacherous route ahead.

Though I thought I had a good understanding of the path, it quickly became apparent that I had not fully comprehended how dangerous it could be. It had been over a decade since I had last trodden this path, and the journey was more challenging than I had anticipated. Nonetheless I felt a sense of urgency to cross the river quickly and consider the other side of the river as the real starting point of my journey. Little did I know that the path that lay ahead would be fraught with peril and adventure. As I began to journey without delay, I had purposed my intention, and that intention was to beat darkness and be over the river before the sun sets. For a short distance towards the river, I walked with some guys that advised me not to risk walking all the way. That sounded like advice from a caring heart because there was a huge probability of encountering elephants that dominated the nights from the Mupfure catchment area to Nyaunde.

Besides all these dangers, it had been more than ten years since I set foot in these dusty meandering pathways, and any attempt to find my way through the dense woods that night would have been absurd. Even walking during the afternoon would have seen me getting lost, I had lost memory of the area completely. With all this to think about and finalize, I did not stop, instead, I quickened my steps, with the advice of the strangers still ringing in my ears. My walk with those guys was only brief, but their words caused me to keep trying to picture where I was going to spend my night.

My ultimate plan was to walk as far as my legs could take me before it gets dangerous and once it becomes unsafe, I wanted to later find a home, any home near the road and ask to spend a night.

As I descended into Mupfure catchment, the sun, now a round huge orange object was shining its last, slowly dipping behind the majestic mountains, sending out a fiery orange hue spreading from the horizon across the sky, setting the clouds above, the entire valley and all objects ablaze with a warm glow. The birds in their numbers and kinds, sounded like the most grateful creatures as they bade farewell to the day with thankful choruses of beautiful melodies, filling the air with song-like sounds.

As if that was not enough, a gentle breeze also whispered through the leaves of the trees, creating a symphony that echoed through the air. It was a magical evening, beckoning all to come and bask in nature's serene beauty, soothing away the stresses of a long day. I kept walking while constantly checking on the sun until half of it was hidden from my site. Finally, as I crossed the river itself the sun was no more to be seen, darkness had not entirely enveloped the atmosphere, but it was approaching faster than my liking.

As I crossed the width of the mostly dragging sandy dry riverbed, I pushed harder against the drag as my feet dug one step after the other. I also felt and cherished the blowing of a gentle breeze, sweeping through the leaves of the trees, creating a mesmerizing symphony that echoed into my ears. The breeze was so cool over my skin, so tempting, so inviting me that I kept drawing in deep gasps of refreshing air whose smell was a mixture of fish and strong mint-like coming from the trees ganging along the river edge. As I took each step, my mind was transported back to the day when this very river almost snatched me away from this world. The irony of it all was not lost on me as I made my way across, the spot where I had almost lost my life, just a stone's throw away. But I was determined to keep moving, inching up the slope, past the trees that hummed with the sounds of buzzing insects, all in a mad rush to stock up on nectar and pollen.

I hurried my steps trying as much to quickly drift from the river. As I did so, the sounds of buzzing insects were also fading away quickly. All these I did while my mind was at work for a solution. I kept trying to push the next step harder as I walked, almost getting to a jog.

As I pushed along, my mind was consumed with finding a solution to my dilemma, I had no clue that fate was about to intervene with a surprising twist. Imagine my astonishment when the solution I had been seeking, one that I had not even dared to imagine, came trotting behind me in the form of a donkey-drawn cart. The cart was moving at an impressive pace, five times faster than my own quickest walking speed.

Normally, donkeys were not my favourite animals, but at this moment, I felt an overwhelming urge to kiss them. The donkeys were not racing, they were moving steadily and consistently, their rhythmic jog a soothing balm to my anxious mind. Without hesitation, I approached the cart to inquire about their destination. As luck would have it, they were headed towards the same area as I was, and they even knew one of my uncles.

I wasn't about to be left behind, and thankfully; I knew the golden rule of hitching a ride: never slow down the pace of the cart. With this in mind, I confidently hopped on board, smoothly and effortlessly.

As the cart went along, I marvelled at the unexpected turn of events. The journey was swift and seamless, thanks to the donkeys and their steady pace, and the newfound companionship of my fellow travellers. So astonishing how the donkeys went almost the whole journey on a jog, navigating their way, manoeuvring every stump and ditch. Whenever they tried to slow down, all they needed from the guy controlling was a clicking sound he made with his mouth, and they would resume the jog.

The guys in the cart turned out to be heading to a village close to Uncle Benji's, where his elder brother, Pawadira, lived. Although I had been hoping to reach Uncle Benji's Village, I was grateful for the lift and the fact that I was now closer to my destination. Uncle Powers was no different from his brother Benjamin, they all saved equal purpose in my life. Uncle Powers had a soft-spoken voice that reminded me of Nelson Mandela. I had grown up making fun of him, along with my two sisters, who often mimicked his way of speaking and teased him for giving customers too much change when he owned a tuck shop. But as a grown- up, I no longer found pleasure in such jokes and teasing. In fact, I wasn't in a teasing mood at all.

By the time we arrived, it was almost 10 o'clock at night. The darkness was all around us, but after such a long journey from Mupfure, my eyes had adjusted to the low light. My approach towards the homestead was a little hesitant and cautious because I wasn't sure if they kept dogs, vicious or not. I called while at the gate, and a woman came outside. "Who is it?" she inquired. "My name is Sifelani" I spoke back. Immediately she remembered me, it was Mainini Erineri, the daughter of Uncle Pawadira. We attended together school at Nyaunde, she was older than me, the same age and in the same class as my sisters. Such an unexpected, expected visit, they knew it was a requirement for me to pitch up at some point soon. To some extent, they were thrilled to see me after a very long time. There was no need for me to announce why

I had visited them, it was quite obvious, that only a few days ago they buried my mom, and I was not there, I had come to pay my respect and see where they laid her to sleep.

After a long and exhausting day, the night seemed to pass by all too quickly. Before I knew it, I was being led by a young man to Uncle Benjie's place. As the daylight broke, I scanned my surroundings, trying to recall familiar features of the landscape, but everything seemed different from the memories of yesteryears. The forests around the villages appeared denser, and that was the most striking difference. The once-familiar sights and sounds of my childhood had been replaced by an unfamiliar and somewhat disorienting landscape. As my attention got drawn by the lush forests surrounding me, I couldn't help but wonder how the inhabitants of this land had managed to cultivate such a thriving ecosystem. In stark contrast, places like Guruve and Chiweshe lay barren, their residents forced to resort to burning cow dung in lieu of firewood.

As I arrived at Uncle Benjie's homestead in the early morning, I felt a sense of familiarity wash over me. Despite the passage of time, the place felt like home. I had assumed that introductions would be necessary, but to my surprise, everyone greeted me warmly as if I had never left. As soon as he laid his eyes on my figure, he greeted me with a smile. "Hi, my friend" I was a little surprised at how he was so sure. "I am well Sekuru" was my answer with a smile. Soon after my arrival, my uncle Benjamin, who needed no prompting to understand the purpose of my visit, swiftly ushered me through the formalities as he showed where my mother was laid to rest, just beside her father, Phineas Hwatetepa. I had only encountered my grandfather, according to my remembrance, once when I was a mere toddler, and my recollection of his appearance was hazy at best. However, my mother had entertained me with countless stories of his wealth, particularly during the colonial era when the sterling pound was the accepted currency.

My mother's recollections of her father's wealth were vivid and intriguing. She recounted how they would spend an entire day seated on the quarry's threshing floor, with piles of cash spread out around them to bask in the warm sun. He was so concerned about the effects of moisture on his fortune that he would frequently unbundle the cash and lay it out to dry. In addition to his stacks of paper money, my mother also spoke of his vast collection of metal containers brimming with gleaming silver coins. Despite his wealth, my grandfather never indulged in lavish spending. In fact, my mother and her siblings grew up just like any other children, with no special privileges or luxuries to speak of. Grandpa seemed to derive his joy from the mere act of accumulating wealth, an unusual trait in someone with such vast resources at their disposal. This is the man she now lay next to. Even beyond the grave, his view of money and life remains to me and many others a mystery only he could provide an answer to, how his family suffered when he kept probably a million pounds in the house, one would wonder what purpose that money saved, we would all think when one earns, they look after the family, buy clothes, nourishing food, but that was not the case with my grandpa.

For a moment I stood there with my uncle, side by side in silence, looking at the grave as if to search for answers. I did not know what to do, perhaps because there's no formal training on how to handle such kinds of things, neither had I had a privilege of observing someone doing it. So, for a good ten minutes, I stood there, head bowed low, thinking, and trying to picture the woman who raised me through toil and grinding laying six feet under, surrounded by cold earth just in front of me. Such is life, only memories of her would linger in me and others for the rest of our lives. Like everyone she had high hopes to see the kids she loved dearly come to do something meaningful, but in her case, it was not to be. I had no flower to drop, I felt only my presence was enough. My uncle was in no rush to hurry me, but after a long moment of silence, Uncle Benji told me a few words to say aloud, and I did just that and that was it, all done.

Each time, during the few days I spent with my uncle, I would wake up in the morning and look at the heap of earth, letting it sink in me this was now my mom's new home. It was hard to register deep down that the woman who taught us songs, and tambourine, the same who carried me on her back when I got sick at nine years – now has taken a rest beside her father.

I hung around for a few days at my uncle's place, lasting more than what I had intended. This after encountering childhood friends from Nyaunde including my favourite teacher Sir Buddha. We had not much to share with my former mates, but once they mentioned there was going to be a soccer tournament, oh how they pleaded that I should hang around to experience the jamboree. At first, I was not convinced, but once they took me around, that tournament was the talk on all lips. Old man, women, and kids spoke with an exuberant that quickened my mind back to the vibrant sporting days around the same area. Once I saw that energy I was convinced to stay.

In this community, there's still that unquenchable flame I witnessed during my childhood, a sport-crazy craving that the passing of time failed to quench, and it felt like nothing I had seen. Ultimately that day arrived and impressed me beyond my imagination, it was such an eventful day, a day also fruitful to those of an entrepreneurial mentality as they came to market all sorts of merchandise.

During my short stay, I also took time to visit my uncles in Chehamba, Lawrence was also there, spending two days with uncle Rori, playing soccer in training with his team. Uncle Rori looked great, highly well-built and possessing the same energy of a bullet that made him prominent when we were young. No loss in celerity of movement, his soccer team highly depended on him just like his good old days at school, a man of sober habits just like me. It was truly good and refreshing to meet Uncle Lawrence after some time, and it was a few days well spent.

Chapter 22

A new era without mom

After the expiry of my set time, I made my way back to Mhangura, knowing Mom ran her race, knowing all too well she invested her all in us, all of what she could afford. Knowing and understanding also that she took high risks making efforts to see us grow.

On the journey day, I woke up as early as 04:00 to walk the long journey nonstop from Nyaunde to Obva, knowing how much the scorching sun was going to drain me. This time, there was no God-sent luck in the form of jogging donkeys like that lucky night. I was going to tread every inch, enduring, and absorbing all the heat. If I had much choice I was going to delay and begin the walk a little late in the afternoon to arrive after sunset or at night. Arriving at night meant no long night to wait for the bus, but just a few hours before the bus comes. However, the idea of leaving noontime was not the best to follow because of two reasons.

Firstly, for me to arrive at night meant starting the journey when the toasting sun was up at its Zeist. Secondly, I did not want to risk seeing the sunset before I go over Mupfure River, for fear of bumping into elephants and risk getting trampled.

My arrival in Obva at 14:00hrs meant there was no escape from sleeping on the Veranda of one of the shops. The bus to Chinhoyi was only coming the following morning, most frustrating was seeing the bus passing, knowing I had to wait for the same bus until the following morning. I had no choice but to be patient, to sit there eating the last of my food prepared for me by Uncle Benji's wife. After that, the only entertainment I could find was of young guys that were dancing to the sounds of Sungura music playing loud from one of the shops. I watched them while I wondered why they come only for dancing. As the sun quickly dropped into the horizon my mind tried to picture how the night would be, considering the pose by bloodthirsty mosquitos waiting in numbers to drain me during the night. Without a blanket to cover myself, all the mosquitos nearby could probably smell a great feast to quench their thirst.

After a few hours of loitering and sitting, the night finally arrived, throwing my fears into reality, as the time for the mosquitoes to rule approached, I didn't know whether to brace my mind or my skin, or both. While I contemplated upon this, my uninvited friends wasted no time, and they approached me in swarms overnight. With that reality now all over me, the thought of catching a little sleep deserted me entirely and I stayed on guard overnight fearing such numbers could drain gallons of my blood and cause me a cardiac arrest hahaha. The fear of catching malaria became a constant nagging bell beyond any bruises on the skin, so I fought to have as less stings as I could get. It was indeed one of the longest nights, how the clock ticked so slow while I longed for dawn to approach. Finally, time afforded me justice and I began to see a few people appearing, with the hope of catching the same bus, soon they set a fire over the road, mainly to keep the mosquitoes away. Before long the sound of salvation graced my ears, the bus, sounding to me like that of a long-awaited saviour, and I was glad at last to see myself on the bus in the early morning hours. What a relief, a relief that felt like Independence Day as the bus carried me away, liberating me from the tenacious little mosquitos. The more the bus picked up speed, the more I wanted it to keep tearing away from the hungry mosquitos whose whistling lasted in my ears long after leaving Obva.

Ultimately, I was back in Mhangura. But I wasn't sure what to do next, it was time to make some movements. I wanted to be where I could find opportunities, looking at Mhangura, it wasn't that promising, and there was a kind of life I pictured. And from the look of things, there was only one place to try, and that place was Harare. Upon arrival in Harare, I was met by a surprise, a coincidence divinely directed. Uncle Oliver had been trying to find me for another job in Mutare, another short-term contract. This felt like something that had been divinely directed, the coincidence of making a journey just at the time an opportunity was open for me. I welcomed the news with open arms and said yes to the invitation. However, my excitement got halted after I learned of an obstacle I needed to cross over, I had no money to reach Mutare, and the people closest to me were reluctant to assist me, and neither could Actor. Everyone was just saying there's no money. Later that evening I noticed Actor sneaking in the dark with friends, hiding away from me, I saw him taking Harmony and other friends to a movie, and I reminded myself to mind my business and not intrude on other people. I knew that wasn't the end of the world. The next morning, I walked to Warren Park which is quite some walk from Tynwald to try my luck with Augustine and borrow the money I wanted. Augustine was always willing and ready to help me provided he had the money. So, after seeing him, he helped me out as in previous times and I was ready to travel. I did not even have to return it because he simply helped me out, giving me more than the amount I had asked for.

Then another glitch, another obstacle, this when I thought all was set for me to go. There was another set of news that followed to cast a shadow on my excitement. Uncle Leonard had heard the news and without knowledge I was back in town during the time of the call. He had sent Stanley, one of his brother's sons to go and work there in my stead because he thought I was out of Harare and unreachable, but he was wrong, I had taken a divinely directed journey to the capital.

What was I to do? I had no answer to that, and for a moment felt hard done. But just when I was feeling down, Fox made a follow-up call. Uncle Oliver was determined to help me despite my place being taken already. A follow-up message came the following day that he wanted me to make my way anyway, even though he had no proper plan, I only took the journey in faith. The next morning, I was on a bus with all directions given. Arrived in Mutare for the first time without much struggle even to find the place where the company was building a dam. So, I got welcomed by the man we called Fox because of his love for martial arts.

When I woke up the following morning, I got pushed into a plan that required me to go and ask Brendon Rally for a job when there

284

was no vacancy at all. Brendon was the son of the General Manager at Tarcon, a guy of my age, a privileged one though, looking impeccable always, preferring mostly side pocketed pants in Khaki and clean white shirts even in those dusty environments. I had to summon some courage to approach him and ask for a job. Again, it felt like God was just going before, paving the way. Beyond what I expected. My courage paid off, fortunately, Brendon remembered me from the Ngezi road project. Truth is, there was no vacancy available, nevertheless, to everyone's shock I was made the foreman of a newly created sect. Not only did I get a job when there was no vacancy, but that move created job opportunities for 15 new people that had been loitering around. I never expected things to turn in such a way, and neither did anyone, good as things seem for me, that turn of things to the positive aroused in some people feelings of jealousy.

Word spread to Harare without delay: "a certain unknown young man had been made foreman." And those in Harare anxiously hung on awaiting my arrival. Some thought it had something to do with Juju while others thought God led me. By the time we took that bus at the end of the month for our routine break, we arrived at the company head office to an eagerly awaiting bunch at the workshop, people asking to see this young man. But it's something that I failed to figure out what the big deal was all about. I did not consider it anything worthy of gossiping about in any way, and for that reason, I got surprised at why people thought it was newsworthy.

My days in Mutare were a little calmer compared to the time I was in Mhondoro. At this time, I had every reason to be a well-disciplined person. I went there at a time when all the important people I could look up to were gone except for one, and that person was very sick and her life hanging in the balance. I went to Mutare knowing deep down I had to be much disciplined in how I conduct myself, I had to find a way to teach myself. Discipline to me was never a challenge because I had learned to draw my lines from childhood.

When I went to Mutare, the passing of my mother was still vivid in my mind. We were all trying to settle into the new reality with a lot to handle. So, it was also a good thing to continue alone for a little while, I was happy alone and I never complained or felt sorry for myself. Teaching myself not to buy things unnecessarily, I understood the task before me was huge.

The people I considered important people in my life had passed away, and now my sister's life was hanging in the balance. My brothers in Mhangura were still young, Mandela was a little grown but had a tendency of wandering away from home, always on the move doing what he believed to be the work of God. I thought he was doing a disservice to himself, and I was right, many times Amos and Para went away to search for him, and find him, but on two occasions he slipped away from them when they got to Chinhoyi. Paradzai was still young and now starting to learn to do things, even though he was that young he was already into relationships and wondered where he got such guts from. Owen the youngest among us was still little but very vigorous, exhibiting as much potential. He seemed to be a gifted guy, everything he touched seemed to blossom in a small way. I understood my responsibilities so well. Even though I knew juniors were looking up to me to come up with something, there was one immediate and pressing issue.

My sister Vaidah had gotten so ill, so worse in Norton and she got worse by the day until my uncle ferried her to his rural home to be cared for by his wife. Immediately worry clouded my mind once I remembered my days of toil in Guruve, but without a solution to offer, I kept going with my day-to-day duties, praying every moment in my heart for my sister to be well. I wondered what best I could do, but I had no solution or answer to it. Soon my second sister left Mhangura to go and help look after her. I remember soon after receiving my first pay cheques, taking a memorable, emotional trip from Mutare to Guruve to go see my ailing sister.

The safest reliable way to journey to Harare from Mutare was by train, an adventure in and of itself, and I was thrilled to have the opportunity to experience it with my talkative Uncle Stanley. The train journey was nothing short of amazing, with breath-taking views of Zimbabwe's lush landscapes and stunning countryside. As we chugged along the tracks, Uncle Stanley regaled me with his hilarious stories and infectious laughter, making the time pass by in a blur of joy and excitement. By the time we arrived in Harare the next morning, I felt as though I had made a new lifelong friend.

Once we arrived, I was eager to explore all that Harare had to offer, starting with my shopping expedition. Armed with a list of grocery stores, I set out to find the perfect nourishing items for Sisi, who was unfortunately bedridden at the time. Guided by my intuition, I picked out a wide array of fresh fruits, vegetables, and other healthy treats that I knew would lift her spirits and aid in her recovery.

Navigating the streets of Harare was a thrill, the vibrant colours, and the lively sounds created a feast for the senses. It was a welcome change of pace from the tranquillity of Mutare, and I relished every moment of it. All in all, the journey from Mutare to Harare was an unforgettable adventure, filled with laughter, joy, and the excitement of discovering new places and experiences. As part of my ever-increasing preparation for a possible soccer trial or opportunity, I splurged on a Red and White soccer training short. Little did I know that it would soon come in handy! With my sights set on success, I refused to let anything hold me back.

The groceries I purchased were essential for Sisi's recovery, but they were heavy! Determined to see my mission through, I packed everything into my trusty Adidas bag and embarked on my journey to Mvurwi. The bus terminus was a familiar site, filled with the hustle and bustle of people from all walks of life. Despite the scorching sun and tired faces, there was an air of excitement and anticipation in the air. Guruve residents flocked to this small town for their shopping needs, creating a vibrant and energetic atmosphere.

As I waited for my bus, I couldn't help but notice the vendors selling all sorts of wares, from fresh produce to handmade crafts. It was a testament to the ingenuity and resilience of the people, even in the face of adversity. Despite the frustrations of waiting for transportation, I knew that the bus was my only sure mode of transport. While we waited, it was so easy to tell the atmosphere was charging by the minute and it was never going to be easy to get into the bus because the numbers kept swelling and there was a chance the bus would arrive from Harare with little to no space.

Finally, when the adrenaline had been silently building within the bulk of the frustrated mob, the bus appeared, and as soon as it arrived, just as I expected, there was commotion all over, pandemonium, people wanted to go, moms shouting between the confusion of pulling a child, belongings, and muscling in. Each one trying to be the one who gets to go, nobody was prepared to be left behind including me. For that reason, I also pressed on to gain entrance, and with my loaded big bag of groceries weighing me down, I still pressed. At last, I was in, or should I say I was standing on the second step pushing my way in when the driver saw such commotion, he began to move the bus slowly as a way to lose the pressing mob.

Suddenly I felt like being weighed down and the weight was way too much to that of the groceries, then I realized two guys, touts had gotten hold of my bag, dragging me down. I could not hold on, meaning they successfully pulled me off the bus. I wanted to know why among many pressing people, I was the only one who got dragged. Of course, those guys would have not guessed I was on my way to see my sister whom I valued much, if I missed the bus, I had no other transport, and neither did I know someone to ask for overnight accommodation in Mvurwi. I wanted to know why. The only response I got from the other guy were insults as if he was possessed, they both tried, by all means, to belittle me to the point of grabbing the collar of my shirt, the bus was still there and many people from my area and some from Disi or Drongo, which was a farm nearby where on the bus watching with worry through the windows of the bus.

I was not looking for trouble, I held on to my Groceries and made sure also to keep feeling my wallet. Knowing I wasn't going to go with this bus, I pulled away from these guys. Surprisingly they went a step further and spat at me, and the next course of action from me came without even thinking, all hell broke loose and, in a blink, I found myself fighting four men. Despite their numbers, they were no match for me. I was in the prime of my youth. Remarkable in physique, towering over them at 1,900 mm tall. They failed to put me down but only took turns to hit the ground. One of them held on to my pair of trousers, the only one I had taken for the journey for that matter, he knew exactly what he was doing. His intention was to embarrass me; hence the guy turned my trouser into a skirt. And in no time as I walked away, I wished the ground could open up and hide me, I was sweating in embarrassment as I was made a spectacle and many people who never saw the fracas wondered if I was okay. Luckily, I caught a pair of compassionate eyes at a place near Mvurwi bus terminus called Shamwari Joe, a man and a lady called me in, their minds dangling in between a willingness to help and satisfying their itching ears, wanting to understand the whole thing but I remember saying very little as I was already worrying about how to make my way home. Thank God for the idea of buying red soccer shorts. I quickly changed into them and made my way up the road with my bags, ignoring the pain from my bruises.

As I walked, my mind raced, trying to come up with a solution to my predicament. I thought about hitchhiking with the cars heading from Mvurwi to Mucherengi, walking the main road past the Grain Marketing Board or GMB, past the GMB to the turn-off. But no car came by, and I carried on past the GMB turnoff. Here, I waited, hoping for a Good Samaritan to drive by, but there was only silence. Just when I had lost all hope, a group of men came walking from Mvurwi. They enquired about my journey and expressed a willingness to help. They were farm workers from a farm located less than a kilometre down the road, on the other side of the dam canal. My heart leapt with excitement at the prospect of help. I was familiar with the area, having roamed these places at night with my uncles in search of game. One of the men was a clerk at the farm, and he offered me a place to sleep if I couldn't find transport. I desperately wanted to go, so I waited for another hour, but still, not a single car passed. My simple reasoning told me that I was not going to find transport, and I had to decide. I summoned all my courage and decided to follow the clerk while it was still relatively early. The thought of what lay ahead filled me with excitement and anticipation as I picture the situation ahead.

Surprise, surprise! I found myself facing the farmhouse, but it was not the farmhouse I was looking for, it was a little scary and frustrating. I minded making moves that would alert any dogs and be mistaken for a thief and invite trouble upon trouble, it felt like I was already in too much of it. I tried another road which I thought would circle the farmhouse and lead me to the compound, once again I was wrong. I found myself facing the farmhouse again from another angle. Eventually, I decided to walk away and find a place in the Jungle to sleep amidst the tall grass in the fields near the main road. Honestly, I did not know what to do. I began walking down a wide farm road that cut across a field with very long grass. The load of groceries I carried made me feel tired, but I knew I couldn't keep wandering in the darkness without a plan. I had to make a decision.

As I looked around, an idea struck me; I would sleep in the field amidst the thick, tall grass, the same type used for thatching. I felt a sense of assurance that nothing was going to happen. I whispered comfort to myself that the dense grass would act as a shield, making it hard for anything or anyone to guess my presence. I made my way into the field and found a spot where the grass was thickest, laying down my bags and flatten the grass to make a bed out of the grass. The long, swaying blades of grass towered over me, creating a sense of comfort and protection. I couldn't help but feel a sense of excitement at the prospect of sleeping out in the open, surrounded by nothing but nature. I was now grown up and not dreaded by the night like my boyhood years.

The night was pitch black, and filled by sounds gracing my ears from a not too distant farm across the tared road. As I settled, I couldn't help but feel hungry and tired. So I pulled out a two-litre fizzy drink called 7 UP and a loaf of unsliced bread from my bag. The refreshing drink and the soft bread were a welcome relief, and I ate to my satisfaction. After finishing my meal, I decided to lie down and rest. The tall grass towered over me like a protective shield, and the distant sounds from the nearby farm caressed my emotions, threatening to lure me into a peaceful slumber.

As I lay there my mind drifted to the challenges I had faced on my journey. For what felt like an eternity, I remained completely still, poised and ready to spring up to any potential threat. My breaths were steady and measured as I lay there, gazing up at the dazzling stars overhead. At that moment I felt as if my mind was being nudged that no other human knew or imagined my presence amidst the towering grass. Besides me and God, the only other beings that seemed to acknowledge my presence in the tall grass were the celestial orbs themselves, shining and staring down upon me amidst the towering blades of grass. As I continued to breathe and listen intently, I detected no movements in my immediate vicinity. The only sounds I could discern were the continual enchanting melodies of the apostolic people emanating from a nearby compound on the farm across the road. Their soulful singing was soon joined by the pulsating rhythms of Gure drums, creating a captivating and lively atmosphere that filled the air. Not knowing which sound to listen to, it was as though two contrasting cultures were locked in a contest of the bands, each striving to outdo the other with their respective musical exploits. As I laid there in the midst of the vibrant soundscape, a new energy began to surge within me. The thought suddenly occurred to me that I was not meant to sleep in the bush. But why? What was the reason behind this intense feeling? It was as though some unseen force had drawn me to this place for a specific purpose.

As these thoughts swirled through my mind, I couldn't help but imagine the potential dangers that lurked in the shadows of the surrounding wilderness. The mere possibility of encountering a deadly black mamba or being attacked by a powerful constricting python or even a stealthy and elusive leopard, sent shivers down my spine.

Growing up I heard stories of encounters where men stood toe to toe with a Leopard. I have had two encounters with a leopard during our night hunting adventures with my uncles, it's an imposing animal that makes one think twice. It takes something extraordinary to withstand a leopard attack, it's very nimble and has deadly claws that can deliver deadly blows.

With a renewed energy I rose to my feet and began to make my way toward the source of the vibrant sounds and flickering lights that beckoned from a distance. The wide road stretched out before me, leading me ever closer to the main tarred road. But as I drew nearer, a sudden surge of adrenaline flooded my veins, causing my heart to race and my hair to stand on end (though I must admit, I didn't have much of it to begin with). My eyes were drawn to a car parked on the side of the farm road, and I couldn't help but feel a sense of alarm at the sight. Immediately stories of people being beheaded for paranormal rituals came into my mind. "What if it's a private meeting and I am mistaken for a spy?"

Despite my instinctive fear, I forced myself to remain calm and composed, determined not to give in to panic. As I approached the car, I braced myself for the worst, fully expecting doors to fly open and assailants to come pouring out. To my surprise, nothing happened. The car remained still and silent, and I continued on my way, my senses heightened and my nerves on edge. Though I couldn't be sure of what was going on inside the car, I couldn't shake the feeling that I had stumbled upon a private meeting or some other clandestine gathering or secret society members conspiring on a subject of their choice.

The idea of being followed by strangers in a car sent shivers down my spine, and even as I crossed the main road, the thought lingered in my mind. But then, I spotted a line of towering trees that acted as a shield against the orange field, beyond these pine trees lay a fireguard that doubled also as a service road for the sprawling orange fields. In normal circumstances, one would feel safer walking in the open, with a clear vantage point to detect any potential threats from a distance. However, that night, logic gave way to fear, and I felt more confident in my ability to defend myself against a wild animal than a human predator. Plus, walking in the open would expose me, making it easier for my pursuers to track me down. The voices and the drums were getting louder, and so were the lights also flicking brighter, I was getting closer. That made me feel like I was drawing closer to safety. But beyond my guess, while the excitement was still building within me, immediately I got stopped in my tracks, right in front of me was a dam standing between me and the compound. How was I to reach the other side of the Dam? It was huge, and when you are midway you find it hard to guess which end is the dam wall. I kept also in the back of my mind that any attempt to cross or linger around these Dams may invite much trouble. The chances of encountering a hungry crocodile patrolling were very high.

I was not a stranger to the jungle, my fear above everything was encountering huge snakes, the type that makes sounds in the knight. Such as those that produce a strong stench that can fill the surrounding air or getting to wrestle a powerful python with the ability to spring up and constrict even more powerful animals than me. But most of all the ultimate poisonous and aggressive Black Mamba. I knew how to walk and listen and detect any signs of danger. I knew also that sometimes the body can detect and react to certain dangers without you even noticing or suspecting them.

There are also certain alarms one has to learn to listen to, these can be birds. Some birds can tell you the presence of a snake and if you are to approach you can make your approach knowing what you are expecting to encounter. And there's another type of bird which calls you to a beehive, that one knows every beehive within its territory. If you walk during the day and become hungry, you can even make sounds to attract it, and it doesn't take five minutes to feature and lead you to where honey is. Some make alarming sounds signalling the presence of either people ahead or wild carnivores. But the most interesting one is when you walk on rainy nights, the frogs are extremely interesting. Assuming you are approaching a river or any water-catching place, you can hear their sounds filling the night air from a distance, but once you hear them going quiet, then you need to approach with caution, their silence means the presence of something. As you walk, be it night or day, your mind pays alertness to all these and more, so that danger may not catch you by surprise.

Now as I froze for a moment, all I could do was stand there and think. The Dam looked huge and indeed it was huge. A minute passed and another minute followed, I was standing there in silence, only hearing the sounds coming from over the Dam. The water in the dam itself was very calm like the night itself, reflecting the countless stars above. One thing I hoped for as I decided to approach the compound from which the sounds came. I hoped the gatherings perchance were all night which was going to afford me a chance to slip into the gathering and spent the night in the safety of their shield.

However, as I stood there, one thing sounded obvious to me, and I knew in my heart there was only one thing left to do. Finding a spot to sleep, I was not afraid anymore to spend a night in the bush as in the days of childhood I was no longer a stranger to the jungle. I had the privilege to have many people teach me hunting, and that turned my timidity into bravery. I hunted with a rifle, I used to do a lot of target practice and could hit targets with pinpoint accuracy. Bamnini Fletcher in Guruve together with Uncle Leonard. Not forgetting my grandma, yes, my granny from my mom's side taught me hunting and many things, remedies, from anti-venom to many other things.

As I was finalizing withdrawing away from the Dam in fear of mosquitos. A sound echoed from somewhere beyond the trees ahead of me, a baby sound came into my ears, I could tell it was coming from very close, so I lifted my gaze, looking a little forward, just in front of me. For the first time since I stood there. I saw a hut, then a second one, there were people guarding something valuable, water engines probably. I walked towards it, voices coming from inside. I called as I approached the huts, three, four times and a response followed. Thank God my wandering led me to a place where I finally found people. I laid out my story and how I ended up here, and the young guys listened with increasing willingness to each following sentence. We continually talked on for a while and slowly began to realize these guys knew where I was going, they knew everybody. These guys were neighbours to my Granny and all my relatives, and these guys knew me, they called me by my name "Sifelani" They asked how all this while I had failed to recognize them, and for the first time it appeared as if a veil had been removed, my eyes were just opened, I looked at them once more and recognized them. I recognized their voices. How I failed to recognize the people I had seen and interacted with countless times; I do not know. These were Mainosi's sons, Kachana was there. Mainosi was known in the area for his many wives and countless kids. Indeed, he had them. I remember one of my uncles called Cheza Gamba would light-heartedly upon getting drunk say; "I do not want many kids like Mainosi, for the first to wake up is the one to find a shirt, otherwise he who works up late spends the whole day without a shirt". And for real on countless days, we met these young guys wearing only shorts, but of course, I would never know if they roamed shirtless because they did not have any at all. Eventually, we went to sleep, sleeping very uncomfortably and also receiving a few bites from things I did not see, bed bugs maybe, probably bigger ones I don't know.

The following morning, I made my way to the main road. As luck would have it, a small truck carrying gum poles pulled up beside me, heading in the same direction. Without a second thought, I jumped aboard, grateful for the unexpected ride. But my elation was short-lived. As we approached Haureni farm, I realized that the truck wouldn't take me any further. I faced a daunting prospect: walking at least six kilometres to my destination, lugging my heavy bags of groceries along the way. As I travelled along, my spirit lifted when I remembered a shortcut that would take me past the Mavare River. The sound of the rushing water beckoned to me, promising relief from the oppressive heat and sweat that clung to my skin. Without hesitation, I veered off the path and made my way to the riverbank, where I washed away the remnants of the previous day's fracas and basked in the cool, refreshing running water.

My arrival was a complete surprise, and everyone was beside themselves with worry - especially my ailing sister, who had been alone at home when I arrived. But just moments after my arrival, my sister Zodwa appeared, having rushed to care for her sibling in her time of need. It was a touching gesture, and I was grateful for her presence. As I spoke with my sister Vaidah, who was in a state of shock and disbelief, I began to realize the full extent of the panic that my disappearance had caused. It turned out that several people had witnessed my altercation the previous day and had spread the word, sparking concern among my loved ones.

My uncles and their friends had become increasingly agitated and had even gone so far as to wait for the very same bus that had caused my troubles at Mucherengi School. When the drivers finally arrived, they were in for a rude awakening. The bus was stopped for two hours, and the drivers were threatened with severe consequences if they didn't provide an explanation for their behaviour. But such is life, we come across such small obstacles to derail us off course.

I recall how I contemplated making a U-turn starting in Mvurwi to the time I tried to sleep amidst tall grass, but one thing kept on giving me energy. My sister was in more trouble and needed me more than before, upon looking and thinking about my trouble through this treacherous journey. The troubles seemed small compared to how much my sister needed me, I was that dear brother in whom she had over and over confided her deepest sorrows. Now she looked forward to seeing me and having a sibling's chat. I am glad I overcame that spirit of giving up, now that I was looking at her, I could see how she direly longed to see me. I looked at her and felt my heart sinking, how she had deteriorated that much I don't know; she spoke with me and showed much concern because of the troubled journey I had, and I wondered why she felt so much for me while she was in much trouble than I had imagined.

As I sat with my sister, her face etched with worry for her young son, Simbarashe, I couldn't help but feel the weight of her burdens pressing down on me. She grew weaker with each passing moment, her thoughts never far from her precious child. As I watched him play innocently outside, flitting back and forth to check on his ailing mother, my heart ached with a deep sense of sadness and helplessness. The emotions I had been absorbing like a sponge since the trouble in Mvurwi came crashing down on me all at once, and I knew I had to excuse myself. I stumbled out of the house and made my way to a small pit latrine toilet, where I wept in secrecy.

What could I do? The answer was painfully clear: not much. I had come, I had seen my sister, and I had given her words of strength and comfort, along with food and money. But reality has it the next day I would depart, and the weight of my departure hung heavily on my heart as I made the long journey to Mutare. Sad to say that was the last time I laid eyes on my sister. Two weeks later, I found myself in Mutare, working on the Dam Project. Standing on the dam wall, gazing downstream, and I witnessed a tree fall inexplicably. I exclaimed in disbelief, but no one around me had seen a thing. A man named Tawanda approached me and ominously declared, "You can't see that. It means someone in your family is dying." The following day, my worst fears were realized when Augustine, who had been working on fixing machines in Mutare, arrived with his brother Truther to deliver the devastating news of my sister's passing.

So, the same day I found myself on the overnight Train from Mutare to Harare. I went on to join other mourners gathered to bury my sister. She was buried, marking the end of her expedition. All she left us with were reminiscences of her goodness and a tender son who never understood a thing. Simbarashe was just an innocent soul that required the tender love of a mom. My sister who is the second born was given the responsibility of caring for the young boy, she took him to Mhangura and began to live with him. Simbarashe was finally an orphan. Finally, and officially, all the people that had a natural direct impact on me in a greater way, all very important people that had provided a shoulder for me were all gone. Nonetheless, it was alright, there were still other relatives willing to give me a push as I climbed my way. So, after the burial of my sister, I hugged my many cousins from Chiweshe, as always, Swisdai is always there, Benson, Blessmore, Pishias, Brian, and our eldest coolest brother Golden. After that, I made my way back to Mutare and carried on working until the end of the project.

Once again, I found myself back in Mhangura which had become like my drawing board. What was I to do next? I did not know. I had not managed to save money enough after the completion of the Dam project in Mutare, it was far from the amount required to process a Visa to South Africa, so I knew I had a long way to go. It was in Mhangura where I would seek ways to navigate my way forward.

Living in Mhangura was an eye-opening experience for me. The community was a melting pot of people from various backgrounds and upbringings a new community as it were, a community newly formed as a result of the government's land acquisition. Fortunately, I had already connected with a few friends who made the transition easier. One person who quickly became a close companion was Albert Nyadzayo, the son of Mrs

Nyadzayo, the woman who had reached out to my mother and expressed a desire to meet me upon my arrival in Richmond Mhangura. Albert, or Ali as he was known, was a discerning friend who was selective with whom he interacted. Although Mhangura was predominantly a farming community, our aspirations were different. We were a little more ambitious and desired a different life than what was readily available to us. While others talked of nothing but farming, we dreamed of other things, and we felt an edge to make our mark on the world in our own small way.

As time passed on, Kudzanai, or Kudzi a cousin to Albert joined us. I quickly realised he was much more enlightened than me and Ali, he knew a lot of things, having worked as a bank teller before. Apart from these two, I also engaged closely with my neighbour called Kadonzvo whom I spent many years without asking him his first name. When I realised this, it felt embarrassing to think of asking after all those years, but I guess it is not my fault, in our societies, we rarely call married people by their first names. People begin to be called by their surnames as soon as they get married, so who was I to ask him his first name when I could just follow what everyone was doing?

Once we started to know each other and days passed by, asking his first name became a cold case. With my neighbour, we planted tomatoes as a joint venture at some point, worked daily, and did a lot of things together without being bothered by knowing his first name. He was a nice guy and still is, we exchanged books and ideas, it was mainly him who found books and gave me starting with one thick volume novel called The Carpetbaggers which turned to be an exciting book, it is from this book I fell in love with one character and ended up picking up a nickname, Nevada Smith. After that first one, he introduced me to one of my favourite writers, Mr Frederick Forsyth and it became a habit for me to finish one thick volume after the other. I would read from morning to sunset, especially during the dry season, if they don't see me at the soccer field, people would assume I had gone somewhere yet I was only in the house reading. Naturally, I tend to get withdrawn and also don't seem to find pleasure in many things that entertain others, I do not find real joy in sitting in front of the TV.

Another interesting character that became closer to me was Partson Makosa. Partson was an intriguing character who quickly became a close confidant of mine. Our conversations were nothing short of captivating, as we delved deep into the meaning of life. Partson had a remarkable sense of humour that never failed to leave me in stitches, and he possessed a rare gift of eloquence that allowed him to speak with great finesse until the small hours of the morning. I can still vividly recall the times Partson would visit my abode and we'd sit by the crackling fire outside, enveloped in the warmth of the flames. His soft-spoken demeanour was a stark contrast to his limitless capacity for conversation, which seemed to flow effortlessly from him like a never- ending stream of wisdom and wit. Our discussions were so engrossing that time seemed to stand still, and it wasn't until the late hours of the night that I realized how long we had talked, and it would require me to wave him away.

I have fond recollections of my brother Mandela joining us by the fire on a couple of occasions, but his presence was fleeting, as he couldn't help but succumb to the infectious humour of Partson. Partson had a distinct way of speaking that was so comical that even those hearing him for the first time would be reduced to tears of joy.

As I listened to Partson speak, I couldn't help but imagine how entertaining it would be if a camera crew followed him around, recording his daily escapades. He was a larger-than-life character who had an insatiable appetite for gambling. His prowess in games of chance was unparalleled, and he had a mysterious knack for winning competitions like the OK grand challenge. He was a man who refused to work, instead dedicating his life to pursuing his passion for gambling. Partson was a unique individual who was a rare find in a country that didn't have much of a gambling culture. He was not ashamed to call himself a gambler when it was common people in that nation castigated it, he had no problem trying to teach anyone about it no matter how much friends or family despise it.

Trying on several times to convince me to try and join gambling, but I would repeatedly say to him, "Gambling is not for me, I have never won anything in my life, and neither do I consider myself a lucky person." Whenever he spoke about Gambling, you could easily see passion building up. Partson was a man with a clear vision of what he wanted in life, and he often talked about his desire to go to South Africa or Florida, where he could pursue his passion for gambling on a grand scale.

He shared with me his experiences of going to the Borrowdale racecourse in Harare to watch horse racing. As he approached the racecourse, he would feel a sense of agitation and excitement building up inside him, causing him to break into a sprint, leaving his companions behind. His stories were endless, and he had an uncanny ability to make even the most mundane events sound glamorous. At times, he would brag about his gambling prowess, vowing never to be outdone by people coming from Nigeria to live comfortably in the Avenues in Harare, while Zimbabwean citizens relegated themselves to places like Epworth or the dilapidated Mahosekwa flats. He was a man of determination, always striving to achieve his goals, never content with mediocrity.

I tried to surround myself with these people, the likes of Ali, Kudzi, Partson, and a few more, gathering time and again to share and sharpen brains and I considered our conversations important and edifying. The guys were ambitious, always looking for ways to break free from the limitations of our surroundings, doing a lot of reading, at times just for the addiction of it. Kudzanai and Albert were my go-to people when it came to discussing books.

After we had all read a book, we would gather together and engage in thought-provoking discussions about the plot, characters, and themes. However, Partson was not one to involve himself with reading, but he had a deep love for history. It was during these discussions that he would share his knowledge of the Nazis, the beginning of World War 2, and events related to the Balkan states, such as the Sarajevo Township. These conversations were enlightening and played an integral role in keeping my spirits up during a challenging period in my life.

As time went by, Ali got married and began to spend more time with his wife. Despite this, I would still reach out to him and disturb their peace, not realizing that newlyweds needed their space. However, they never seemed to mind and would always make time to talk and laugh with me.

Their kindness and generosity in putting up with my constant presence left a lasting impression on me. As time passed, I found myself spending more and more time with Kudzi. Our discussions grew deeper as we explored ways to innovate and improve our lives. Despite his own struggles, Kudzi remained determined and resilient. During one conversation, I couldn't help but burst into laughter as we reminisced about a time when life had humbled us both in different ways.

Despite the challenges he faced, Kudzi had a wealth of ideas on how to overcome them. However, with no funding to turn his visions into reality, he had to resort to desperate measures. In one moment of desperation, he made the difficult decision to sell his battery-operated toothbrush just to raise some cash for a project. Sometimes, desperate times call for desperate measures, and this was certainly one of those times for him.

Those were the kinds of situations we found ourselves in, we toiled together and shared these experiences while finding a way to keep believing. These hardships never deterred us, we remained resilient and kept hope as a burning fire, reminding ourselves that we had the potential to do better.

One other thing was an obsession we shared, it was an obsession towards finding ways to make work lighter in an environment where people believe in working tough and are encouraged to desire tough work. I did not subscribe to the idea of overwhelming myself with hard work under the roasting sun. By the communal standards, we weren't hard workers. In Richmond, market gardening was commonplace, a lot of people were doing it, and we also wanted to venture into it without overwhelming ourselves and pushing our bodies to the limit, so we had to find a way of doing it commercially without using watering cans because it was watering that constituted the hardest part. We knew that we needed a smart solution for our market gardening venture, especially since we had no water pumps to draw water from the dam. After days of consideration, we realized that the answer had been hiding in plain sight and was right in front of us all along, "siphoning" This simple, silent, and eco-friendly method was the perfect solution to our watering needs. However, for the siphoning method to work effectively, we had to position our gardens behind the dam wall. By taking advantage of the gradient of the dam wall and running pipes down the slope, the water in the pipe would continually pull more water from the dam.

When word got out about our innovative gardening method, many people began scrambling to grab a portion of land on the downside of the dam wall to start their own gardens. I was fortunate enough to secure a plot next to Kadonzvo's, and together we started our tomato project. Kadonzvo is also an interesting character, he is always remembered by how he does things by the book, in his garden everything gets pre-calculated, beginning with measuring the ground to the last centimetre and the plant ratio is estimated according to spacing. Even the yields were estimated, including how many tomatoes per plant, how many leaves per green leaf vegetable plant, fruit sizes and so on. As we moved into the second season of gardening, I had no idea that my garden would soon become a pivotal part of my life. It was simply a way of living for me, but life had other plans in store. The garden quickly became a source of refuge and, eventually, my main source of income. But beyond that, it became a place where I could vent my stress and frustrations.

There was a time when things became particularly difficult for me. My sister was persecuting me, and it was a challenging time. Thankfully, I had supportive friends who stood by me, and Ali's mother from the Seventh Day Adventist church became like a second mother to me. Although she never discussed my troubles with me, she made it clear that she was there for me. Despite her own wishes to talk with me, she chose to remain silent and instead provided a source of courage and comfort. That made it easy for her to invite me to a weeklong crusade popularly known in the Adventist Church as efforts. It was there that I was provoked and intrigued by the preaching of a short man called Huggins Mpfana, from that effort I began to follow more discussions and studies from the Bible.

While that new chapter was introducing itself into my life, I kept fighting that dark moment that made me feel unworthy to be alive. Things get a little painful if they originate from a very unlikely source, but in this life always be ready to expect the unexpected. I am not a person who plays victim or self-pity. Nonetheless, it is natural for people to feel sympathetic when they notice a pressing problem, I had problems of my own and people naturally wished me well, so who was I to forbid people to feel that way?

It's still a mystery to us why my sister's once-loving demeanour towards me turned into a raging hatred that consumed her like a ferocious beast. Her seething anger was so intense that she even threatened to poison me at one point. It was a nightmare living with her. I could feel her eyes on me, full of venom and contempt. Her gaze alone was enough to provoke me to a fight, but I refused to stoop to her level. I had known her all my life, and I knew better than to underestimate her. My sister is not one to make empty threats. She speaks her mind with conviction and follows through on her actions. Before the poison threats, she had already tried numerous tactics to drive me out of our family home. It was as if she was consumed by insatiable greed, always wanting more than she could possibly have.

Dealing with someone like my sister requires a boldness that is not easily shaken. But even with my courage, I knew that I was walking on thin ice. One wrong move could set her off like a ticking time bomb. She would rather watch a thing sit idle or rot than share. She wished we could all die for her to have the home to herself. If my sister could manhandle me, she would have done it. Despite all her efforts, I remained steadfast and calm yet vigilant. Since I knew the threat was food poisoning, I took drastic measures to make sure I eat the food I cook and prepare, I purposed not to touch anything of hers or to do with the family.

My sense of determination was provoked in a much greater way, and I said yes to the call. At the escalation of it all, I recall how I woke up one morning and walked the journey from Richmond to

Geluck, having no money to hike, I simply walked all the way, a distance of 20 km. I was determined. At Geluck is where Amos's Mom lived, she is my mom's sister, in other words, I considered her mom, and she was the right person to go to when I longed for that motherly care. Talking to her had always brought a certain level of comfort and peace.

As I arrived, she listened to my story together with her husband who was a traditional healer, and I told them I only needed a kick start. So, mom organized things that gave me a kick start, and soon I started and gradually fend and look for openings of any kind.

Chapter 23

Finding a church

At 23-24 years old, I was fully aware of the things that demanded my attention -- the serious matters that could make or break my future. Clothes, on the other hand, seemed trivial in comparison. They didn't have the power to kill or harm me, so I paid little attention to them. As a result, my wardrobe deteriorated rapidly, one item at a time. My shirts began to wear out, and my shoes started to fall apart. But I remained unfazed, focused on my priorities, and disregarding the rest. Eventually, I found myself with several shirts and only one pair of trousers, with no jeans in sight. Yet, even then, I refused to let it get to me. I carried on, minding my own business, and paying little attention to what others may have thought of me. Their opinions held no weight in my life.

At this point, I was now making serious church attendance with the SDA church. Thanks to Ali's Mom for the invitation to that crusade. I carried on attending because I found many things intriguing about how they taught the Bible.

With only one pair of trousers to my name, I had to be resourceful in making sure they were clean and presentable. I would wear them all week, washing them on Friday evening and leaving them to dry overnight. To speed up the drying process, I would wake up early on Saturday morning to put charcoal in the iron and press them. Sometimes, despite my best efforts, the pants would still be damp by the time I needed to wear them. But that didn't stop me from going to Church. I would put them on while still wet and begin the short walk to the Church which was conveniently located nearby.

As I made my way to the Church, the warmth of the sun and the gentle breeze would help dry my pants to completion. And by the time I arrived at my destination, my trousers were once again dry and ready for another week of wear. It was a simple solution to a small problem, but it was one that worked for me.

It felt like I had finally found a good Church in the SDA after a few years of wondering. In no time I began to realize how my newfound church began to influence my thinking, and it was the first time a Church caused me to ponder much on many life subjects, unlearning many subjects that I used to generalize while learning to speak from the Bible's point of view. As I navigated the changes in my life, it became increasingly important for me to adapt and assimilate to my new way of living. The church, with its powerful influence, played a significant role in shaping my outlook and worldview, and I willingly embraced its teachings from the Bible.

To ensure my survival, I relied heavily on my garden for income, sustenance, and nourishment. In many ways, the garden became the centre of my existence, serving as both my pantry and kitchen. I must confess, it is somewhat humbling to admit that I lived there in a literal sense, but it was a necessary means of survival that helped me persevere through challenging times. At that point, I felt reluctant to keep my food and cook at home, so home only became a place where I go to sleep in the evening or simply during lazy afternoons. I reminded myself to be on the alert side of things in case threats by my sister come to get real. My young brothers and my immediate young sister Sheba had to find a way of managing things well, keeping their heads low and playing dumb while also on the lookout with me. I knew it would only be a matter of time before their roads and my sister's cross. Honestly, many things played against me, I was going against the flow of the current and it felt overwhelming at some point, nevertheless something in me gave me energy, and my confidence was never entirely eroded. I remained calm and behaved normal, never carrying my head like a ton of bricks, or dragging my feet in grumblings.

As I became more involved with the SDA Church, I found myself drawn to a young woman named Emma. She was petite, with a fair complexion and soulful brown eyes that seemed to sparkle with intelligence and depth. I felt a strong urge to get to know her better, for she was not only beautiful but also a devout member of the church.

In the Adventist community, it was easy to spot the type of woman I was looking for, as they often separated themselves from the common trends of the world. Emma was no exception; she was fully committed to her faith and demonstrated a deep understanding of its teachings. I was smitten with her and decided to take the initiative to get to know her better. However, in the rural setting, traditional dating activities such as going out for lunch or to the cinema are not possible. Instead, I had to rely on creating strong bonds through meaningful conversations.

Despite the limitations of our environment, I was determined to pursue Emma and see where our connection could lead. Indeed, pursuing a relationship in a rural setting can be a challenging endeavour. The cultural attitudes and expectations surrounding courtship can be vastly different from those in urban areas. In many cases, women may be hesitant to engage with a man who expresses interest in them, especially if it is perceived as being too forward. As a result, persistence and determination are essential qualities when it comes to pursuing a romantic relationship in a rural community. It often requires a delicate balance of pushing forward while respecting the cultural norms and values of the community. In many cases, women may appear disinterested or even unapproachable, but this is often a test of a man's sincerity and commitment. It is customary to engage in a prolonged period of pursuit and courtship, where both parties have the opportunity to assess each other's character and intentions. This process is believed to weed out those who are not serious about a long-term commitment and ensure that both partners are fully invested in the relationship. While it may require more effort and patience, the end result is often a deeper and more meaningful connection between two people.

The moment Emma said yes, I felt like I was on top of the world. But that feeling was short-lived. Just two weeks later, Emma changed her mind and said no. I couldn't understand why. It felt like she had found out something about my family that made her change her mind. To make matters worse, Emma didn't even have the decency to tell me herself. Instead, she sent Rodrick, a young neighbour who went to the same school as her, to deliver a letter to me. As I read the letter on a late Wednesday evening, I felt humiliated and embarrassed. It was like sinking into quicksand. Rodrick had clearly read the contents of the letter before giving it to me, and I couldn't help but wonder what he thought of me. But I knew I had to pick myself up and move on. Even though Ali and his mom thought I was good for Emma, I knew that the relationship was over, and Emma had her reasons, which I may never know. Despite the pain, I had to carry on.

Chapter 24

Getting arrested

While I thought I was going through struggles, as if all these things were not enough, beyond my wild imagination, my sister was hatching a plan to pour more misery upon me and further damage to my soul.

This time it was not only me, but my young Brother Para got caught in the middle and paid the price of being in opposition to Sissy. The experience was not small talk, and it did some temporary physical damage and imprinted emotional scars that required a long run to heal. It was and still is difficult to understand what manner of spirit got hold of her. She houses within her bitterness, hate and anger of the utmost type. They say too much of anything becomes monotonous, and it truly is.

Long story short, ultimately her plan saw us getting arrested. At one point I considered her the vilest person I know, and even now there are times I feel so. She was not happy the boys were now voicing their unhappiness over her conduct too, she felt challenged and went on to frame us for theft.

She told an overwhelming story to the detectives at the Mhangura police station. Soon enough, events began to unfold at a rapid pace and the police arrived, unleashing a violent and humiliating experience upon us. Without even bothering to inquire about our identities, they descended upon us with the clear intention to torture. These detectives were nothing short of demons in human form, relishing in the act of beating and belittling us. Although their names were never disclosed, I pray that I am granted the capacity to forgive those two vile detectives for their callous actions. They subjected us to great indignity by forcing us to wear gunny bags over our heads while we were handcuffed, using us as objects of ridicule.

I vividly recall the moment we arrived at the Mhangura police station, stepping down from the back of an open truck, still bound and gagged by the itchy, dusty gunny bags. One of the officers at the station inquired about the reason behind our peculiar attire, to which one of the taller detectives responded callously, "I'm not sure, maybe they're crazy. Why don't you ask them?"

What a despicable way to treat suspects without even giving them the chance to speak. As if the initial humiliation wasn't enough, the police subjected us to even more torment during the three days they detained us while they prepared their case for court. I remember summoning up the courage to speak out, telling them plainly that I had nothing to say and to write whatever they wished. Unfortunately, my boldness only served to fuel their cruelty, as the interrogator, a female officer named Dudzai, sat there with her two male counterparts, using torture as a means of extracting information from us. Despite their efforts, we had nothing to offer them in terms of pleasing answers. She sat there, watching as her colleagues took turns flogging us mercilessly under our feet with a doubled electrical cord. Their twisted plan was to leave no visible marks on our bodies while causing us excruciating pain under our feet. But when someone repeatedly strikes the same spot, the pain becomes unbearable, and at times, it feels as though your feet have been completely severed from your body.

When the flogging under our feet failed to yield the desired results, one of the officers left the room and returned dragging a large metal coffin. They forced both of us into the cramped space and locked it shut. It was a terrifying experience for me, as I found myself in a coffin for the first time and I am certain that my second time in one would be permanent. The inside of the coffin was sweltering, and we were sweating profusely, struggling to catch our breath as we shouted back at the wicked officers outside. As the coffin remained closed, we could feel it being dragged along the ground, making us feel as though they were going to bury us alive. This barbaric form of investigation leaves a lot to be desired, especially in this modern era. Some individuals are simply unfit to serve in such positions of authority. Despite the horror of our experience, we were fortunate enough to survive the ordeal and emerge from it alive. But it pains each time I recollect and imagined the same coffin had carried countless decomposing bodies.

Ali paid us a visit while locked, and so did the other ten people from our village who came as a delegation in our defence. Everyone had a feeling that my sister had crossed the line. After that visit by the delegation from our village, among which I was told some shed tears when news broke that we were arrested. This response helped to open up my eyes to see how much people loved me around our neighbourhood. After the village delegates, Amos visited us also during the night hours, I did not know he could be so convincing and respected, but I will never know how he convinced them to be granted permission to see me. From the time the ten people came over to the evening visit by Amos. I knew independence was inevitable.

Those three days spent in police custody felt like an eternity, with day and night blending together as I sat in my cell, isolated and alone. The overpowering stench emanating from the toilet chamber in the far corner of the room only added to my misery. Without any way to tell time, each hour felt like an endless stretch of time. During the day, I would stand by the door and peer through the peephole with one eye closed, watching as people bustled about their daily business outside, cars whizzing past. I longed for the freedom to join them. For hours on end, I would stand there, yearning for a freedom that I had taken for granted before. This experience made me realize that freedom was far more golden than money, and it was the one thing I needed above all else. I began to envision the possibilities and opportunities that could open up for me once I regained my freedom. All other things would simply pale in comparison to the value of being free.

The following morning, we got released, Scot free, without a charge and with nothing to sign. Amos was waiting, his mom joined, she shed tears the moment she saw us. I was feeling a surge of energy in me time and again. A push that made me feel like I could kill my   sister upon seeing her. I am sure Amos was reading my mind, he couldn't leave us but asked that we come with him, and it worked because after two days I was calm.

After the coffin incident and our release without charge or apology by the police. I stopped speaking with my sister for three years and she couldn't care also to speak with me, sometimes spitting when she saw my face while trying all sorts of smaller dirty things during this whole time. This happened while we lived at the same homestead.

For three full years, there was no exchange of a single word between us. We could meet at any other space away from our home, but never making an attempt to speak to each other. One thing she never tried as daring as she is, was to come into physical contact with me. By then I had grown very tall, strong, and imposing. Then there was a turning point, it took something compelling to reach a point of turnaround. My sister became very sick, ending up in the hospital, a time when none of her dear friends and advisers were not willing to help. When she was taken to the hospital in Mhangura, I enquired from my young sister who had taken her after compelling feelings gripped my heart, looking how my little sister looked overwhelmed by the task. She was too young to handle being stuck with a sister in the hospital with no money for her to get treatment. In some medical places in Zimbabwe, they do have a tendency of admitting a patient and ask for payment for each day they spent in care, ironically one would only be paying for their mere presence. It doesn't matter how many days one spent. Medication can only be given when money comes.

It was with that understanding I felt compelled to help and save a life, giving them money to pay for medication, but I did not go there in person. Ali tried to persuade me to go but I had other ideas, so Ali went alone to see my sister while I took a bus to one of my sister's enemies, an enemy in the person of Amos's mother.

She was the Mom I could go to when I felt heavy-laden, but my sister had vowed not to have anything to do with her. Many times she would look the other side when she sees her. This was the person I took a journey to see, I went there with the confidence that she would come forward to help. After listening to me, her husband was still alive, he encouraged her to go and see my sister.

Long story short, in the end, my sister was out of the hospital, alive and thankful. Auntie Regina did not only go to see my sister, but she went a step further and took to her home for further care. Imagine your enemies teaming up to find a way to rescue you in your darkest moment. Any person would have learned a lesson, but my sister being my sister never runs out of drama in life.

Chapter 25

Losing Actor

While days were cruising, I was getting stressed by my lack of progress and that made me feel like it was time for me to do something with my life.

The environment around me offered very little hope and very few options. I was not making any progress. Everything I was trying to work on could not yield the desired positive outcome. At some point I joined hands with Oliver Rabson, an aspirant of premier football like myself, together we began going to train football with Mhangura FC a team that had slid down to the second division. But it was just to maintain shape.

Following the harvest, I made my way to Harare while Oliver returned to Shabani. Little did I know that a sombre experience awaited me, one that would leave a lasting impression and a weighty responsibility. Nevertheless, I accepted this responsibility with open arms. Upon my arrival in Harare, I was informed that my cousin Actor, was gravely ill and lying at death's door in the Harare Hospital. Despite the heart-breaking news, I made my way to the hospital to visit him. I found him lying in his sickbed, his frail body barely able to muster the strength to engage with me. Although he was unable to sit up, he forced himself to converse with me solely to express his delight at my visit. As he expressed his joy at seeing me, I felt a wave of sadness wash over me. The sight of my cousin, lying there in his sickbed, was a stark reminder of the fragility of life. I couldn't help but wonder what had led to this sudden decline in his health.

Despite his weakened state, my cousin spoke with a glimmer of hope for his recovery. His words echoed the same wish and prayer that I held in my heart: that he would pull through and emerge from this ordeal stronger than ever before. Though I desperately wanted to offer him words of comfort and assurance, my tongue felt heavy and my mind blank. Instead, I silently prayed for a miracle. Unbeknownst to any of us, including my cousin, his time on this earth was dwindling. In less than two weeks, he would take his final breath. Yet, even in the face of such a bleak prognosis, he clung to hope and the belief that he would once again walk and live a full life.

When I left Mhangura for Harare, I had intentions of proceeding to Bulawayo to try my luck with work. But after this encounter, I decided to delay. I had to wait a little while, so, I decided to go back to Mhangura and try to raise a bit more money for my journey and most importantly to help him because he had requested that I help him with some cash. I returned to Mhangura, but I never thought that would be the last time to see him. For some reason when I left the hospital, I did not feel that assurance in my heart that he would be well, but I felt my heart surrendering to the possibility that the worst may happen. Before I left for Mhangura, I learned Actor's wife Hazvinei was pregnant, and in the last trimester, but I failed to see her. Their life together had been filled with complexities of sad stories, they had a boy child at first, but unfortunately, the child died while still an infant. I can recall the time Actor narrated to me how a child died in his arms on a train while they travelled to town to see a doctor. That was a very sad experience. I tried to imagine how it felt for them, but honestly I could not feel the pain as much as they did. So, they made a second attempt and Hazvi conceived. Here she was, towards giving birth, yet she had to deal with her husband's sickness.

Life is at times so unfair, when one is faced with such huge troubles, they are never spared, other day-to-day troubles do not relent, in fact, in many cases they become more aggressive.

I got the impression that in the last two weeks of his life, Actor seemed to have been simply waiting for the birth of his son. When the good news came that his wife had a baby boy, I was told he only smiled and gave the boy a name, FLETCHER, named after Actor's father. Nonetheless, he never got to see the boy because he breathed his last, leaving the new-born fatherless. While he was breathing his last, everything got ripe for me to take my journey back to Harare via Norton. I took that journey with the hope to see him and give him the money he asked for. Unfortunately, everything was too little too late, the news awaited my arrival and as soon as I landed in Norton. I was told of Actor's passing. My stepmom had already made her way to Guruve. What a sombre moment especially for me, having grown so closer to Actor over recent years. From the time we started attending school together at Nyamhondoro to the moment we lived together in Harare. That made it feel like a personal loss for me. Actor was so young and exhibiting a lot of potential, it was a huge blow, but above all my sorrows, I felt much for Hazvi who a few days from labour was, now attending the funeral of her husband, while clinging on to her new-born Fletcher who resembled his grandpa in a very great way. Not forgetting she was nursing the bruises from the excruciating labour time. I kept checking on her, but she hid her pain and showed fewer signs of it, no emotion or cracking. She wasn't familiar with most of our relatives, the only people closest to her were me and Truther the brother to Augustine.

As always funerals are always brief, and the next moment working people are in a rush to get back in time for work, back to their places. It was the same here and we knew as per our family custom we would be gathering after three weeks to do the formalities and see who was to take responsibility for looking after the child and play a father figure role. Time fled so swiftly, that three weeks felt like three days, and before we knew it, we were heading back to Guruve. I was late due to a misunderstanding; however, the formalities were done, and luckily upon my arrival, people were still gathered. As soon as I arrived, I could tell something was in the air, there was a way certain people looked at me; that talking eye filled with gossip, a look which always has something to say – while some greeted me with ear-to-ear smiles, with some overzealous aunts choosing to hug me as if I had been rescued from an earthquake. Some aunties called me aside with a big smile to hint at the developments. I wasn't surprised that they had given me the responsibility of looking after the child, I knew beforehand that things would turn out like that. What I did not know was many among the gathering would encourage me to take Hazvi for a wife, it sounded like a great and easy suggestion, after all, I wasn't married and without a girlfriend.

Later on, that evening, one of my cousins named Collins briefed me in the presence of Uncle Fletcher and the rest of the guys. I recall him pressing me hard that evening, and there was silence everywhere, even the ladies went all silent as they listened from within earshot, with ears itching to hear my response to the proposal of taking Hazvi to be my wife. I said no in the presence of everyone despite others urging me to do it. I wondered why there was such a push, I simply said no and refused to explain myself sounding a little rude. Hazvi also wasn't for the idea, I was not the person who would approve, at least then. But it would be untruthful if I deny how tempting and appealing that was, I mean, during that time I had no girlfriend, and then came something that seemed like manna on a silver platter. But above all I felt Hazvi was also too overwhelmed to engage in such. After the gathering, we all parted ways and went our ways. But I made sure to pay visits now and then to see Fletcher and Hazvi. These visits I paid without anything to offer the two, nonetheless, I was never deterred by such

Chapter 26

Under the mine/ Girl crush

It was important for me to resume the plans I had when I parted with Oliver Rabson as he made his way to Shabani. The plan at that point was to try to find a job and work again. I could only think of one better-placed compassionate person in Uncle Chamu. Uncle Chamu was a warm-hearted tall cousin of my dad who lived in Bulawayo Turk mine where he occupied a position of influence, so I felt like imposing myself in his presence would see me landing a job in the end.

As soon as I arrived in Harare, I enquired through Uncle Fletcher who had direct contact with Chamu, the next day I was in the Bulawayo train dreaming with eyes open. Things moved with speed and in no time I found myself on my way to Bulawayo Turk mine as a first-timer in the city of kings, luckily I was not going to be an alien at Turk Mine because there were other close young relatives apart from Bamn Chamu and it made settling a little easier. Bamn Kodza and Uncle Edgar were all working at the same mine.

When I got to Turk Mine, I waited a week before commencing work under the mine. Now I was working, but there was now an issue constant at the back of my mind, unlike previous years, the bells of love were now ringing constantly in my mind. My heart was now telling me to find someone, and at that stage, I felt like it was time overdue and told myself to have one anyhow. From the time I began working there, I kept my eyes open, looking around for any girl that could appeal to my heart and become my girlfriend, but I found none, I was not impressed. I liked down-to-earth good-looking girls who valued themselves, especially those with a light or not very dark skin. But it turned out my search was equal to searching for precious metal. It was highly unlikely that I could find an unlucky beautiful, down-to-earth girl in an environment that had more men than women. So, with no one in sight, I dropped the whole girlfriend thought aside and focused on getting settled into my new environment.

After I told my heart to sit back and relax, it turned out that my heart never got to relax. Maybe because I felt the vacuum every day, an empty space. Maybe the issue could not be entirely suppressed because I felt lonely by the day, and because of that, I began to have a crush on a girl on TV. That's abnormal by any standards, imagine, a TV girl that appeared and appealed to millions, I am sure I was not the only man who liked her. She was popular and featured on the nation's single TV channel several times a day on various music videos. Their videos were among a few that had an alignment with the revolutionary party. Because they had a message resonating with the drive of the ruling party, they were given a lot of airplays on TV and radio every fifteen minutes. Other people better knowledgeable called these short airplay jingles.

Then there were also countless moments where they got airplay for full songs on Television. These were the prime days of Jonathan as a Minister of Information, at that time Jonathan had become the breath of TV and all state-linked media, shaping broadcasting in a new way. Jonathan also had a hand in the band called Pax Afro, writing songs and some say he sang in one of their videos, never appearing on video but doing only vocals.

This new method seemed to have been a well-thought method by the brilliant professor, creating a new method to condition people's minds for the tough times and the new political and economic environment the country was getting into. To be honest, his methods seemed to work because people had only one TV station and subconsciously those Jingles became embedded in people's minds that even enemies of the revolutionary party found themselves singing those popular jingles involuntarily. Close to them was also a group called Tumbuka Dance Company which for a short time took the airwaves by storm, dancing alongside the Pax Afro band. Besides being close to the government, that music group seemed like the real thing, and they looked organized, playing songs that appealed to the emotions and in a way portrayed an Afrocentric way of music and dance that anyone could easily love. The kind that every Zimbabwean would easily relate to, taking people's memories to the good old days of rural Jiti dances around the fire.

Their songs appealed to and made you forget about the political environment around them, and I was no different I also fell victim to the enticement and I remember one of their songs called working under the Mine, a song that seemed to be speaking to the things I was experiencing. I was new to underground mining and struggling to adapt to the conditions. Pax Afro in their song "under the mine" sang to my newfound experiences and I wanted to hear them daily.

It was through my daily observations and attentive listening that I stumbled upon the captivating lead singer of the group, Yulith Ndlovu. Her graceful and alluring presence was impossible to ignore, and I found myself drawn to her in numerous ways. From her soulful singing to her effortless charm, she possessed a unique magnetism that left an indelible impression on me. Yulith's vocal prowess was nothing short of remarkable. Her smooth, resonant voice had a way of transporting listeners to another realm entirely, evoking a range of emotions with every note she sang. But it wasn't just her voice that was mesmerizing - it was her poise and simplicity that truly set her apart. Dressed in unassuming attire, she exuded a sense of effortless elegance, complemented by a dazzling smile that lit up the stage every time she opened her mouth to sing.

As I watched her perform day after day, I couldn't help but be captivated by her magnetic aura. She possessed a rare combination of talent, beauty, and charisma that made her outstanding. What a temptation she became to me, and I wanted to catch the first-morning bus to try and find my way to her. Of course, assuming that she had also a down-to-earth attitude housed inside her beauty.

I guess I was still normal and not going insane, but I had never imagined myself losing sleep over some girl on TV whose appearance and smiling were no doubt a magnet to millions of men that watched the same TV. Wasn't this a weakness? Boy oh boy! Poor me, how could I? Wow, to ever imagine a high upmarket girl on a popular countrywide TV? How would I go there and what would I say to her, assuming I had gone and found her? Poor me, doing this when I was just looking forward to my first salary under the mine. Oh! It sounds like an embarrassing tale told by an idiot, but it's a good thing that nobody knew about this foolish infatuation, I was the only one who knew how much I burnt inside, and I was the only one who knew about my losing sleep on several nights. What a weaker version of me that I had to fight.

My weaker side is going all out when I need something. So I get convinced and think ahead, going all out. I can't help it, maybe that is the downside of not falling for ladies too easily that when my mind gets awakened I love with all my heart. I close my eyes to the whole world and put on blinkers and keep my focus.

So, during that time I badly sought a way to get the contact number of Yulith even though I didn't have a cellular phone. But at the end of it all, of course, I was daydreaming.

While all this madness and daydreaming were taking place, I forgot one thing, a few too many, that was a possibility of a bunch of high-profile guys to go past before I even get closer. Secondly to imagine that band was so dear to Jonathan Moyo, honestly, I was dreaming with my eyes open, and trying to swallow a whole elephant.

After only a month of working underground, I left the mine to everyone's disappointment, the   bosses, and the coaches. I left because the conditions underground were asking too much from me to adapt, I don't know why I was experiencing a lot of nose bleeding even without a headache. But above all, I felt like Turk Mine. Also, for some reason I did not like the idea of settling there, it felt like a place that would not help push what I had in mind, so I decided to go back to the drawing board and that place is called Mhangura.

Chapter 27

Without a plan

After a short stay in Mhangura, I found myself in Norton. This time I had no particular format and plan. Very much uncomfortable, imposing myself on the scene.

The only certificate I had when I arrived was a baptismal certificate confirming my adherence to the Seventh Day Adventist Church. The SDA was also the only place I knew I could quickly find a second home for it can be hard to start a new life in a new environment.

I have been a newcomer a few times and I can tell it can be a very difficult thing to get to a new place and network. In Norton I knew the only way was to build my network around the people from Church, nonetheless, church people are people and they can as well make it hard to break into their established circles. I couldn't wait for the Sabbath to come.

As I walked into Katanga Church in Norton, I don't recall the attire I had adorned, but I wasn't clothed in splendour, for splendour in my world was a taboo. However I had anticipated a warm reception, a welcoming embrace that would make me feel at home. However reality struck to my dismay, I went unnoticed. Perhaps it was a lack of hospitality at Katanga SDA, or maybe I had failed to make my presence known amidst the throngs of countless smiling faces. It could also be that everyone was too preoccupied with their own affairs, a behaviour I myself have exhibited countless times.

For the next two weeks, I attended the church, yet no one acknowledged my presence. I was a mere speck in the sea of unfamiliar faces.

It was not until the following Sabbath that a hospitable fellow, close to my age, finally greeted me. The man who stood amidst the sea of unfamiliar faces to extend a warm welcome was Tichakunda Tagwirei, also known as "elder." I was taken aback at first, as I never imagined someone so young, only 24 or 25 years old, being an elder. It wasn't until several weeks later that I learned Ticha was a layman, much like those I had encountered back in Mhangura. When the term layman in the church first fell into my ears, I was given the impression these were pastors in training, but as time went on I realised only a drop out of the sea of layman ever get promotion to be pastors unless one takes the initiative to go to college.

Lay people are the unsung heroes of the church, tirelessly involved in the work of God. They are akin to runners for the pastors, carrying out much of the grunt work, mobilizing gatherings, preaching, and teaching.

I was reminded of the short man who had preached to me, leading to my conversion. Lay people like him often pave the way for pastors to baptize new converts, playing a crucial role in the growth of the church. Despite their tireless efforts, lay people in the Seventh Day Adventist Church go largely unappreciated and unrewarded. They receive no salaries for their selfless service and depend entirely on the generosity of others for their livelihoods. Unfortunately, this support is often sporadic and inconsistent.

Ticha was one such layman, a married man with a young child. I only met him on my second week of attending church, as he had been absent during my first two weeks. It was then that I learned of his circumstances and the challenges he faced as a dedicated layman. Despite these difficulties, he remained committed to his work in the church, driven by a deep sense of purpose and conviction.

During my fourth week at the church, an announcement caught my attention - a youth social gathering at Vimbai Secondary School. I had never attended such an event before and had no idea what to expect. Nevertheless, my curiosity was piqued, and I decided to attend as a first- timer. I felt it was important to attend gatherings like this, not only to quench my curiosity but also to pursue a potential relationship.

With a high concentration of youthful girls in the church, it felt like they were ours to lose or choose. Traditionally, girls from this church preferred someone within the church community. As I scanned the crowd, I knew exactly what I was looking for – someone truthful, not only well-behaved but also stunningly beautiful, talking of beauty, I had in mind the girls in the Pax Afro music group or even better.

From the very start, I couldn't help but be captivated by one individual in particular. Her appearance was distinct; perhaps not as elegant as the models you see on television, but there was something about her that exuded an air of confidence and assertiveness. It wasn't just her physical beauty that drew me in, but rather an intangible quality that made her all the more alluring.

My eyes first fell upon her while she was leading the congregation in song during an afternoon program at the church. Her voice was melodic and pure, and her movements were graceful yet powerful. With a little bit of inquiry, I learned that her name was Chido Murawu. While she may have appeared shorter than me, she was still of average Zimbabwean height. However, it was her singing voice that truly set her apart. Gifted with a sharp, needle-like tone, her solo performances were simply breath-taking. Listening to her sing was like hearing a voice meant for the celestial choir in heaven.

But Chido's talents didn't stop there. She also possessed an insatiable desire to participate in various church activities, bringing an infectious energy that radiated throughout the congregation. Her passion for worship and serving others was truly inspiring, and it was no wonder that she was highly regarded within the church community.

Social Sundays were a much-anticipated event for young people, as it offered an opportunity to connect and network with their peers. It was a time when we could let our hair down and express ourselves freely, away from the watchful eyes of elders and the formal environment of the church.

Unlike the prim and proper appearances of churchgoers during regular services, Social Sundays allowed for a more relaxed and casual atmosphere, where people could dress down and let their true selves shine. That was the goodness about the social gathering, unlike the church where there was always an unspoken code of conduct that seemed to permeate the church environment.

The popular saying: "Walk softly in the sanctuary," encapsulated the prevailing air of decorum that was expected of all attendees. Every step, every gesture, every word spoken was expected to be executed with utmost respect and reverence for the sacred space. It was a jigsaw piece that fits perfectly with the overall tone of the church, where propriety and respect were held in the highest regard. But not on a day like this, when we knew the sanctuary and its categorized Pharisee-like elders and deacons with eagle sharp eyes to nit-pick and correct the slightest of ill behaviour were away. It was a day to forget all these, putting behind us the holy walk and becoming ourselves. Because of this gathering, I slowly began to know people, the first person to greet me was a girl named Rumbi, her father was a church elder, a devoted man who shaped his life and family around Adventism, almost walking softly even outside Church parameters. We were just a mixed bag of people of different temperaments, some preferring pomp and visibility while others looked humble and talked less, some never uttered a word at all. Among the quietest, some were new like me while some were newly baptized, and still trying to get a foothold and build a network in their new environment.

The following Sabbath brought even more exciting news — there was going to be a camp meeting in Mhondoro. I had never been to one before, and my only frame of reference was the vivid image I had imagined in my mind from the stories told by others. Despite my lack of experience, I was eager to attend the camp meeting and witness for myself the profound encounter with God that so many had described. From what I had heard, it was an otherworldly experience where one could almost imagine God and angels walking and mingling with the congregation. The prospect of being part of something so awe-inspiring and transformative was truly exhilarating.

A few newly baptized guys wanted also to go to their maiden camp meeting just as much as I did. From the time they announced the camp meeting preparations, there was a certain level of hype that gripped the Church, causing some of us to crave more for such a gathering. It was going to be a new experience for us all.

From the talk by the people with a camp experience, they gave the impression that if the second coming of Jesus happens during the camping week, many sounded convinced they would literally enter heaven, and with that understanding, I wanted to be there at all costs.

I was at this point working with another old man doing thatching on a big church in Knowe Norton. From the small earnings I had gathered, I managed to fund my trip to the camp meeting. Teaming up as a bunch of lonely guys with no family to camp with, we grouped and pulled our resources together.

Ultimately making it to the camp as a group, we were quite a number. Among the guys I camped with was a short guy who usually came to church in blue jeans and a red T-shirt, he was a slow and lazy talker with a serious problem of acne. His name became known to me as Allan. I shared the same blanket with him at the camp. What became outstanding for him about that particular camp was how it became an endurable camp as he struggled with a stomach bug. I was a little scared, but eventually, we had a great camp meeting.

As the camp progressed, girls from all walks also attended that camp in numbers too numerous to count, some in prayer groups would openly say how they were praying for life partners, and many among my crew had the same prayer request, yet for some reason at the end of the camp meeting, we all went back empty-handed.

It was after the camp meeting that I and a few guys began to slowly gel together. We started mixing up a bit more with guys from Church. Allan or Sir Adza as we called him became much closer to me from the time we shared a tent and blanket. I realized he was just as healthy as anyone despite his Acne problem. Soon another young man called Mischek became part of the pack, Tichakunda the elder and layman made himself friendly to us, we were all zealous, all curious to learn more of the Bible. His closeness to us helped him to advance his agenda of luring us into an evangelism team.

Now the feelings of pursuing sport began to fade away because of my ever-increasing adherence to the Church and its teachings. The church was now playing an influence on how I ruled my life, kind of taking centre stage, putting pointers to the things and directions I should follow. Things were happening, some without us planning, I found myself together with Allan and Mischek involved in evangelism programs. I felt like it suited us so well since we were all not employed, and I think the Church also viewed us that way.

Our journey continued with a newfound sense of purpose and passion. We had found a place where we could vent our frustrations and make a difference in the world, and we were determined to make the most of it. Unlike other guys with jobs or in college, we had the time and energy to devote to Church programs, and we did so wholeheartedly. We practiced strictness with the Sabbath and adhered to all the teachings in the Bible. And as part of our evangelism team, we even had a few girls, including a young woman named Moline. She was dark, short, and absolutely beautiful, with a smile that could light up a room. Her short hair and punctuality were just a few of the things that made her stand out. Moline was always carrying a notebook to jot down points during every teaching and sermon - a true student of the word. Her two sisters were also part of the Church, and they were both married. The other girl in the group was Chido, my favourite girl at first sight. She was passionate and willing, sometimes held up by commitments at home where she stayed with her married sister, but generally a person we could count on. Bubbling with a can-do attitude, and ability to take the reins and lead in song, also speaking with admirable confidence before a congregation. There was also Lloyd, a light-skinned young man that many looked up to, a kind of busy guy who always tried to share his time between work and church involvement, he was a boilermaker apprentice at the Hunyani pulp and paper, a close buddy of Mischek, very close to each other. Soon Mischek's heart began beating towards Moline, finding himself setting his sights on the ever-smiling Moline. When he began to pursue his quest, I got convinced from my own judgment they seemed a good match and I supported Mischek. Mischek began to push, but none among us could take a guess that a disappointment was brewing inside Lloyd's heart, and before the relationship could materialize, Lloyd jumped in and snatched Moline away from Mischek to the demise of their friendship. But honestly judging, I felt like Mischek was not going to win because circumstances on the ground, economic and otherwise, favoured Lloyd. In the end, Mischek threw in the towel but, sad that Moline and Lloyd would not last long.

Now that Chido my favourite, the soprano singer was regularly featuring among us, I found myself drawn by her positive energy, daily drawing closer and closer. She however had no idea how I felt about her, but in return, she liked speaking positively about me, and I counted that as a plus on my side, it was only towards me that she made good comments time and time. We were not entirely consumed in spiritual matters to the point of forgetting we had lives to lead, we now and then tried to make some income, and I and Allan were almost always together. At that point, the only means to an income between us was his father's lawn mowing machine that he used to make some bucks by cutting grass for whoever would call. Most of the contracts were his father's, nonetheless, I helped him whenever I could and it was from the little money we got, that we used to sustain our small things, from Sabbath meals that we prepared at his home to meals on Social Sundays that we were doing as frequently as we wanted.

At the back of my mind, there was always a consistent thought that lingered, the idea of wanting to end up in South Africa. During that time, people from Zimbabwe required a visa to enter South Africa. Raising R1000 for the visa may sound like a joke now but it was then an uphill task. From the days I mingled with Sign Chuma in Mhondoro to the time of sitting around the fire with Partson who gave me a sightseeing book for Cape Town. I knew Cape Town was the kind of place I wanted to be, everything looked blissful, but I needed a plan to end up in the land of bliss. So, I decided to try the long March to freedom, setting my sight first on Botswana, an idea that seemed realistic.

I began to work towards going to Botswana, but in reality, it was never a walkover especially considering the difficult corner I found myself trying to break free from. I did not have the money to go and make a living on arrival, let alone bus fare to reach there, the odds were against me. I pulled some funds together and made my way to Bindura where my cousin lived.

I first saw Swisdai when we were all very young, I was at my father's place in Chitungwiza, and Swisdai had just lost his parents, so he was looking for a way to kick start his life, looking for some money to go back to school. My father then took him under his wing, going with him to Kadoma to work in the same company that he worked for. Swisdai was ever determined and never lost focus. After working for some time, he was able to go back to school. Ultimately going back to school and progressed until he became a person to be counted on and relied upon at his workplace. What a man with a positive attitude, always jovial and able to ignite a dull moment. He had the kind of energy that could light up a city. He was living in Bindura, now a married man working at Bain's new Holland and steadily growing. For days I stayed with him hoping to borrow some money to go to Botswana. But I was unlucky and had to return back to Norton. My time to make a move was long overdue, I needed to force something to change my life.

My friend Allan was now stationed at his sister's hair Salon, in the same shop by the corner, she allowed a guy named Frisco to put his computer and do music piracy, burning on Compact Disc. Allan became the guy that copied music for people at a fee. It was a place I found myself hanging around many times. His sister did not mind my presence neither did Frisco. Truth being spoken, they respected me even when I had no penny or direction only because of my attitude. In friendship we became one big family when other guys became part of us, those that felt like we belong in the same boat, Blessed, Caspa, and the Huchu brothers. Blessed and

Caspa we're doing carpentry in a rented workshop, giving us an option to a place we could hang around while discussing many life subjects, including of course girls. Some names were thrown in there for discussion, some for approval or disapproval.

By this time, I had made it clear to them all that my heart beats for Chido and the guys felt it was a good thing to try. So, knowing that wishes don't wash dishes, I started making a move, starting point was easy for me, there were countless opportunities to engage her on any subject of choice. We both took part in various church programs like Church music, youth music, church prayer band, and the youth program. She portrayed attributes of a likeable person, always jovial and energetic mimicking her no- nonsense sister in many ways.

By this time Chido had grown much closer to me, I had as well-known of her failures in relationships because mainly guys failed to stand her strictness. Some guys in Church called her *sister white*, and she at many times was at liberty to empty herself to me. I felt all those things played to my advantage, I mean, after knowing all her tricks, she appeared defenceless.

It had been two years since I set my sight on her and liked her, I had asked my questions and she seemed to tick the boxes. All that was left was to hit the striking note.

Our prayer band usually met on Sabbath mornings and Sundays too. Chido, her sister, and the sister's husband were all part of the prayer band, and they came from home as a pack. But going back, she was at liberty to take separate way home and many times during our friendship, we would walk together. Sometimes it was the two of us while other times it was me and Mischek walking her home.

There was one Sunday afternoon, when it was only me and her, as we walked past Calfa towards Mbuya Bona School. A school named after the mother of the former president of Zimbabwe. It was while we walked on the road near this school that I finally told her, telling her probably the things she had been waiting to hear in a while, who knows? But she did what all girls usually do, she was so good, so clever in talking and she spoke convincingly. She said no, but indicated how much she enjoyed the talk, to the point of asking if we could use the longer route if I was not in a hurry. Of course, I wasn't. So, we had a long chat, and after much talk, we parted ways.

Want to know how I felt? Of course, she was a clever talker, she tried to be clever in speech, yet she gave me a hint. Glad I was able to pick it up, had I not, definitely I was not going to have the courage to go back. After that we had a few other moments of engagement on various programs and subjects, and again one good Sunday morning as we left the prayer band in haste to prepare for a Social Sunday event taking place at the Hunyani pulp and paper sports field. When we left the Church I felt Chido had something to say, but, I did not want to give her a chance to speak with me. She was good at hide and seek, and in turn, I decided to play my cards differently when it felt obvious that I was going to walk with her. She found herself isolated. Mischek and I took the same route, leaving her to walk home alone. She quickly saw how I made a deliberate move, and being who she was, she was not to let that happen, she only walked a short distance before calling me to come with her, making it as clear that Mischek was not to be part of us, she wanted me alone.

Well, it was all well, probably not so well with Mischek who had left his route to walk with me halfway down my journey, nonetheless, he had to walk alone, knowing what had been happening between the two of us. It was just a cat-and-mouse game now happening between us that she probably enjoyed while I was getting frustrated. "I just called you to tell you I don't love you" that was all she said. I looked at her and all I could do was laugh. "I know, but thanks for letting me know" So, the discussion was over, I knew she only wanted to provoke me, but having known her I thought it was also my chance to play her and make her curious and on the edge. Knowing that we were going to a Social Sunday, I told her I had to rush and prepare, we agreed and parted ways. I did not doubt that she was beginning to ask herself if she had done it too much to my discouragement. Social Sundays never disappointed and we anticipated a great gathering as usual, filled with games of all sorts, a place for people to express themselves without trying to portray that holier behaviour. We loved Social Sundays, they made us know each other a little further than what we usually saw on a Sabbath day. I mean, Allan and I were too observant of the things that took place around us, sometimes in a flash. How do we remember one dance move by Rumbi? A girl we had always known as this calm daughter of two soft parents, of which the father was an elder in the Church, but she pulled that dance move it was such a shocker to me. She made our day, and we were to remember that dance forever. I knew Adza, in particular, was following up on the progress between myself and Chido, observing the behaviour of the two of us.

On the day, despite being a sporting person I deliberately chose to have less of an active part in the games.

When they began with soccer with boys and girls playing in mixed teams, I chose to be on the terraces cheering, making us two cheerers on the stands. Allan always took part in sport, he never kicked a ball in his life, so that made two of us be on the terraces.

Chido had chosen to play, but in no time, she pulled out to come and sit by me, Sir Adza took notice, and he pulled away to give us space as he went on to cheer from the touchline. Eventually, Chido convinced me to go and play, and we played on the same team. As we played, each time I touched the ball she expected me to pass it to her, and Sir Adza would not help but laugh from the touchline.

After a thrilling game of football, we all gathered together for some post-game activities. We were determined to make the most of our time together, and so we played game after game, talked, and shared all sorts of delicious foods. But as the day began to wind down, we all knew that there was one more game that had to be played - a game that was a must-do for everyone, no matter what. It was called Sarura Wako, and it was the perfect way to seal up our day of fun and bonding.

In this game, we formed a circle and sang together, cheering on the person in the middle as they danced around in circles, looking for someone to choose. Everyone took their turn, whether it was just for fun or as a signal that they were interested in someone else. For me, there was only one person I had my eye on - Chido. But it seemed like everyone else knew it too. Whoever entered the middle, the girls would avoid choosing me, while the guys, even just for fun, avoided choosing Chido. Despite the playful nature of the game, it was clear that there were some unspoken rules in play. And as we all laughed and sang together, I couldn't help but wonder what was in Chido's mind. The moment that Allan and I had been waiting for finally arrived - it was Chido's turn to choose someone in the Sarura Wako game. As I watched her dance around in the circle, I couldn't help but wonder what was going through her mind. Would she choose me?

Despite the signs of jealousy that had been creeping in, I couldn't shake the feeling that this was a crucial moment - a chance to measure how she truly felt about me. And as the song continued, my heart raced with anticipation, hoping she would set a decoy. But then, to my surprise, Chido chose me. It was as if the whole Social Sunday had been organized just for us. Everyone in the group erupted in cheers and whistles, and it felt like the perfect end to a day of fun and bonding.

As I looked around at the smiling faces and heard the laughter ringing out, I knew that this was a moment I would never forget. But we were okay, there was nothing wrong with all that, we were just part of a big team, making contributions to the fun. Surprising how after this incident she still carried on playing hide and seek, and I knew there must have been a third hand, and I was right. There was someone elderly watching, and upon seeing us together several times, they went on to give her advice. Her mind was torn between what she wanted and what people of experience told her. I was not employed, and neither was I at the college or varsity, my only hope was to land a job somewhere in a foreign land and start building from there. She partially gave it a chance.

So, she said yes, a hesitant approval, nonetheless an approval, one that upped my energy and willingness to hit the ground running and prove myself worthy. I felt compelled to brave the weather.

Chapter 28

III – prepared

Mischek and I had made the bold decision to leave Zimbabwe behind and try our luck in Botswana. For me, at that moment there was one thing that mattered more than anything else - getting married and starting a new life.

Over the years, I had watched many of my former classmates tie the knot and start families of their own. And as I approached my adulthood, I couldn't shake the feeling that I was falling behind somehow, obviously not in competition with pals, but it was a response to my own cloak. I had made efforts to approach life with care and caution since childhood, it seemed like I was constantly getting knocked down. Lady Luck had deserted me long ago, and I was left with nothing but my own determination to keep moving forward. And so, with little idea of what to expect, we set out on our journey to Botswana. We knew that life itself would be our teacher and that every step we took into the unknown would be a test of our faith and resilience. But even in the face of uncertainty, I felt a glimmer of hope. I hoped that trip was the one to afford us a chance to take control of my destiny.

Francistown is a small city located in Botswana, in close proximity to the Plumtree border that separates Zimbabwe and Botswana. Plumtree, the Zimbabwean side of the border, derives its name from the area's presumably straight trees, but I never bothered to investigate. On the other hand, the Botswana side named their border Ramokwebana. Despite the numerous obstacles and challenges, we encountered along the way, we finally arrived in Francistown, brimming with energy and a sense of accomplishment. Although we had a meagre sum of only twenty Pula, which was equivalent to approximately $4 at the time, we remained undeterred and looked forward to sending a favourable report back home. We held high hopes that we would soon be congratulating ourselves on a job well done. However, our arrival was met with a hostile reception, not just towards us, but towards all Zimbabweans. It seemed like brutality was the icing on the cake for Botswana law enforcement, which was even more prevalent in Francistown than in other areas.

One significant difference between Botswana and other countries like South Africa is the nature of the hostility. While Botswana citizens are generally good-natured and harmless, the police and soldiers were present everywhere, looking agitated and ready to punish. Meanwhile, South Africa has an alarming rate of violent crimes and a general public that harbours strong feelings of hatred.

In Botswana, the security forces could easily identify Zimbabweans, mainly from their humble dress, among other things. It felt like a curse to be a Zimbabwean, considered as the lowest of citizens by people in whose country we roamed in search of a better life. The feeling of being unwelcome and unwanted was palpable, and it made us realize how difficult it was to integrate into a foreign society. One could not walk a long distance without encountering either the Police or Soldiers. At night they knew places where Zimbabweans logged and they came raiding fiercely with an astonishing appetite to brutalize.

Mischek was so unfortunate, by only delaying to open his bio page of the passport, he was given a clap in the night. Such kind of a clap caused his ear to ring bells days after the incident. What a trip! So unfortunate for Mischek, this came to him while we still had it fresh in our memories of how he lost his small suitcase in Kwekwe while on the train. As the train got in motion leaving the station, a thief jumped in a grabbed the suitcase vanishing into thin night air with all his clothes. Fortunately, he kept his money and passport in his pocket.

While we least anticipate anything, when the guy was still trying to recover from this, another demoralizing incident strikes in the night. The police knew these places where people took refuge and, in the night, went to raid one after the other because they were many. The conditions in these places were not great.

Men and women slept in the same wide room with nothing to divide between. The word privacy had no place here, meaning you had to be a person of a certain mentality to withstand pressure and last longer or simply succumb to the enticement. The ladies cared less and could dress or undress, going half naked or applying lotion, scattering breasts all over, and each time you turn your head that early morning, (your eyes would catch site of fallen soldiers) a derogatory term used for sagged breast, and there we were subjected to naked breasts without brasseries everywhere, the kind that took away our appetite of seeing naked breast, however, we got captivated and looked on, surprised, not only by naked breasts but by seeing other men not paying attention and we knew they were used to this and probably fed up. That was too much for two innocent guys whose lives revolved around church, prayer and fasting. We felt like the place and these small incidents were dragging us by the nose to the bottomless pit. We prayed to God to take us somewhere else, we had prepared to face challenges but failed to imagine an experience like this one, it was beyond our preparation.

By sunset the following day God indeed took us someplace. We had one plan which felt better than watching sagged breasts uncovering before us. We agreed to camp in the nearby bushes around Francistown, to sleep in the bushes by night while coming into the city by day to look for work. We had everything figured out, like bathing, we had seen a river flowing with clear water and we knew where to go and bathe. This plan saved not only the purpose of taking us away from bare breasts, but we would also save Ten Pula each night, meaning we only had to make sure we bought our brown loaf and Drink Opop, a powder that could be diluted with water. For days we lived on bread and Drink Opop, the bread was so filling that we only needed a loaf per day, unlike our first day in Botswana, arriving hungry, with a Zim mentality of sharing a loaf in half or just finishing your own loaf. It's a thing that was very common between us, it became a routine, buying unsliced bread that we would simply tear like vultures devouring a carcass. We were ruthless towards bread, and because of that we had many days that we never ate at home.

Life did not welcome us so great in Francis Town, though we weren't strangers to hardships, we simply diminished in front of unfamiliar things we walked into, falling short of survival tactics in this environment during our short stay. But we were never worried when we were going through these things, how we felt comfortable when we were homeless away from home. I remember how we sat hidden in the tall grass just by the edge of an army barrack, watching troops patrolling the boundary of the Barrack fence without noticing our presence. That was very risky, but I can only see how risky it was now, what if we were seen and mistaken for spies or enemies?

When days were passing without significant change, we pinned our hopes on the power of God hoping he will send our way a solution. Pressing forward I remember on a weekend, Saturday, as usual would only be meaningful when we found the Church, and we did. It was after the Sabbath when we ended up at the pastor's house, and it turned out he was a senior pastor, the head of their conference. We approached him with hope and never cared or knew what discomfort we were bringing, after telling him our story he gave us a place to sleep one night, and the following morning gave us work that we spent the whole day doing. After that, he blessed us with P50 and told us to use that to return home. So, we left his place with Pula 50 knowing it was not enough for one person to take a bus home.

We tried to seek for solutions to our immediate problem and found none. So, we looked at each other and exchanged those looks as we watched success drifting further away. And in no time, we found the courage to make use of P50 to go home and indeed we made our way back to Norton with nothing to show. People were surprised by our sudden return, of course they scorned us, and some made it worse by making a mockery out of the whole thing insinuating that we were deported. Mischek tried to convince them clarifying we did not come back because we got kicked out but for other reasons. I did not have the time and energy to argue or to try and explain myself. I had bigger things to worry about. That failure probably discouraged the girl who gave me the energy to take that journey and soon she caught the eye of another guy named Phillip, he was a good guy in the sense that most of us agreed, he was in a sense most of the things we all aspired to be. A good accounting job he had, living in Knowe with his brother according to our knowledge. Phillip used to come to our Sunday music gatherings or socials driving top-of-the-range cars, changing them from time to time while we could only imagine what driving felt like, we looked like dwarfs in comparison to him from the outlook. Rumours of him having registered his own Company were already rife among Church people, and soon he moved out and began living alone while I, his competitor was just ambitious and hopeful for a better future without a proper outlined plan to get there. I mean who would blame the girl for choosing him over me? Phillip's only problem was being scared to confront the girl. Like many guys, he was intimidated by her confidence and assertiveness.

Many in the Church called her *Sister White*. Phillip sought a friend's help, those that took it a privilege to be closer to him, guys like Elvis who volunteered to do the dirty work for him and convinced Chido to jump ship. My only option was no option but to carry on living and look to the future. I am sure everyone could understand through proper reasoning if anyone made me their last choice, and I had such an understanding too and only blamed myself for lacking vision and a plan to see myself out of the tight spot.

As I continually tried thinking about a way, this time on my own seeking another plan that could bring some change into my life and see the wheels rolling, nonetheless I had no proper plan on how to get out of my situation. The other thing that was going through my mind was a myriad of questions on why I was unable to come up with a plan, I wasn't sure if I was just denying that reality seen in me by those people that did not believe in me. I would spend a lot of moments during the night trying to crank my mind into a thinking mode. Many times I felt like I would give in and succumb to circumstances.

Chapter 29

Lessons from Zambia

One day my uncle Fletcher told me Augustine was in town from Zambia, so I sought a way to call him and freely expressed my desire to go with him to Lusaka.

I wanted to go with nothing specific that I would do there, my spirit was agitated and simply wanted some movements and a refreshment to my mind. I needed to do something or go somewhere. Augustine was more than willing to take me to Zambia without seeking to know why I wanted to go with him, as a matter of fact, he expressed a delight to have me around him. At least in Augustine, I had somebody who understands my desperation and desire to see a bit of movement around me. Usually, people feel bothered by having someone who has no clear plans, but Augustine saw no problem in taking me across the border, not when I had nothing specific to hang around for. From another angle, this pushing and movement were meant to quench my agitated spirit. It brought a bit of positive energy in me and caused me to keep believing.

Going places does always have its advantages, it opens up eyes in a particular way. I packed my thatching tools because at that point, the only other thing I could think of after football was to use my newly gained experience, thinking if a chance could arise, I could use my acquired skill, a skill that I wasn't proud of, nonetheless a skill that I could use if an opportunity arose. I packed the tools. Each time I think of that time it feels a little embarrassing to me to relate how I carried thatching tools to Zambia. On this same point, I am surprised that Augustine took from a positive point and whenever he tried to encourage other people on being courageous and prepared, he gave my example, of how he felt I was prepared to face life. He could be right, and I do not dispute it. Only when I was feeling low and embarrassed that of all jobs listed, I could only do thatching. Nonetheless Augustus interpreted that as courage and determination. It's a good thing to be positive and build upon the present. I found the Zambian environment to be very conducive for a person like me. The country's peaceful and friendly atmosphere made me feel welcome, and I enjoyed exploring the local culture and traditions. Even though I could attest to these positives, the country's economic opportunities were limited, and obtaining a work visa was not easy.

Nevertheless, these challenges did not make my stay in Lusaka boring at all.

Augustine lived in Long Acres, an area characterized by high walls and tall trees that give it the appearance of an affluent neighbourhood. Not far from Augustine's place was the American Embassy, which stood out from other buildings and embassies with its unique design and architecture.

Despite the economic challenges, I enjoyed my time in Zambia and felt grateful for the opportunity to experience a different way of life. The country's natural beauty, welcoming people, and vibrant culture left a lasting impression on me. To kill my time and boredom while in Lusaka, I spent a lot of my days watching DSTV, with VH1 being my preferred channel for its music selection. At other times, I found myself wandering around the city, observing, and admiring the sights and sounds around me. Street vending was commonplace, and I was particularly fascinated by the guys who pushed modified wheelbarrows, replacing the regular wheel with car wheels, after which they give a name "fibala." It was awe-inspiring to see how much weight these wheelbarrows could carry, sometimes even surpassing the weight of an actual car. It looked like a litmus test to the strength and determination of the people who used them. It's hard for me to forget how these guys would push their loads under the scorching heat of the Lusaka sun, panting, gasping, and sweating while constantly replenishing themselves with bottled water. The thin face towels they used to wipe away sweat was commonplace in Lusaka during the hot season. I cannot do justice to Zambia without mentioning the country's diverse and delicious African cuisine, the warm and welcoming nature of its people, the love for formal wear in Lusaka, and the widespread use of English as a common language due to the country's linguistic diversity. It's impressive to see how women in Zambia hold on to their cultural African values despite being educated. Speaking of food, my first taste of fried chips made from sweet potatoes was in Lusaka, and I must say they were delicious. I also fell in love with some of their organic products. However, what I crave the most is Chikanda, an alternative to meat made from various plant seeds. It's a dish I could eat with much gladness any day.

During my visits to some of the shanty suburbs in Lusaka, I was pleasantly surprised to find a sense of community and togetherness among the people. There were no incidents of crime or violence, which made my experience even better. All in all, my experiences in Zambia were overwhelmingly positive, and I was able to see the country's good side.

Chapter 30

Meeting Obert

After 2 months I returned to Norton to resume our normal routine. The routine included gathering at various points with Church friends, Allan, Mischek, Blessed, Caspa and the Huchu brothers, gathering at Frisco's, at Blessed's carpenter shop. We also carried on with church business. Talking of church business, at this point, we had become like an evangelism team for the district. The district of Norton had five Churches.

We were based at Katanga Church which happened to be the first and Mother Church to all other churches in the area. Still being led by Tagwirei, who ministered to the whole district, hence it made things easy for him to move with us to other Churches for efforts and crusades. We began helping a sister church conducting Bible studies in homes around Knowe which is considered a low-density area in Norton.

When we started working with Knowe church, it is here we encountered this short, dark, talkative young man with a little limp, only a little younger than me. He looked very young then. Soon he began to talk, and we learned through him of his recent relocation from Harare to Norton and was renting at the house of the elder of Knowe Church. This newly relocated man introduced himself as Obert Jongwe.

In life, you come across people who are gifted in talking but this one was beyond anything I had encountered. I remember the only time we had to say anything before him was before introductions, thereafter, he did all the talking, it felt like he could ask a question and answer it. But we all liked him at once. Obert was married with one young child. His wife then was going to college while he spent most of his time at home. He had so much time at his disposal that he volunteered to join us in conducting Bible studies, his situation was different, and he was not desperate despite spending most of his time at home.

His small, rented dwelling looked packed with furniture of good quality. He could feed our whole evangelism team every day, this he did after noticing the insufficiency of what the Church of Knowe had organized for the team. His house and everything that he had seemed like they all belonged to some big guy doing great stuff and not him. We were all curious but found guts to ask him how he earned his living, later he told us he was an artist and sells art with Galleries in Harare and one in Cape Town called Rossouw based in Hermanus. We listened to this guy a lot, but it was difficult to remember the things he said because they were so many. He is a talker, the kind that feels sick if he doesn't speak out. We stayed in touch with him until we became closer, especially to me and Allan, and he made efforts to reach out to us even outside of evangelism work. We became free to engage him at any time. Our conduct was not entirely evangelism, each one was trying a way to take off from the ground. I kept sneaking out to Zambia now and then to learn a few things from Augustine who at that point was trying to establish something of his own.

So, it was like that for me; Zambia, Norton, church, and camp meeting preparations at that point and soon the camp itself. After the camp I found myself going again to Zambia, this time I tried buying clothes for resale in Mhangura, I was pushing myself as I felt like I was losing precious time, there was a hunger inside me that required me to find a way to satisfy it. I tried many other things that were also commonplace in Zimbabwe. Several times I made my way to Botswana to buy merchandise because Botswana was a closer neighbour with plenty of Chinese-operated shops. In doing this I was aiming to raise money for my South African Visa, with Cape Town in mind.

My friend Obert had already sponsored his uncle and Brother to go to Cape Town to search for work and they were already working, sending back glamorous reports, painting a picture of an abrupt rise in their way of life.

I vividly recall the challenges I faced in raising the R1000 amidst the relentless onslaught of inflation that ravaged Zimbabwe in 2007/2008. The economic landscape was in turmoil, and the value of the currency was plummeting at an astonishing rate. The foreign exchange market was a volatile and unpredictable terrain, with exchange rates changing at a frenetic pace - up to 10 times a day! I can still recall the frustration I felt while attempting to purchase foreign currency on the black market at the bustling East Gate centre in Harare. The exchange rates were exorbitant, and I found myself hesitating due to the exorbitant prices. Undeterred, I decided to venture to the Road Port, which was a mere four-minute walk away. Alas, when I arrived, I was met with a staggering exchange rate that was even higher than the one at East Gate. Feeling despondent, I made my way back to East Gate, convinced that it was the better option. However, to my dismay, the exchange rate had already skyrocketed, and it was becoming increasingly challenging to secure the foreign currency I needed.

The situation was dire, and I found myself trapped in a never-ending cycle of fluctuating exchange rates and mounting frustration.

Chapter 31

Going to Gaborone blindly

While I was in Zambia, a daring idea began to take shape in my mind, and I embraced it. Despite my tendency to seek guidance and support from others, I decided to keep this plan to myself, not mentioning anything even to Augustine. This time, I was determined to embark on an adventure alone. With a newfound sense of courage, I resolved to travel to Gaborone, Botswana, without any assistance or companionship. Although I knew Augustine had always supported me, I felt compelled to take this risk on my own. I feared that he may try to dissuade me from the idea or worry excessively about my safety. I was determined not to let anyone, or anything hold me back.

Departing from my usual routine, I purposely took the afternoon bus from Lusaka to Harare. Despite the long journey and the fact that I would arrive in Harare at night, I remained resolute in my mission. As the bus rumbled towards the border between Zambia and Harare, my heart swelled with anticipation and excitement. I was about to embark on a journey that would test my limits and push me out of my comfort zone, but I was ready for whatever lay ahead.

Finally arriving in Harare, I felt a rush of triumph and exhilaration. I kept encouraging myself to carry on with the idea. Although the road ahead promised uncertainty, I was determined to face it with unwavering courage and determination, knowing that with faith it was possible to overcome any obstacles that lay in my path. So, I took off from Zambia knowing the bus would arrive in Harare at midnight, and everything went just as expected.

I arrived safely at midnight in Harare's Road Port where I mingled with various people packed at that place for various reasons. There was a wide foyer with permanent, fixed smooth metal benches spread all over, so nobody really cared why you are seated and for how long.

While I sat there waiting for morning time to make my move. I observed overnight more buses arriving mainly from South Africa, so people were always there in numbers. I chose to linger at the benches spread all over the wide waiting area, sitting there waiting for dawn to fall when most minibuses starts operating. I did just that, hanging around until 04:00 hrs.

Finally, the hours of anticipation came to fruition, signifying that my plans were about to be set in motion. Next, I found myself boarding a minibus headed for Mbare bus terminus, with the intention of catching the Gaborone-bound bus which was scheduled to depart before 06:00hrs. By avoiding the morning rush hour, I was able to quickly settle into a seat on the bus en-route to Gaborone - a city where I knew no one, had no contact information or any points of reference. Stepping into unfamiliar territory, I knew I would be surrounded by countless unfamiliar faces, buildings, streets, and an overwhelming number of new experiences. Despite this, my intuition assured me that I would be able to navigate these new surroundings with ease.

As I made my way towards Gaborone, I couldn't help but feel a sense of excitement and anticipation. This was going to be my first time in that city, and I was eager to explore all that it had to offer. Although the prospect of being in a new and unfamiliar place was daunting, I remained confident that I would be able to navigate my way.

My arrival in Botswana Gaborone the following morning was as per expectation, without any problem but feeling very exhausted, having been on the Lusaka bus the previous day after which I found no rest. Now the Gabs journey was three to four times longer, making me feel highly exhausted and only wishing I could find a place to sleep. Despite being exhausted, I realized that arriving in Gaborone was not enough - I still had a long journey ahead of me before I could finally rest. This was just the beginning. My first task was to secure a place to live and begin my new life in this unfamiliar city. This time around, unlike my previous experience in Botswana with Mischek, I was acutely aware of the potential dangers of sleeping in the bush, and I made a firm decision that it was not a viable option for me.

Gaborone, in comparison to Francistown, is a bustling metropolis. Upon my arrival, I immediately sensed a feeling of relaxation in the air - a stark contrast to the constant sense of hostility that permeated Francistown, where it often felt like you were being watched at every turn. With a sense of purpose, I scanned my surroundings, searching for someone that I could turn to for help. It wasn't long before I noticed a group of men and women dressed in white - unmistakably members of the Marange church from Zimbabwe, who were well-known in Botswana for their forex trading expertise. Realizing that they might be able to offer some assistance, I approached them with a sense of cautious optimism - hoping that they would be able to guide me in my search for a new home in this vast and unfamiliar city.

As I arrived in Gaborone, I couldn't help but feel like an outsider. At this point, I was the only person who knew about my journey to Botswana, as Augustine was reluctant to check up on me, assuming that I was in Zimbabwe. Meanwhile, people back in Zimbabwe believed that I was still in Lusaka. However, all of their assumptions were misplaced. I had made it to the heart of Botswana and was now on the hunt for a place to stay, armed with only 120 Pula - my last bit of money.

Following directions from the Mapositora people at the bus terminus, I eventually stumbled upon a place to rent, known locally as "kwagogo". But by this point, I had only 100 Pula left in my pocket. With this money, I paid 90 Pula for a month's rent and was left with a mere 10 Pula, which I used to purchase milk and mealie meal - or "parish", as it is known in Botswana. Despite my limited resources, I felt a sense of relief knowing that I had secured a roof over my head and a meal to sustain me. It was a promising start to my new short stay in Botswana, and I remained optimistic about my adventure.

As I lay in my new home, surrounded by unfamiliar faces and with no blanket to keep me warm, I couldn't help but feel grateful for the small blessings that I had been afforded thus far. Although I was still a stranger in a foreign land, thanks to the calm Botswana weather and the good timing. Also, in terms of the differences between Francistown and Gabs. At least this time the ladies lodged in a separate room, unlike my first encounter in Francis Town.

When I arrived in Gaborone, my mind remained uneasy because I wanted to be in SA ultimately. All these movements were makeshifts in preparation for what I really wanted to do; hence I did not last long, only worked for a month to raise money to buy electrical gadgets for resale in Zimbabwe and Zambia to speed up the raising of R1000.

Again, I took a trip to Zambia, this time I was going to sell some electrical gadgets as well as help Augustine like my previous visits. He had started his own company supplying and programming scales, a job that took me to places in Zambia. At this time Augustine was now married to Chichi a humble Zambian lady, he also rented another house that only a maid occupied. So, I went on to join the maid, a move that turned out to be quite a test for me, staying with a single of the opposite sex was by all costs a temptation. Nonetheless, I was able to stand resolute, even though the desire would at times push me to just follow the feelings.

I have tried all my life to avoid things that would embarrass me, and in that case, I knew if I had engaged in something stupid, there was no way I would have been proud, it was a guaranteed embarrassment. The maid told me she was preparing to get married soon, yet she surprisingly tried to Initiate Sex with me. Was that a big challenge? Uhm, not really, I knew what I wanted so it was either I get what I want, or I don't get anything. So passive resistance works wonders for me and also minding my business. Thanks to life experiences that have taught me to mind my business. At that point, I had a clear reason to say no and remain faithful. I had met Caroline, a graceful and fair-looking lady from Katanga Norton, who had become the new love of my life. Despite being miles apart, I remained true to her, and loyalty was my middle name while sincerity was the icing on the cake. I made a promise to her, and I showed it through my actions.

My involvement with godly business in Norton played affirmation to my character, giving me more reason to say yes for yes and no for no.

When you go around evangelising, you don't end up doing the opposite of what you encourage others not to do. I wanted to stay true to the things I told others. Not underplaying the impact of my upbringing, from a tender age I had learned to stay away from things that had the potential to bring an undesired outcome.

I am not saying the maid did a bad thing, if anything, it is normal for a person to exhibit intentions to the opposite gender if they consider them desirable. Despite what I felt, thought or what she did or didn't do, it remained nonetheless a temptation. However, there was another person who stirred my emotions in a much stronger way, causing me to think twice. I remember spending time with Janet, Chichi's sister or, to be more precise, Augustus's sister-in-law. It was impossible for me to be around Janet and remain unaffected. She was incredibly beautiful and appealing, a real temptation that made my heart race. I struggled to resist my attraction to her and had to fight my own feelings. At times, I found myself imagining what it would be like to be a Zambian son-in-law. It was difficult not to consider her as a potential girlfriend or even a wife. I mean, who wouldn't want to wake up to that melting smile?

While on two occasions Japheth went naughtier by trying to cheer us into kissing each other in front of him. I mean, everything that a person of my age longed for, seemed to present itself as a beautiful package in her, and everyone around me felt there was something wrong with me. Janet was a real headache for me, nonetheless, I managed to remain restrained. Besides Janet, there was again another girl I encountered while we went about the scale business, with Japheth Nyati in the mix, Japheth was a fellow Brother-in-law to Augustine, married to the sister of Chichi. One of the prominent places we used to go was an Abattoir called

Majoru where a fair young Coloured lady worked. That girl went to her lengths in expressing how she wanted me for her boyfriend. Each time I remember her I feel like I broke her heart even though we never had a love affair. I remember the whole team, saying they thought she was good for me. Some weekends we went there with Augustine and his brother Truther to service scales and weighbridges. The lady was hospitable towards us, treating us like kings in their canteen. I remember everyone on the team including Augustine urging me to go all out for this young lady and everything felt compelling.

But my love for Caroline and commitment and belief was stronger than any enticing smile. I had loyalty springing from the depths of my soul. I should also point out how it isn't fashionable to stay truthful and resolute when at times it felt like I was being stupid and overdoing things.

That young lady was disappointed in me and so was the whole team, but I was just staying true to the things I believed in, never intended to embarrass, or bring emotional pain to any girl. It was for the same reason I stayed away from things like double-crossing. Soon the Zambian temptations were going to be forgotten as I went back with a thankful heart for the hospitality.

Chapter 32

When I least expected it

When I returned to Norton, I visited my talkative friend Obert, who had just returned from Cape Town. Sadly, he had separated from his wife, but it never looked like a big thing because he made it seem so. As usual, we talked about life and progress, telling me how flourishing his art was in Cape Town. In turn, I briefed him on how things were going with me, and how it had remained a struggle to raise the R1000 for the Visa. Oh, how it again sounds ridiculous now for any serious person to stall in raising a thousand rand. Of course, it sounds so because times have moved, however, during those days it was a mountain. So, after listening to me, he offered to give me R1000 to buy travellers' cheques. At last, it was happening, my dream of heading to South Africa was coming into reality, moving a step closer to my wish.

Those days we watched a lot of SABC TV and admired the glamour on the news and their films, we were all getting the impression that life is glorious in South Africa. The kind of glamour that overshadowed the ugly reports we all heard. Everything about South Africa in comparison to how hard life was getting each day in our country, no matter how we looked at it, all seemed like SA had things to die for. To cement this assumption we had to simply go to the Road Port in Harare where buses from South Africa load and unload. Taking a sit on the benches, observing, how other Zimbabweans coming back were carrying loads and loads of heavy goods wrapped in all forms and shapes leaving me to only wonder what could be in their heavy luggage.

Their dressing as well spoke well about the place they came from, nothing looked amiss, and you could easily identify them among other people. So, as I sat there, I would imagine what life was going to be if I made it to South Africa, I couldn't help but imagine myself being the next guy coming back with such goodies. It seemed like destiny was now just before me to shape it in the way I see best. From whatever angle we looked at life, listening to stories about how much people earn, and calculating daily expenses against the minimum wage, it still gave us hope that we would make it, I felt like there was no way I would fail to afford breakfast daily. South Africa offered more hope than we had imagined. TV made it worse by portraying things beyond our imaginations.

With everything set, my visa finally in my passport I finally kissed Caroline goodbye leaving for Cape Town, the place I had read about a lot, a place I wished I could reach and experience. I left Norton having assured Caroline that as soon as I began working, we would marry and live happily together. I meant every word and had determined in my mind to do just that. So, I said goodbye to her, obviously with tears on her cheeks. Off I headed to South Africa. A land of a diversity of people, languages, and beautiful ladies, the land of the good, the bad, and the ugly. I arrived in Cape Town and got welcomed by Peter Jongwe, the uncle to Obert. I had known Peter and became closer to him while we still lived in Norton. The guys that lived in the house at corner Regent Road in Woodstock in Cape Town could be well positioned to tell a better story, especially about the house they lived in. Woodstock is an old suburb, only a stone's throw away from Cape Town City Centre. Though most of the houses in Woodstock looked older, this particular one stood prominent, in a state of disintegration, making it a perfect shelter for people like us coming from either war-tone countries like DRC or our own Zimbabwe with its ever-increasing economic problems. Regent House was a tight dwelling accommodating a lot of people, but for a person like me, having once existed in Botswana where six people slept on one bed, and worse those days in Francistown with Mischek in the bushes, I did not see any major problem with living at Regent.

There was another thing that stood out, one thing that particularly caught my attention while inside the house, the pungent aroma of fish emanating from the cooking of the couple hailing from the Democratic Republic of Congo. Their culinary endeavours lasted a considerable amount of time, but the true issue lay in the overpowering scent of the dried fish from their homeland which asserted itself prominently and lingered long after the cooking had ceased. Despite the persistent odour, we made a conscious effort to attend to our affairs. Great to say many of the guys if not all the Zimbabwean guys that lived at the Regent House were also from Church, I mean the SDA Church, making it so easy to gel with these strangers. Soon they ceased to be strangers but brothers and friends I could have confidence in, some if not only one was married but his wife still in Zim. This was the place where I initially had the pleasure of meeting individuals such as John Mabuto, a composed and candid gentleman. Simba Makombe, who frequently occupied the communal kitchen with his significant other, now his wife, was also among the group. Clever Kahari was present as well and let us not overlook Uncle Peter and his nephew Joachim. Joe, as Joachim was commonly called, along with Peter, both of whom were related to Obert, proved to be invaluable in making my stay a bit more manageable. Without their assistance, I would have found it quite arduous.

Teaming up with the Regent guys for a church outing on Saturdays was a breeze. The church in question was referred to as Salt River, and upon my introduction to it, I discovered that the older members of the congregation, mainly comprised of Coloured individuals, would often boast about the fact that they were worshipping in the oldest standing Seventh-day Adventist church building within the republic. It was within the confines of this historic church building where I encountered a number of individuals who would later become dear friends and integral members of my community. Among them were Aaron Motsi, Brighton, Tapiwa Furawo, Lawrence, Jerimoth, and Timothy Nkata with more pouring in as time progressed. Our community continued to swell with this influx, more individuals from both our home country and Malawi. Some of these guys included Peter Mutenure, and Admire in a wheelchair, I saw also Edwin Anderson coming in, and they kept coming and adding to the Church. Grace and her sister Gelline were already there upon my arrival, later came Kidwell, Prince, and a whole lot more.

Upon my arrival at Regent, I was met with the unfortunate news that the base was set to close, leaving each individual to fend for themselves. At the time, I was unemployed and found myself seeking refuge at a local establishment known as Dolly's, situated on Albert Road in the Woodstock neighbourhood. Dolly's was in close proximity to Gympie Street, a location notorious for drug-related activity and gangs. One would think twice before venturing near Gympie and Page streets, as young men brandishing knives would often follow and rob unsuspecting individuals of their belongings.

I remember my first encounter with robbery vividly. On my way to Cape Town, with only a R20 note in my pocket and no mobile phone at the time, I passed Gympie Street. In a matter of moments, two young men with sharpened knives began to follow me closely. It was the first time in my life that I had been threatened with a knife, and I knew exactly what they were after. Without uttering a word, I surrendered to their demands as they searched me and took the R20 note, the sole bit of money standing between me and destitution.

It is safe to say that my life would have been significantly more difficult had it not been for the unwavering support of individuals like Peter and Joachim. These two gentlemen proved to be instrumental in helping me get on my feet as I faced a rocky start in Cape Town. Although Peter was not residing at Dolly's, he consistently lent me a helping hand, while Joachim, whom we affectionately referred to as "Mkoma" or "Brother Joe," stood by my side throughout my struggles. Despite his reputation for having a short fuse, Joe showed me nothing but unwavering respect and admiration, sharing valuable lessons from his past successes and failures.

Chapter 33

Settling in Cape Town

The decisions I made during my formative years played a significant role in shaping my experience at Dolly's. It was a place that had the power to lead one down a path to ruin. The inhabitants of Dolly's were primarily young people, with a handful of adults scattered about. The lifestyle at this establishment was characterized by recklessness, and it was not uncommon to see people arrive at Dolly's with a completely different demeanour than the one they had after spending a few weeks or months there. Many individuals who frequented Dolly's became feral, their behaviour and attitudes mirroring that of wild animals.

Looking back, I find it remarkable that I was able to reside in such a place and emerge from it as the same person, if not better and more disciplined. At a certain point, I found myself at a crossroads: **An allure of new life dangling a banner in front of me, there was temptation for me to** easily succumbed, allowing pleasure to guide me. After all, I had the freedom that comes with being away from home and past the age where parents could compel me into good behaviour. I could have followed the lead of my peers and engaged in reckless behaviour to enjoy life to the fullest. Yet, I chose a different path, one that demanded discipline and self-control.

At Dolly's, turmoil reigned supreme, and some individuals were willing to do anything to earn a quick buck. The atmosphere was rife with sexual immorality, trading of stolen possessions, and other illicit activities. Despite the mayhem, I was thankful that drug use was not prevalent among Zimbabweans back then. The most common activity at Dolly's was the buying and selling of stolen cell phones. I recall one particular individual who would purchase up to thirty phones at a time and ship them back to Zimbabwe for resale. He was able to accumulate enough capital to start an informal money transfer business, charging an exorbitant 20% fee on each transaction. Although his fees were steep, many of us had no other options, as obtaining proper documentation was a challenging feat.

For me, abstaining from such activities was not a difficult feat. I have always been someone who can withstand peer pressure, even when I am the only one who chooses not to participate. I waited patiently for the right time to do the right thing, fully aware that doing so would be slow and painful. It took me six long months to land a job that paid just enough for me to survive, but I was grateful, nonetheless. I began by purchasing the cheapest cell phone that my limited funds could afford. Although it was not the latest model or the most advanced, it was a start. I was determined to work hard and earn an honest living, even if it meant starting small and working my way up.

During my time at Dolly's, young women expressed interest in me, with some being bold enough to confess their feelings outright. As a young man with the freedom to choose my path, I was tempted by the allure of a lifestyle filled with pleasure and indulgence. Despite these temptations, I remained focused on my principles, increasing the frequency of my prayers, and setting aside two times each night to pray and listen to instrumental hymns. Eventually, I found the courage to wake up early on Saturdays and Sundays, before anyone else went out, I would get up and summon courage to preach in the stillness of the morning. Afterwards, I would pray, and this routine became a regular occurrence that people began to expect and look forward to.

As a result of my commitment to my faith, I earned the respect of my peers, and many young women were drawn to me, some genuinely interested in learning from me and praying with me. While some may have pretended to share my love for godly things to get closer to me, I was not easily fooled, and I could discern the genuine ones from the pretenders. My promise to Caro still stood as a driving force and I resisted all the enticement in the best way possible. More than doing it for her, I loved keeping my word and my side of the promise, making sure to call her every Friday through a payphone using an international calling card.

Caro and her family did not have a cell phone at their place in Zim, but with the way I felt for her and the amount of determination I had, I used to call their next door and ask to speak with her, going on like that for a while. I stayed true to my promise, stayed true to myself, and did not want to be a hypocrite. I believed in following a clear pathway believing God would cleanly bless me, so, I never felt like being left behind. Soon Caro's sister Lovenes joined me, after asking me to assist if she could come and try life in Cape Town. My answer was a yes because I believe in helping others, and she seemed like someone trying to change her life having also previously came to me when I was in Lusaka. This time she braved the storm together with her boyfriend, for that courage I liked her spirit, and in turn, she liked me a lot too. Before long she began working and after some weeks, I called her man where I worked, and the two started with their journey while living also at Dolly's. Time was moving, and we had a few problems with Caro, but ultimately, we were together after I paid a visit to Zimbabwe.

Chapter 34

No glamour in our start

Life is full of surprises, and sometimes it takes sheer determination to overcome the obstacles that come our way. Such was the case with Caro and me. I can still vividly recall the day we moved into our small room in Guguletu. The landlady was taken aback when she saw us arrive with only three bags, some blankets, pots, and a two-plated stove. We had no bed, no furniture, and certainly no fancy belongings. But we were determined to make the most of what we had.

As we settled into our new abode, we couldn't help but feel a sense of awe and amazement. The landlady had expected us to arrive with a truckload of belongings, but we had defied her expectations with our minimalistic approach. We asked ourselves if there was anything wrong with the way we had moved in. But deep down, we felt like we had everything we needed to start a new life together. We had no bed but it was all well with us. We never saw a problem with that. But time would make us understand why she was concerned, Thabisa the landlady knew the RDP houses in Guguletu during winter would bring up moisture and a lot of colds. So, she sent her son Thando into the ceiling space to take down a thick foam rubber for us to use as a mattress and we were more than thankful.

This is how we started our life together as Mr and Mrs Masamba. From that day and many, many days to follow, we never experienced a dull moment, I felt like for the first time in my life, I was happy, Caroline became my friend, the kind that I never had, and we would joke, poke, and tease each other. We were never embarrassed to invite friends to our empty dwelling and make them sit on our two plastic chairs while we talk and laughed together. How beautiful it is to witness two people in love, supporting each other through thick and thin. Caroline and I were no exception. Despite the challenges that came with our new life together, we remained devoted to each other and never let anything come between us.

One of our frequent visitors was Caroline's sister, Lovenes, and her partner from Woodstock. They marvelled at the love and harmony that radiated between us. Not once did we argue or quarrel, and Caroline never once frowned or complained. She was carrying our first child, and her joy and excitement were palpable. She longed for a boy and made no secret of it, and although I shared the same desire, I never commented on it, knowing that the most important thing was for our baby to be healthy. We were blessed to have the help of Thabisa, a kind-hearted South African woman who took a keen interest in Caroline's pregnancy. She offered invaluable advice, ensuring that we were well- informed about the stages of pregnancy and what to expect. I, too, paid close attention, trying my best to understand what Caroline was going through.

To supplement Thabisa's guidance, I even bought a book solely dedicated to pregnancy, and we followed its recommendations closely.

Finally, the big day arrived, and our first child was born without any complications. It was an emotional moment, and we were overjoyed to welcome our little bundle of joy into the world. Our love for each other had created something beautiful. With no scan results we all thought it would be a boy, we deliberately opted not to go for a scan. However, our anticipation was wrong, our firstborn turned out to be a bouncing beautiful girl. Nevertheless, as soon as the child was born, we loved her in a very particular way, to be honest, the love came naturally for I did not know or plan how I would feel when the child is born.

I surprised myself with how much I loved the child and cared for her. I named her Blessing. How beautiful she was, I had not seen many babies being so cute. A first addition to the family, now had two people around me.

So, after welcoming Blessing, she had a response of her kind to the love and care we gave without measure. Her response was countless sleepless nights from day one, Blessing was always agitated and full of energy, capped by persistent crying and Thabisa would wake up after midnight to try and help us calm her. I remember some days I stayed up until 02:00hrs, we were not sure why she was like that. Even after trying all suggestions to no avail, Caroline ended up thinking if we could get medicine to make the baby sleep.

Family dynamics can be challenging, and it's not uncommon for different family members to have differing opinions on certain matters. This was the case with Caroline's sisters. Caroline had two other sisters residing in Zimbabwe: When her eldest sister planned a trip to visit us, I was informed only after she had already arrived at the road port to catch a bus. Initially, I saw no issue with her visiting us, as Caroline had a strong bond with her sister. However, things took an unexpected turn when Lovenes, Caroline's other sister, expressed her disapproval of Clarisa's visit. Lovenes believed that their sister was not the best person to have around, and she even went as far as trying to block her sister from coming to visit. I was unaware of Lovenes' actions until she put my name in the mix, insinuating that I too was in agreement with her decision to prevent the sister from visiting. This was not the case, and I was displeased to find my name being used in this way. Despite the unexpected drama, we were able to resolve the situation and make the most of the sister's visit. As with any family, there were ups and downs. Eventually, she arrived, and we had to make space and a plan to accommodate her. Lovenes was right. If I had the power to turn back time, I would have participated in blocking her. After just over a year with Caroline, we had not had a single argument. However, just two days of her sister's presence was enough to see us arguing for the first time! I immediately noticed a problem and began trying to convince Caroline to see things my way, but I was wrong. Some people know how to turn something good into something ugly. Slowly, things began to change, new traits and habits started to appear and grow. I am a patient guy, I also knew my sister in law was going to be with us only for a season and thereafter find her way to life. Being who she was, she simply used the short time she had with us to awaken in Caro some energy of a different type, a seed of decay would slowly, silently grow.

Lovenes the sister-in-law I had always loved and her also considering me dear, had no choice but listen to the person with first-hand information. A very bad and corrupt seed had been planted into the heart of my wife. But one thing that helped my situation was at that point I was at the peak of my commitment to the things of God. However, this seed would persistently grow, undercover slowly, silently though, nonetheless, it never stopped. Prayer continued to be part of my daily life and I also tried to live my life as a prayer and sermon.

It takes a great deal of strength and conviction to stand by one's beliefs, even when it means turning down lucrative opportunities. I learned this lesson the hard way when I was presented with a series of financial opportunities that conflicted with my personal values. The year was 2010, and the Soccer World Cup Tournament was set to take place in South Africa. I was approached four times to star as the main character in different sporting commercials that would have brought me substantial financial gain. However, each time, I had to turn them down, knowing that they went against certain principles I lived by. Some might have seen my decision as foolish or naive, but to me, my beliefs were more important than any amount of money. I refused to compromise my integrity for the sake of financial gain, even if it meant sacrificing potential opportunities that could have had a significant impact on my career and finances. I also became part of a study group investigating the bible every Sunday, led by a brother named Sydney, the presence of Brother Sydney Jones helped us much, and our eyes began to open to some truth in the depth of scripture, and we ended up forming a ministry called Primitive Firm Faith. The same Sydney Jones was concurrently studying with a group of young guys at Riverside SDA Church and those guys also went on to form a ministry called AMEN, which became a success.

While we focused on studying the book of Daniel mainly and began to write a commentary, we did despite falling short of publishing the book. So, these things within the Church kept me focused, and was not overwhelmed by any negative occurrences especially at home, in fact, for a long time I felt like, or should I say it seemed to me there was no problem at home, kind of fooling and comforting myself. My commitment and interaction with these things helped to arrest the status quo and, in the end, we lived as though there weren't any problems. I was not earning much, but I kept pushing and making sure we have the basics. It was a job that kept us going, but that less-paying job soon ended after a little scuffle in which I got frustrated in a split second and the next day I was without a job.

When I lost my job, I began to advertise on Gumtree. Fortunately, people responded well, giving me calls for small maintenance jobs. It was during this time that I felt like I can dream and learn to stand alone while I pursue life. I had a challenge though, with transport, you know as an Artisan especially in the Plumbing and Electrical field, having a vehicle is a must, but I did not have one, yet I kept pushing, the positive thing, I was not terrified or embarrassed. However, these calls were not coming in greater numbers, only a handful. Had they poured in as they do with other people I have seen, it could have been a big problem reaching many places, especially places where public transport does not go. In order to travel, there were times I would call a brother from church named Fungai, he was working independently doing wooden decking and wooden houses, he would take me to some of my jobs, his help did one big thing for me, that's bringing a bit of dignity, I remember once or a few times I called Brighton Matake and he also helped me get where I was needed, these guys gladly helped me and I felt thankful.

One day while I was wondering where my next call would come from, I received a call from a guy called Marcus, doing renovations with his company UK2CAPE. He was not a stranger to me, I had previously worked with him while I was still an employee at PJ Plumbing. He wanted me to do like a subcontract for him, I gladly said yes and considered that as my first meaningful job, some kind of an oasis in a desert. He liked my work and my pricing, and I liked also how the money seemed useful, compared to the time I was an employee at PJ where the next pay check came when the pockets were dry. Marcus began to call me to more of his jobs, making him the man I mainly depended on. Soon he gave me two more jobs and one of them introduced me to an Afrikaans gentleman called Arno, a very soft and calm guy.

From this point, my mind began to believe I could buy a car or do something, but travelling easily was top of my priorities. There were times when things would go quiet. During such times I carried on posting on Gumtree for one or two jobs. I don't consider myself a lucky person in life, jobs were hard to come by, so I joined one agency in trying to find ways to cast my net wide, here it paid off a bit, I got called by a man called Cas Lehana living in Johannesburg while owning some small properties in Cape Town.

I innocently undertook his work to satisfaction, obviously as someone looking to make an impression. Finished everything well but never knew in paying me he wanted to short-change me, but in turn, he did the opposite and overpaid me. R15 000 he paid into my account instead of the R1500, he wanted to pay me lower than I priced him. My first instincts shouted to my reasoning, obviously, "Take the Cash, change your phone number, go get yourself a vehicle and travel easily to your jobs, this is God answering your prayer".

But like my experience with Moline Dhakwa in Kenzamba that dark stormy night, another side of me withstood me from doing such a thing, I told myself "God has a clean way of pouring his blessing on me". Ultimately, I obeyed this timid voice, the same one that has always caused me to lose things. Long story short I paid him back to his surprise, and from here onwards, whenever he had something to be done, he would call me, and at times when he came to Cape Town with his talkative wife, whom he always travelled with, a talkative German wife who after this incident wanted to know more about me, asking whatever she felt was necessary to know.

I carried on pushing until I bought myself an old Opel Monza, a car that was in bad shape with no bumpers, lights, and a few more things. The most positive thing about the car was it would start and go without a problem. I worked on the Monza finding used parts from car junkyards to make it roadworthy, jobs kept coming very slowly, and Marcus also continually called me each time he wanted help. Introducing me also to guys like Scot George and Shannan, these two happened to have lived in Zimbabwe in the past. Knowing these new people was as well progress, and my confidence was slowly growing.

One has to understand where I was coming from and the sizes and amounts of drawbacks I had experienced, I mean for a guy who at some point considered having shoes to cover his feet as the most important need, to now buying a Monza, it felt like I could do more, and to me or another person who knew me and has seen my life growing up, those years of uselessness, such a person will understand why buying an old Monza was such an important moment. Remember we grew up being chased away by friends that felt our company or presence would strip them of all dignity and value. Slow as things were, we kept pushing, trying to make progress, and in a short space, I upgraded my Monza to Mazda 626 with a good engine and everything.

It was here that the scarcity of jobs intensified. Strange things began to happen, such as the things you cannot control, so I tried to stretch my mind in trying to think and as well absorb the stress. The more I tried to absorb my stress, the more I would not get any work, at times going for 2 weeks. What was I doing wrong? Became the question that dominated my mind, I had not received a report of bad workmanship; all my jobs had no comebacks. I felt an edge to do something to intensify my search.

With that energy and determination. Caroline began to help me distribute flyers, targeting 5000 flyer distribution per week, meaning by the end of that month we had distributed 20 000 fliers. We used to go out, the three of us, our little child Blessing at this point was now walking, she would also with much excitement ask to be lifted to push that flyer into the letterbox. After the distribution of flyers, we kept our phones charged, expecting to get more calls, but we were wrong. We waited while I continually post also on Gumtree and the agency. No calls at all resulted from flyers distribution, not even one, so strange for a place like Cape Town.

Then, one day when I was at home with Blessing, Caroline started work at Maverick MTN. Because I had time and a car, a guy that I knew named Tafadzwa asked me to take him to Phillipi, a place in Cape Town where a few grocery wholesalers are located. He intended to buy groceries for his Tuck shop. Since I was not busy, I agreed to go with him, but I never assumed what a bad day it would turn out. Our shopping was so quick and without any other business, we had to do the obvious and head back home.

In my wildest guess and dreams, it never smelt like something bad was brewing around us. But a lesson learned, in life, expect the unexpected because life doesn't fall short of ways to throw curveballs at us. As if my stress levels were not enough. When prayer felt like the breath of life to me and all things around me were in a way a constant reminder of how I should live.

On my way from Phillipi, as we were only a few meters from Tafadzwa's shop, on that drizzling mid-morning weather, when the blowing warm air from the fan in the car was playing a distraction to the dreary weather outside, causing Blessing to fall asleep surrounded by groceries in the back seat of the car. As I listened to the acapella group Vocal Union's CD, I felt a profound sense of nearness to God.

The music resonated deeply with my soul, and I savoured every note. Just when I thought nothing could break my reverie, Tafadzwa asked me to make a quick stop at a friend's shop to collect his bread. However I stayed in the car enjoying the soothing music and warmth of the blowing fan. I had no idea what was about to happen next. In a shocking turn of events, I was jolted from my peaceful state by an annoying knocking on my car window.

My first instinct was to unleash my irritation and put the person in his place, but when I turned to face them, my blood ran cold. What I saw before me was nothing short of terrifying. A gun, a devastating weapon that takes away life in an instant, was pointed directly at my forehead, mere centimetres away from my face. I had never experienced anything like this before - the power and lethality of the weapon can sent your mind into a frenzy. In that moment, I knew that my life was in grave danger. As soon as I saw the gun pointed at my head, my mind raced with adrenaline. It was as if I had rehearsed this moment a thousand times before - I knew exactly what to do. Slowly, deliberately, I surrendered and unlocked the car door. My movements were choreographed, intentional, and I didn't dare deviate from the script. In the blink of an eye, I was yanked out of the car, and Blessing remained asleep, blissfully unaware of the turmoil unfolding around her. The soft strains of the acapella music continued to play through the car speakers, a stark contrast to the violence playing out before me. But even in the midst of this chaos, I saw an opportunity. A window of opportunity, so small it could be easily missed, flashed before my eyes. I could hit the attacker, make him fall, and take the gun - but it would require unwavering diligence and precision. My mind changed to safe mode instantly when I saw the other guy at a distant with a second gun. So, they took my cell phone, and I watched them pile into the car while my child was sleeping, violently driving off while a worship acapella song was still playing, driving off with my child.

When that happened, I fell into an instant moment of madness. Every action that followed did not require me to think. I was consumed by a savage frenzy and felt as if I had been transported into a trance. My mind was a blur, and my actions were driven by pure instinct. In a matter of seconds, my world had been turned upside down.

My heart nearly stopped when I realized that my child had been thrown out of the car but thank God she was only three hundred meters away. I watched in horror as my car disappeared into the distance, and I knew that I had been completely and utterly hijacked.

In that moment, I cried out to God, wondering what I had done to deserve this. The sense of helplessness and despair was overwhelming, and I felt like my whole system was shutting down. The faces of the hijackers were etched into my memory, their rough and ugly features a testament to the evil that lurked within them. I couldn't help but wonder if they had any capacity for remorse, or if they were consumed by darkness and wickedness. For days and months to come, the haunting melody of the Vocal Union song played in my head, accompanied by vivid images of the hijacking and the twisted faces of the criminals who had robbed me of my car and my peace of mind.

Through my experiences in life, I have come to realize that choosing to do good not only brings inner satisfaction, but it can also have a profound impact on one's physical appearance. However, despite this positive aspect, it was hard for me to forget the faces of the people I encountered during the hijacking incident. Sadly, this is a contagious issue in South Africa, specifically in the townships where poverty and neglect are rampant. The more neglected and impoverished an area becomes, the more violent crime, selfishness, sexual immorality, and recklessness it tends to breed. It's a vicious cycle that's difficult to break, and it's heart-breaking to see so many people trapped in these circumstances. In these areas, it's unwise to underestimate a seemingly harmless person walking down the street. Boys, even at a young age, frequently carry knives and do not hesitate to use them in fights instead of relying on fists like we did growing up. This is a sad reality that highlights the dire need for more resources to be allocated to these neglected areas to uplift the people and give them hope for a better future.

It's common to see South Africans, even from a young age, carrying knives and scissors, and many of them seem to be quite skilled in their use. It's not uncommon to encounter someone asking for 2 Rand while standing near a shop or corner, and unfortunately, this behaviour can become a way of life. Once they adopt this way of living, they often avoid working altogether. Then they begin to move around in groups of three or more, hunting for any vulnerable people they can pounce on and strip them off their belongings. Once they settle for this life they strive to find guns which are sold cheap and illegal. From here, these groups set out to dominate the surrounding areas, such as Nyanga, Khayelitsha, Guguletu, Samora, and many others. These groups are numerous, making it extremely dangerous, especially for vulnerable foreigners who become easy prey. The way people conduct themselves in these areas is not entirely surprising given the circumstances. Drinking and partying are the main activities that men and women live for. Unfortunately, this often leads to unsavoury behaviour and incidents of violence. It's a pity that the refuse scattered all over the place is also a common sight. Even when the city council provides large bins for people to throw their rubbish, they often disregard them and scatter their waste around instead of disposing of it properly. In truth, these areas are not for the faint of heart. One must be vigilant and aware of their surroundings at all times to avoid becoming a victim of the rampant crime and disorder that permeates these areas.

South Africa is home to some of the most stunningly beautiful girls in the world. It's a shame that such beauty is not always accompanied by brains. Sadly, many of them view themselves through a lens of self-deprecation and cheapen their worth. In these places, it's not uncommon to see young women waking up in the morning and carrying a bucket of urine and poo to pour into the nearest storm water drainage. It's a stark reminder of the harsh reality faced by many in South Africa's townships. Having lived in these areas myself, I can attest to the fact that life there is beyond anything that words can convey. It's a far cry from the glamorous portrayal often depicted on South African TV. The harsh reality of life in the townships is one of poverty, crime, and disease. It's surprising that diseases like Cholera and Malaria haven't ravaged these areas, given that many of them are built on swampy grounds. Yet, despite the odds, the people of these communities continue to persevere and find joy in the little things in life.

The guys who hijacked me had grown up in these harsh environments, where survival of the fittest was the norm. In these swampy places, people are forced to do whatever it takes to make ends meet, even if it means resorting to violent crime. Men like these hijackers are the ones to be feared the most, as they are ruthless and have nothing to lose. In general, the people in these areas have become desensitized to violence and crime. It's not uncommon for a mob to kill or burn someone, only for life to return to normal the next moment as if nothing had happened.

The experience of being hijacked left me feeling as though I was trapped in a terrifying nightmare. It's something that I never thought would happen to me, and it made me realize just how dangerous life can be in these areas. It's a harsh reality that many people living in South Africa's townships face every day. Any survey in these townships will definitely reveal how 10 out of 10 who work, and commute daily have in one way or the other experienced violent crime.

When I recounted the events of the afternoon to Caroline, she dismissed it as me being overly dramatic with my jokes. However, it was no laughing matter and far from a dream - such is the harsh reality of life. I often caution the young individuals I interact with that life does not always offer up its rewards easily. In fact, it tends to strip away even the most hard-earned possessions you may have acquired. With my car stolen, my life took a turn for the worse. The absence of my vehicle and phone left me feeling powerless and vulnerable. I was eager to get back on my feet and work, but without a phone, I was unable to receive any job offers or inquiries. For four months, I was unable to secure any work, and this difficult period highlighted just how strange and unpredictable life can be.

While I was struggling, Caroline continued to work, but the stress of our situation weighed heavily on her. She confided in anyone who would listen about the challenges we were facing.

Chapter 35

Partnering in business

During this time, I formed a close bond with a fellow church member who had a passion for business. He was always smiling and had a positive attitude, actively participating in church programs and even teaching others. Beyond his cheerful demeanour, he was someone with a commitment to put his words into action. He often spoke of his desire to pursue his business ideas and one day, he decided to take the leap.

He began by flying to China to purchase suits for resale. Initially, he sold them informally, but eventually opened a clothing shop, which unfortunately did not last very long. Despite this setback, his passion for business never wavered, and he continued to strive towards his goals. Prior to the closure of his shop, I invested in a few shares of his retail business which brought us closer. We frequently met to discuss potential business ventures, and he proposed the idea of launching a removal company - where we could purchase a truck to transport household goods for those relocating. However, this idea never came to fruition. It was through this shared interest that we developed a friendship beyond our church community.

On one occasion, when I visited his shop, he divulged that he had a dream the night before about starting an insurance business that catered to Zimbabweans residing in South Africa. The business would specialize in providing funeral policies. At the outset of our venture, neither of us possessed any knowledge about insurance or funeral policies. Therefore, we had to make numerous inquiries and conduct extensive research. As I had limited mobility and resources, we relied heavily on his car for transportation. On some days, he would venture out alone to meet potential clients, using leads he acquired by conversing with people at his job as a waiter. In order to gauge the market interest, we conducted a survey to determine how people would respond to our idea. Despite numerous setbacks and rejections from established organizations, we persevered. Many of these leaders adhered to conventional business practices, and their scepticism could have easily demoralized us. Nevertheless, we remained undaunted and continued to pursue our idea.

As I was challenged in terms of mobility, my business partner took on most of the legwork, utilizing his car for transportation. After a prolonged and arduous process, we eventually developed a funeral policy which we named Zororo Phumulani after our company. The name comprises two words with similar meanings - the first word, "Zororo," is in Shona, while the second word, "Phumulani," is in Ndebele. Both words denote "rest." Shona and Ndebele are the predominant languages spoken in Zimbabwe. Because the business was formed primarily with Zimbabweans in mind. During that time a lot of people felt they would be in South Africa for a short while, but when time kept on lapsing, there was a big struggle in terms of repatriating someone's remains if one died. So Zororo Phumulani got launched, entering into the unknown, uncharted waters and territories without any prior knowledge, experience, or capital but just a passion.

Yeah, I recall on our day of Launch we had nothing between us. The brother did not have enough petrol in his tank, neither did any between us have a cent to spare, only a willingness to take off was what we had. Then we thought of a person who could assist, and a familiar name came into mind in the person Brighton who seemed to always have a willingness to help. The guy has always been like that, Brighton is blessed in that regard, and even on that day he came through and saved the day.

The launch was indeed a moment to celebrate, however it was a matter of rejoicing on a certain step towards the mark. We quickly realized that the real work had just begun. We immediately ushered ourselves into a multitude of challenges that required pioneering intelligence. We could not rely on traditional methods of operating, as our target market was vastly different from anything else operating in South Africa. Furthermore, we had no capital to work with.

I was still working intermittently, while my colleague boldly quits his job at the restaurant. Our concerns were not limited to Zororo Phumulani alone; we also had to consider our own survival at home. In the absence of a means or budget for advertising, the only viable option for reaching people was through direct contact. However, such an approach has never been a mere matter of small talk, as it demands considerable commitment and financial resources. Consequently, the notion of reaching people in masses began to take shape, as we sought to find a more efficient means of communication. In this regard, the idea of leveraging churches as a platform for outreach came to mind, as it promised to spare us the countless miles of legwork typically required to reach people individually.

Our strategy centred on collaborating with churches and other community groups to engage and connect with people. In particular, the AFM church worship centre, led by Pastor Isidore

Mariga played a pivotal role in the success of Zororo Phumulani. Without his unwavering support, I have no doubt that our efforts would have floundered. The church graciously allowed us to promote our product and make announcements during their Sunday services, an opportunity that we would not have dared to pursue at our own SDA church. Not only did our SDA church lack the platform to showcase our product, but we also received no support from its members outside of the church's operating hours and days. By leveraging the AFM church's reach influence, we were able to connect with a much larger audience and generate more interest in our product. Although church gatherings are a universal occurrence, it is widely known that it is virtually impossible to introduce any business-related matters during SDA church gatherings. This presented a significant obstacle, but we refused to be deterred. As is typical with any new venture, the road ahead was fraught with challenges. Nonetheless, we persevered, leveraging leads generated from our interactions with the AFM Church to reach as many people as possible. Our days were spent juggling between meetings, presentations, and client visits, all while ensuring we had enough to eat at home.

Caroline's job, although not particularly lucrative, proved to be a vital source of support during this time. With no official office space, we were forced to hold meetings in public libraries, McDonald's, and any other place that offered a space to sit and strategize. Despite the difficulties, we were committed to our vision and determined to make it a reality. My friend eventually sold his car, making it another thing that played to our disadvantage, transport. There was now no car between us, and now we relied on public transport, especially when Tich Jorofani also came to join us becoming part of the team, he was not the only one to be added. Before long we added another guy called Moreboys Munetsi, a man with experience in the insurance business. Not forgetting, of course, the last man to join us in the person of Tafadzwa Tazvitadza, he is the same guy whom I helped that memorable day I got hijacked. Out of all this bunch, only Moreboys had a car, not for our use, of course, he was also still committed to his job at Old Mutual.

We operated under a very tricky situation, it is always a given fact that people do not usually want to be the first to join something that is starting from scratch, people go for established businesses, we were nobodies, we arrived at meetings walking, causing any sober person to question the seriousness of what we were trying to drag them into. Despite the challenges, we were determined to push ahead. Convincing people to sign up was no easy feat, but we had no other choice but to persevere. However, after three months, we realized that our progress had been slow, with only 30 paying members to show for our efforts. This was partly due to Zimbabweans' tendency to adopt a wait-and-see approach, which presented a significant obstacle. Furthermore, they bombarded us with numerous questions that required thoughtful and detailed answers. For instance, many assumed that their stay would be short, which made them hesitant to commit to long-term funeral plans. To address this challenge, I suggested that we explore the possibility of forming a strategic partnership with a Zimbabwean company. This would not only help to build trust and credibility but also enable us to offer a broader range of services and benefits to our members. With this in mind, we set out to identify potential partners and began laying the groundwork for a mutually beneficial relationship. This we treated as a matter of urgency; my friend took a bus to Zimbabwe for a meeting with Nyaradzo. They are one of the leading companies in funeral insurance in Zimbabwe, but their response was somewhat sluggish, so, ultimately, my friend called Moonlight funeral assurance over the phone and their response was swift, the next day five of their directors plus one Actuarial guy named Moses were in the plane coming to Cape Town Their negotiations were aggressive, these were guys who had been in business and above that had a political mentality and knew how to manipulate. But ultimately, we found ourselves working with them. Now their presence did bring a great deal of difference both the positive and the negative. On the positive side, we saw a drastic increase in the number of people signing up for our policy. Remember we had been sitting at thirty people for three months working flat out. We kept on trying to find ways to see the business running, bearing in mind we now had paying members whose premiums were not enough to fund anything. We had to dig deep and try other ways of fundraising, and again the results were not great. We went in any direction that we felt would lead to one or 2 people joining, knocking on every door we could think of. And many times, the people we were approaching were better than us. However, there was one door that took us a lot of thinking to knock on it. We needed a way to bring our message home, our home being to the Seventh Day Adventist Church. We knew Adventists could frown and look at us as if we had been rescued or pulled out from a pile of rubble after an earthquake, and I feel they had a right to look at us that way. What reaction could we have expected, these people knew us, people from our local Church. These were people who knew our struggles, understand we were planning to pitch in front of people that at some point extended to us a hand, at which sometimes faced struggles to pay back in time. Some among them had at some point helped us in one way or the other during our times of lack. I remember my friend telling me of a time he borrowed from someone and delayed paying back.

It only took just one well-written text message for him to find the cash and payback. Any brave person would definitely think twice before standing out to make a presentation, thinking about all these made it an uphill task. But, uphill or downhill, we had to find a way to confront our own Church.

For the first time, I saw my beloved friend taking a step back, throwing me under the bus. He is the kind of man who had always stepped forward to pitch at any point, but on that night, he took a step back, relegating himself to the benches, and I found myself on the thicket of a battle, I had no choice but to present. I was not a stranger to presentations, I had countless times presented to the same bunch, but that night I felt my nerves being rocked. Nonetheless, I had to speak.

One other method that we devised, and I pushed much together with Tich Jorofani also to the approval of Moreboys Munetsi was the sponsoring of Shower Power, an Acapella group from Zimbabwe, this we did in a bid to find a way to break into the Adventist circles. Presentations were hard to find in other

Adventist branches and we had to do this and put our banners there and had the projector display the Zororo Phumulani logo and products. That we felt was strategic, but our Adventist friends would only come for the music and cared not about what we were selling. It was a fluke; we ran a loss together with Brighton whom we dragged convincing him to put some money hoping for some returns. This was not the only time we tried this manner of fundraising and marketing, one more time we tried with No Limits because they are local and cheap to transport, and our efforts yielded the same disappointing results.

The presence of Moonlight had its downside. From the time they arrived. An air of discord and poisonous fumes could be felt in the boardroom, I had not been in many boardrooms, but I would love to believe very few ever had such long meetings, nor have I seen documents sitting there unsigned for weeks, it was chaotic, those guys especially Moses knew how to divide and conquer. All these efforts we pushed hoping to strike a note and end up with a way that works. But there was always friction among the members on what best methods to apply. In all cases, it was always one against all.

Soon my friend decided to attack me for reasons only known to him. He began to send some private emails that skipped me and

Tich but shared with other members, the members who came late in the game. The closeness and the bond that once existed between myself and my friend began to crack. I found myself slowly going back to the industry seeing that I needed income, and the company was not making money enough to pay salaries. My dear friend and brother in Christ was now under the payroll of Moonlight.

Chapter 36

Moreblessing

Caroline's unexpected pregnancy brought with it the news of a second child on the way, and we anxiously awaited the arrival of our new addition, hoping for a son. This time around, we decided to take a more modern approach and opted for scans, which confirmed that Caroline was indeed carrying a boy. We prepared ourselves for the arrival of a son, eagerly anticipating his birth.

On the 13th of January, our prayers were answered as Caroline gave birth to a healthy and energetic baby. However, when Caroline called me early that morning while I was working for Marcus in Montague Gardens, her tone was brief and distant. Though she expressed happiness, I sensed a tinge of disappointment as she informed me that we had been blessed with a baby girl. Despite feeling a bit cheated by modern technology or the person responsible for interpreting the scans, I remained calm as I made my way to Vanguard Hospital. I retrieved both mother and baby and brought them home to the delight of Blessing. Our second child was another beauty! In that instant, any disappointment about not having a boy vanished as I gazed upon her. She was as energetic as Blessing, but unlike her older sister, she was calm and never caused us any sleepless nights. The trickier part was coming up with a name for our little girl. I asked Caroline to name her, but she had no names in mind. Finally, a name came to us: Moreblessing. It was a name that drew interest from people who found it amusing and questioned our thought process behind it, I mean from Blessing to Moreblessing. Despite the jests, Moreblessing, who resembled Blessing in appearance, was a calm and collected baby who possessed just as much energy as her older sister.

Despite everything happening around me, my love for Zimbabwe never waned. In fact, my heart burned with a fierce longing to return home. It had been five long years since I last set foot in my beloved country, and this was completely unlike me. The circumstances seemed to be closing in on me, but I knew I couldn't ignore the pull in my heart any longer. I was determined to make the journey back to Zimbabwe to see my siblings and reconnect with my roots. My love for my country was unwavering, and I felt a deep sense of responsibility to be there, no matter what challenges, I was determined to push. At work, it seemed like we were picking up a lot of important projects with Marcus. Going to Zimbabwe was a good thing, but on the contrary, it had its negative impact and only time would tell. When my time to go came, I braved the journey, driving to Zim with only a learner's license. Such a bold move that was bravery. I told a friend, Edwin of this driving experience between two countries with only a learner's license, and he said, "You are a soldier, my brother".

When one drives in SA you don't usually get unnecessary stops, so it was not a hustle at all to drive using my newly acquired international license. This I got last minute after Aaron who had earlier indicated he wanted to go with me changed his mind opting not to journey with me after weeks of planning together. At that point I only had a provisional or leaners license. The international I only produced to ignorant South African traffic cops the few times I got stopped. The South African traffic police had little knowledge of what a complete international permit looked like. It was only when I got to the border and produced it before a lady cop who knew about these cards. I remember how the lady pressed me hard and threatened to arrest me. I tried reasoning with her for a good one hour, she wanted money, and I didn't want to bribe her, at one point I infuriated her when I told her she was the guiltiest part in asking for a bribe. But ultimately, I gave her the money she needed. In Zimbabwe, they had no knowledge of the difference between a learner's license from South Africa and that temporary license given to use while awaiting the printing of your driver's license. I simply flashed my leaners, and they waved me to go. One other thing is I did not have money enough upon taking this journey, if any breakdown was to happen to my car, I was surely going to get stuck in the middle of nowhere, but thanks for the great job I did on building this Telstar, it was performing like a Monster, the engine and every other component of this car performed without disappointment. Even the tires were all brand new, so, from the time I left Cape Town, to spending a month in Zim and coming back, I never had even a puncture, it was just a matter of pouring petrol and checking the oil level. Not even the badly damaged Zimbabwean roads could put it down, the roads were so rough that in many cases the car shook as if it were disintegrating. Upon arrival, I noticed how a lot of things can change in five years. The most significant changes being that of people, the kids I once taught football at Richmond Primary School were now grown-ups, most of which were now married, they were no longer called by their first names but as is the custom in our community, in respect of someone upon getting married or having a child, we begin to respect them and change even the way we call them.

One of the most remarkable things to look up to when one travels from South Africa to Zimbabwe is the cuisine. The taste of the food in Zimbabwe, particularly in rural areas where the fare is pure and wholesome, is simply unforgettable. Caroline herself was impressed by the butternuts she tasted during her visit. In South Africa, butternuts, sweet potatoes, pumpkins, and other vegetables require expert cooking to make them palatable, often necessitating the use of spices such as cinnamon. However, Caroline's experience with the butternuts in Zimbabwe was a revelation. Although she had sworn off butternuts after trying them in Cape Town, she was persuaded to give them another chance. To her surprise, she discovered that butternuts could be delicious when simply boiled, as the ones she tasted had been. These vegetables were piled up, awaiting sale, and it took only a single taste to convince Caroline that she had been missing out on something truly special. I just love the food from Zimbabwe, every other thing you taste from that land is very different from South African food. Talking about food, another country whose food is equally great is Zambia, I love how they sell a variety of greens on their markets.

During my time in Zimbabwe, I took a drive to Chinhoyi to meet Augustine, and together we ventured on a trip to Guruve to visit my cousin Abednego. He was the same Abedi who used to reside in Nyanhunzi, located closer to the tarred Guruve highway. Abedi still lived in the same red brick houses that I remember seeing from the bus window during the year we departed from Guruve. Sadly, Abedi was not feeling well, and it had been a considerable amount of time since I had last seen him. During my stay in Guruve with my grandmother, I visited him frequently. As I reunited with him after several years, I felt a mix of emotions. While I knew that our presence would energize him, I also knew that it would awaken his pain. Upon seeing him, he attempted to display courage, but I could tell that he was in agony. Although I had hoped that he would recover, I was mistaken. It was reminiscent of the time I visited Actor in the hospital, where it was challenging to determine how much time Abedi had left, as his appearance was somewhat deceptive. A few days after that visit, I started on a journey making my way back to Cape Town having overstayed my TIP by a day, accompanied by Yvonne my youngest sister, and Khumbulani my brother, leaving Caroline and the kids behind as they awaited the outcome of passports application for the kids.

We were driving way past Johannesburg using my preferred Kimberly route, at this point I only had the journey in mind. But a message came through to my disturbance, the message was notifying me of the passing of Abedi. He was gone at a very young age, being only 2-3 years older than me, it was yet another heart- breaking moment for the Chamboko family as has been the case since the days of our fathers and grandparents. People are so fragile in our troubled family, they don't last long, their lives are so brief and the leaving is always bitter.

Undertaking the journey from Cape Town to Harare is by no means an easy feat. The sheer length and arduousness of the journey can be difficult to fully comprehend, particularly as one embarks upon the trip to Harare. The initial stages of the journey to Harare are often characterized by euphoria, energy, and adrenaline as the engine is pushed to its limits against the brutal incline from De-dons to the Karoo. The agonizing sound of the car engine at Petersburg only adds to the intensity of the experience. The overwhelming excitement of returning home can often cloud one's perception of just how long and gruelling the journey is. However, the reality is that it is a considerable undertaking, requiring significant stamina and perseverance to complete, especially as a lone driver. Way back was boring because as I had nothing much to look up to but only life struggles. But on my way up I had things to look up to, thinking and recollecting on Mhangura, a place I consider to have practically taught and preached all but humility to me while it afforded me friends of a similar mentality, a rare thing to encounter.

While I was driving way home, the recollections pushed me to a certain level and it was that willingness to reach home that kept me agitated, pushing the adrenalin and the desire to arrive carried me all the way causing me to overlook how great the distance was. Only upon embarking on the return journey did I notice how far life has carried us away from home. What an experience! This time we took turns driving, but I couldn't put myself at ease and sleep while Khumbu was driving. The boy needed more time to get used to the steering wheel, so, I stayed on the edge, each time reminding him to slow down. Yvonne simply sat there, she was travelling this long for the first time and she also failed to sleep for the two and half days we travelled. A long journey it was, nonetheless a safe one, a trip that offers also a great driving experience.

From the Karoo, a vast landscape that appears inhospitable to vegetation, to the rugged mountain pass beyond Beaufort West, we descended steadily toward the flatlands of Touws River. The descent seemed to transport us to another time zone entirely. As we descended, we were immediately awestruck by the breath-taking vistas of the Cape's barren and rocky mountains stretching toward Dedorians. These same mountains towered so high that they were always capped with snow and clouds during winter. While in summer they stand dry and cracking and yearling for a downpour. These mountains are a wonder to watch all year round. They look so dry and lifeless keeping me wondering if they host in them any form of life. This carries on until the road begins to meander in slow curved turns and sharp corners, negotiating its way out of the mountains, this time slopping more steeply. Road signs at this stage repeating every short distance, a reminder to drive in the lower gears. "REDUCE SPEED NOW" The scenery keeps inviting the eye to keep looking to the downside of the mountain where a river, a brook called Hex River reveals the hope of life in its banks teaming with green vegetation. Soon the eyes gets charmed by an outstanding view of the cape grape fields that stands contrasted to the lifeless barren mountains with no vegetation but only disintegrated rocks. Despite their barrenness, the same mountains stood as if they are assigned to guard the vineyards that teem with much grapes as if to preach hope to the barren and thirsty-looking mountains. Such carries on until the mountains shepherded us into the wider flat valley area towards the Worcester where the mountains spread to the left and the right sides, leaving a wider flat plain where more amazing views of organized and well-maintained grape fields attract more attention.

Once we drove past Worcester, we immediately found ourselves entering the ever-lit 4km of tunnel, never minding the reality that above us was the Dutoitskloof Mountain with its millions of metric tons of earth, rock and sparse bushes, all this, at their mercy letting us pass unthreatened. Out of the tunnel, and at last into the Cape Town air.

Chapter 37

A new set of battles

Upon my return from Zim, little did I know that I was about to enter a season of tumultuous misfortune. Although I am well-acquainted with hardship and adversity, each new blow seemed to strike with greater force, rendering previous difficulties pale in comparison. I began to realize that each challenge had been a training ground, preparing me for the ultimate test of my fortitude. Answering the hard questions and making decisions, some that will change life for the good, some that will set you free, and some that can be regrettable is always daunting. But life has taught me that when it is time for decision-making, it never brings any great feeling either way. Sometimes when it is that season of bad luck and misfortune, even the most brilliant of ideas put into a wine press will turn sweet into sour.

As I made my way back to Cape Town, I eagerly anticipated diving back into work and reclaiming a sense of normalcy. But to my dismay, the world around me seemed to have fallen into an eerie silence. Despite the fact that my phone remained powered on at all times, I was surprised to find myself constantly missing calls and receiving no notifications of incoming messages.

It was a strange and unsettling time, as I found myself struggling to understand why my voicemail box was constantly being bombarded with messages from people trying to reach me for work. It was as if a mysterious force was conspiring against me, blocking my path to success, and thwarting my best efforts. This frustrating experience dragged on for months, stretching from May 2014 well into 2015. Eventually, I was forced to abandon my dreams of entrepreneurship and resign myself to the whims of fate.

For a fleeting moment, I entertained the idea of venturing into the motor parts retailing business, a decision that would prove to be a costly mistake. With only a meagre amount of stock on hand, I struggled to attract customers and generate sales. I vividly recall one particular day when a couple wandered into my shop and asked if they could wait around for a friend. To my disappointment, they ended up staying for three long hours, during which not a single person came in to browse or make a purchase. The woman couldn't help but inquire if I ever sold anything at all, and I was forced to admit that there were days when I spent the entire day without making a single sale. It was a crushing blow to my ego and my bank account, and I soon came to regret my decision to invest in this ill-fated venture. In hindsight, I wished I had spent my hard-earned money on something more worthwhile, like providing for my family. To make matters worse, I had sold my car in a desperate attempt to raise capital for the business. This left me with no choice but to trudge home on foot at the end of each long and fruitless day, a daunting prospect given the dangers that lurked in the streets of places like Guguletu.

Despite my best efforts, it had been some time since I had been able to participate in the activities at Zororo Phumulani. The toxic boardroom environment, fuelled largely by the presence of Moonlight, had made it nearly impossible for me to work effectively. But things truly reached a breaking point when I stumbled upon a series of email exchanges that were clearly intended to belittle and undermine me. The fact that these conversations were taking place behind my back only added insult to injury, leaving me feeling hurt and confused. The crushing blow to my very soul came in the form of a mail that targeted me specifically. Its words twisted and distorted my contributions to the initiative, painting a skewed and crumpled version of events. Yet I know the truth: I was there from the very beginning, a soldier in the ranks who did the grunt work alongside my friend. Together, we pounded the pavement, knocking on countless doors until we finally launched the project that would become Zororo Phumulani.

To tell the story of Zororo without acknowledging my presence on the starting line would be a grave injustice. I was there when the funeral product hit the streets, and I made the first sale for our company. I remember vividly the woman who believed in me and became the first policyholder, Thembi Beture. It was a momentous occasion for all of us, a testament to the trust placed in us by Mr Schoeman and the underwriter KGA, and a tribute to my good friend Jorofani, who was by my side through it all.

That mail may have attempted to erode my sense of worth, but I wondered why a friend I had regarded high got to lower himself to such new levels. It was indeed a bruise to my soul, but my spirit did not succumb to what he perceived of me. Despite the intended aim of the dig on me, the fact of the matter remains, and my contributions remained vivid for a witness to those that watched us from the onset.

The most damaging part to my soul was a mail that talked specifically about me, there a distortion to a greater extent, and it presented a much-wrinkled version of how I became part of this initiative. At the point of our first sale, the rest of the guys that came to join us afterwards were not yet part of the company, that's Moreboys Munetsi and Tafadzwa Tazvitadza. All these things and the endless meetings we held at any place we found a gap were just part of the toil I had to face in the initial stages of Zororo, but the distorted emails suggested it was because of many struggles to the point of failing to support my family that saw me being handed shares on a silver platter. This was shocking and heartbreaking to me, but as usual, I am a person who believes in seeking the whole truth, so, I made a phone call and me and my friend had a discussion. Of course, it is a thing he regrets doing, but we all falter in life in one way or the other.

I realized this was one of those times in life when people may find no answer or explanation to why and how things ended up this way or that way, in such instances, it is pointless to press for answers or seek an explanation. If someone says a sincere apology and fails to explain, I am one person who believes in forgiving, whether they mean it or not becomes not my business. But from that point, I found it extremely hard to work around everyone seeing that when these other guys received the emails, from then I felt like they considered me and any of the things I say in meetings of no value because it was not of merit that I found myself in the boardroom. Perhaps the smear campaign had accomplished its intention, but I can only guess. So, when I was going through rough times, I felt like I needed to get Zororo out of my way and my mind. I did not rush into making this decision while still hurt, I knew and understood the potential of the company, but felt like a good environment was more preferred to me than forcing where I was considered of less value, so I left.

Even though the company later grew, while my walk of shame carried on, I still consider my decision the right one. While all this was happening, I had a non-running Volvo S80 bought from Stanford a friend of Aaron. I worked on the car till it came to running condition. I managed to make it start and drive and put in a new window, and it felt like I could now use it to rush and do any job that may arise. This period became one of my driest spells, almost everything stopped. I started looking for employment because everything else had stopped. This of course was a stressful period, but I had no idea there was still more to come. My family life was not spared of problems, some only falling short of separating us.

It is always given that people for no reason influence someone, nonetheless, I am not a people person, I chose my associates carefully and they will be very few in many cases, and it makes it difficult for people to come forward to me with stories. While in the middle of the fracas and this entanglement, a rare opportunity to go to Brackenfell and do a small job arose, I made preparations to go do it with much excitement, energy and willingness. But before leaving I had some time in the car where I sat and talked with Khumbulani. We parked our car in an open space just outside the shopping mall of Charlesville, there were a few cars scattered around that open field. People also sprawled around, informal traders and countless numbers of people were pouring into or out of the shopping mall. Can you imagine robbers skipping everyone and every car as if there was a magnet pulling them towards my car? So, they marched stealthily through in broad daylight, while all sorts of people were going about their normal routines. There was no way I or anybody could suspect that three wanderers were on a mission to come and disturb my life, just to hijack my car for who knows why.

There was confusion in my mind for a little while, but soon as I realised I was being hijacked. A quick flashback of the time my Mazda 626 was taken from me in broad daylight played in my memory. In a flash, my mind processed a thousand thoughts, the picture of re-living the agony after losing a car. I felt like I had to act, three guys, one gun, one screwdriver, I saw a chance. I faked a walk away, a sign of surrender to create a decoy, but bang! I sprang back like a cat leaping toward prey, in a blink I charged for the guy with the firearm, getting him by the neck hoping to take him down with one knock, but my fist wasn't strong enough or he was just a tough guy I don't know. Nevertheless, he dropped the gun, so foolish of me I did all this half-committed so in my panic, I failed to notice the falling of the gun. My assumption quickly felt like checking the gun in his hand and hitting him the second time before he reacts. But the second guy upon noticing the gun had fallen quickly moved in to pick it up. Immediately, it registered in my mind what a bold but foolish and dangerous move I had made. While I waited to hear the sound of the gun going off, I didn't freeze but thought of safety, I darted to place myself at a distance before turning to look back still expecting to hear that ugly deafening sound of a fired gun. Surprisingly he didn't fire, then I froze upon realizing my brother was still standing amidst them. I thought it was over for him, "They would shoot him" was my conclusion. One more moment there was no gunshot but pandemonium as the three robbers rushed to pile into the car to leave in haste. Again, I was robbed, just like that, so senseless and humiliating in the sight of many people of which among the onlookers some knew this was my second time. Was there something wrong with me? I wondered. Why was everything including every good act and every good thing turning sour against me? The car was gone. And

I felt like it was not returning like the first one, but this one returned the same afternoon with no keys, which was still frustrating, painful, and a drawback. I had no spare keys and no money to cut new ones, my phone was taken during the robbery, and I needed a new phone to receive calls if I was to get any employment.

After this experience, I finally closed the embarrassing motor spare shop, same old story, waste of money, money that could have bought the family a few goodies. What was I to do? First things first, get a new phone Sifelani, a cheap one from Pep stores. After that, I developed a new tendency of buying a weekly train ticket to Cape Town to spend some time in the city library using the internet as I searched for work and send CVs. I had finally given up the pursuit of working independently, I could not help trying to figure out what I was doing wrong. I saw other guys coming after me to start working independently, though not so much better than me in terms of work, some calling me to help figure out things, but they were working. I couldn't help to think something was blocking my way.

My situation became visible to the wondering eyes of the people that mattered, those obviously from the church family, but I paid little attention to what people thought. Despite all that was happening I had few good friends, especially those I ministered with within the Primitive Firm Faith. Aaron, Grace, Prince, and Kidwell remained close. They probably understood me a little better. We had a custom of eating together once every month, and they would come to dine some nights at our small, cramped place. Prince was still unmarried, Aaron was a few years like me into marriage with one Daughter named Atida, the same age, and friends with my daughter Blessing. Grace had recently married Henry a brother from our neighbouring country of Malawi. They were all great company to be around. We used to have these rounds as a group where we gather at each other's house and have dinner. From these gatherings, we shared many memorable moments, I mean, who can forget the meals comprised of roasted fish among other home- cooked delicacies? I wouldn't hesitate to do it all over again. Joining those group gatherings felt like the right thing to do, and it still does. But it wasn't just the group events that made my time there special.

Aaron, in particular, stood out as someone I could always count on. He made frequent visits, and I felt comfortable enough to visit or call him at any time, for any reason. Aaron is a strict guy, no doubt about it. But his strictness doesn't scare me away. In fact, it's one of the things I appreciate most about him. When we're together, we can talk about anything and everything - from the serious stuff like life's big questions to the silly things and embarrassing moments that make us laugh. What I love most about Aaron is how easy it is to be myself around him. With him, I can let down my guard and just be me. I don't have to pretend or put on a show. One thing that sets him apart is his unwavering dedication to a systematic approach in everything he does. Whether you ask him to pray or to tackle a complex problem, you can be sure he'll follow a consistent and methodical way of operating. And yet, he's not the only person I know who takes prayer seriously. I've been fortunate to have many friends who approach their faith with sincerity and devotion. Brighton, for example, is one such guy. My spiritual life has always been an integral part of the way I approach the world. When I joined the Adventist church, my thinking and actions became more radical and more intentional. But I've always been wary of becoming too gullible or having my mind clouded by any particular doctrine or belief system. Despite my spiritual grounding, I still had to contend with the practicalities of life. I searched tirelessly for employment, but my efforts seemed to fall on deaf ears. It was frustrating, but I refused to let my faith waver. I prayed constantly, seeking guidance and strength to keep going.

Throughout this journey, I couldn't help but think back to my childhood and the experiences that had shaped me. Some of those memories were painful, but they also served as a reminder of how life can be. At times, it felt like my past experiences were replaying themselves, constantly haunting me. Despite my efforts, everything seemed to fall apart. I found myself at home with a car that I couldn't use because it had been hijacked and returned without its remote and key. Although it was a beautiful car, it sat motionless, deteriorating in the sun and rain, waiting for me to find work and hire a locksmith. Unexpectedly, I received a call from Gary James of Protea Plumbing. He sounded friendly and asked for my CV, which I promptly sent. Two days later, he called again, inviting me to an interview.

Finally, things were looking up. It was a relief to have a potential job opportunity after struggling for so long. I've never been confident in interviews, and I don't consider myself eloquent. However, someone close to me, Aaron, had mastered the art of interviews through his experience with eighteen interviews in one year. He gave me some great tips that I found helpful. I knew my weaknesses going into interviews: I wasn't the most eloquent person and my qualifications on paper might not be the strongest. However, I believed that my skills would speak for themselves. I learned a valuable lesson from Aaron's interview experiences. Traditional interviews can be intimidating, making candidates feel small as they try to exhibit politeness and other desirable qualities. However, Aaron had a different approach. He turned interviews into normal discussions and even took over by asking the interviewer questions as if he were interviewing them. Aaron is one of the many diminutive Aarons I have met in life, but this one is in the league of his own. A wellspring of knowledge, somewhat an addict reader in things even beyond his field of work and Church. A man who strives to stay true to the things he believes and preach. I decided to adopt his approach and practice it for myself. By making interviews more conversational and less formal, I hoped to feel more comfortable and confident in showcasing my skills and personality Aaron's unconventional interview approach paid off during one interview that the interviewer took notice after being impressed by Aaron's persuasive skills that he remarked, "Ever considered going into politics?" However, Aaron didn't take the comment as a compliment. Despite his gift for talking convincingly, he didn't want to be associated with politicians and their reputation for dishonesty.

For Aaron authenticity and transparency are key values that he held dear. He tried to lead a life with integrity and honesty rather than politics and deception. He preferred to lead a life that stood in opposition to the stereotypical politician, one that was honest and authentic. Following his way and approach, I got hired. To my surprise, I received a call from my new employer just a week after I began my probationary period. In the midst of my nervousness, I walked into his office, expecting to be given feedback on my performance, but he had something even better to say. With a gleam in his eye, he said, "I am bumping up your salary now, and after a month, I will bump it up again." I could hardly believe it. This guy wasn't messing around - he clearly recognized my potential and didn't want to lose me. It wasn't hard to see why he valued me so highly. My dedication, commitment, focus, punctuality, and preciseness to detail were all unmatched. I took pride in my work and always strived to do it to the best of my ability. Even notoriously picky clients had no complaints when I worked with them. I was a force to be reckoned with, and my employer knew it. With his unwavering faith in me, I was more motivated than ever to continue exceeding expectations and proving myself as a valuable asset to the company.

As Caroline continued to work at the MTN Maverick, my sister Yvonne was busy pursuing her own endeavours. Despite the challenges she faced, Yvonne remained steadfast and resilient, a testament to her unwavering character. Growing up in Mhangura under the care of my elder sister, Yvonne faced extremely harsh circumstances that punctuated her life with great difficulties. Even as a child, she battled illness, struggling to walk as she was ravaged by tuberculosis that had taken hold in her bones. But thankfully, with successful treatment, Yvonne managed to overcome the disease and regain her health. Though she had faced such daunting challenges at a tender age, Yvonne never lost her unyielding spirit, and she continued to forge ahead, determined to make a better life for herself. Her unwavering strength and courage were truly inspiring, and I felt proud to call her my sister.

When I left Mhangura, my younger sister Yvonne was still just a child, having been left to fend for herself after our mother's untimely passing? Her life was fraught with difficulty, made even more challenging by the harsh treatment she received at the hands of my elder sister. As a result, Yvonne and my younger brother Owen were forced to endure many tough times, struggling to make ends meet while still being so young. Yvonne once confided in me about the horrible things my sister would make them do, things that even the vilest of people would baulk at, let alone a sibling. I was shocked and appalled to hear about the terrible things my sister had put Yvonne and Owen through. Some of the things Yvonne mentioned sounded so unbelievable, like the time my sister sent the two small kids on a dangerous mission to steal chickens in the dead of night. Despite all this, Yvonne remained strong, refusing to let the trials of her life break her spirit. Her unwavering resilience and determination were truly inspiring, and I couldn't help but feel a deep sense of pride for the brave young woman she had become.

As I listened to Yvonne's stories about the appalling treatment she received at the hands of my elder sister, I found it hard to believe that such cruelty could exist within a family. But then again, I had been put in a coffin alive by the very same sister, so I knew that anything was possible. Yvonne's life was marked by constant struggle and hardship, so much so that at one point she had no place to store her clothes in the house. Instead, she had to resort to keeping them in a drum outside, on the peripheries of our yard. It was a cruel irony that this same drum had once belonged to me when I lived there. For Yvonne and me, that drum had become a symbol of our shared history, a testament to the trials and tribulations we had endured. For me, it had served as a place to store my food and pots during the years of my struggles, when I was persecuted by my sister and had nowhere else to turn. But despite all the hardships we faced, Yvonne and I remained strong, determined to overcome the obstacles that life had thrown our way. And as we looked back on our shared experiences, we knew that we had come out the other side stronger and more resilient than ever. During my absence, the same drum that had been brought home from the garden continued to play a life-saving purpose. This time, it was used to store the clothes of my youngest sister, who faced struggles far beyond those of any child her age in the area. The crucial difference between us was that I was already a grown man with a voice, while my sister was still very young and had few options or choices. Yvonne confided in me that she and Owen had pressured my sister into performing these tasks, leaving her with little room to refuse. It was an abhorrent act to send children into danger, especially when they were expected to return with some form of spoils no matter what. The fact that my sister had returned empty-handed was deemed unacceptable and called for serious punishment. As I watched my sister Yvonne go through challenges that seemed more befitting of a drama series, I couldn't help but feel a sense of despair. However, we eventually learned to let go of our bitterness and forgive, even though the hardship remained etched in our history.

When I first brought Yvonne to Cape Town, she was unable to read, write, or even understand when white people spoke. It was heart-breaking to see such potential lying dormant, suppressed by the harsh realities of her surroundings. However, things began to change when she was given the opportunity to work. I was amazed by her tenacity and the dreams she envisioned for herself. It was inspiring to witness her transformation and see her rise above the obstacles that had once held her back. Despite the odds, Yvonne proved that with hard work and determination, anything is possible.

It was a stark contrast to the bleak future that had been preached to her by those around her. My sister had been repeatedly told by our family that she would amount to nothing in this life. This was a sentiment that had been directed at me in the past, and I knew first-hand the damage it could cause. However, Yvonne refused to let their words define her. Instead, she channelled her energy into pursuing her dreams and carving a path for herself. It was a powerful lesson in perseverance and the resilience of the human spirit.

Looking back on our journey, I am proud of how far we have come. Despite the challenges, we refused to give up, and that determination ultimately led us to a better place. What a testament to the power of hope and the unwavering faith and determination, and many times I have said to myself, if only fate had not conspired against us in trying to thwart every progressive move we make, surely by now we could have been a force to recon with.

As Yvonne worked to pursue her paths, we made sure Moreblessing was enrolled in a local kindergarten, where she could learn and grow in a safe and nurturing environment. Meanwhile, Blessing was preparing to attend Grade R at Good Hope Seminary Junior. We were excited for her to embark on this new journey and discover all the wonders that school had to offer. Little did we know that there was something even more special waiting for her.

It was at Good Hope Seminary Junior that Blessing was introduced to the enchanting world of music by a Japanese woman named Maria Botha. Maria was a gifted musician who had a passion for teaching young children how to play the violin. Under Maria's guidance, Blessing quickly discovered a talent for music that she never knew she had. With each lesson, she grew more confident and skilled, her fingers dancing across the strings with grace and ease. It was a joy to see her embrace her newfound talent and flourish under Maria's tutelage. It's a testimony to the power of education and the transformative impact it can have on a child's life. As we looked on with pride, it gave us a feeling that Blessing's future was bright and full of promise. With her talent, determination, and resilience, there was no limit to what she could achieve.

Throughout my work experience, I have been fortunate to gain momentum at Good Hope/Protea, which has provided me with numerous opportunities to tackle and handle more challenging construction-based projects. However, as with any salaried position, advancing in your career requires planning and discipline. Climbing the ranks and achieving success in a salaried position can be a challenging journey, but one has to bear in mind the rewards are more than just a salary and with good vision to progress is can well worth the effort. With each project, I undertake and every obstacle I overcome, I was gaining valuable experience that will help me advance and succeed in my not so glamorous career.

Upon pondering about my future, I decided in 2016 to attend college to further my qualifications. This would enable me to formally register a company and become accredited with certain regulating bodies, but above all, my heart had always had a burning desire to one day migrate to Australia. I shared this plan with Caroline, with the main reason being that we needed to plan for when we would have our next child by God's providence. I told her that I did not want us to have a child in 2016 or 2017. She seemed to agree to the plan, but I soon realized something about women, especially those who belong to a common social group.

I have always joked with friends from Church agreeing planning is often discussed at church by ladies, and once they see a woman in their social circle having a beautiful baby, they admire it and may feel pressured to follow suit. As a result, the husband may hear an announcement about a pregnancy soon after.

In early 2016, Caroline became pregnant, and we said; "Well, let the preparation take centre stage. However, that was not the end of the news, we soon learned that she was carrying twins, which brought a bag of mixed feelings for me. I felt both excitement and a sense anxiety in waiting as I pictured what having twins could really be like. Knowing what was at stake, we began to prepare for the arrival of the twins, which required us to make significant changes to our plans and lifestyle. We had to consider the additional financial costs, as well as the practical aspects of caring for two new-borns at once. We did not know what the experience would be like, but we were determined to do whatever it took to provide the best possible care for our children.

We had a lot to prepare for the arrival of the twins, from buying preparatory clothes to finding a new and better living space, and even changing our car to a seven-seater SUV. As the owner of a reliable Volvo, I knew that the brand would serve us well, despite the high cost of replacement parts. To finance the purchase of the new vehicle, I consulted Gary for help, and he agreed to assist me, allowing me to repay him slowly.

Everything seemed to be taking shape, and I was doing my best to prepare for the twins despite negative talk from some people who thought I was ill-prepared. Their criticism did not discourage me in the slightest. I remained focused on doing what I felt was necessary and put all my efforts into preparing for the arrival of our children.

Chapter 38

A perfect storm

Despite our best efforts and expectations, we never imagined the perfect storm that was heading our way. This whirlwind took the form of Caroline's pregnancy, which kept us in suspense as we tried to figure out what our future would be like with twins in the picture. We anxiously awaited the experience, picturing a house filled with energy and excitement with Blessing and Mobi in the mix.

We both looked forward to having a boy or boys, but Caroline was more vocal about it than I was. I preferred to keep my thoughts to myself for fear of being quoted out of context. Nevertheless, the prospect of having two new additions to our family filled us with anticipation and excitement. We could hardly wait to begin this new chapter of our lives, even though we knew that it would be challenging at times.

Since Caroline's registration, the doctors had indicated that there was a slight issue with her pregnancy. However, we were assured that there was no need to be alarmed. As a precaution, they transferred Caroline from Mowbray Maternity to Somerset

Hospital near the V&A Waterfront. To help with the complication, they provided her with tablets to consume. Given how seriously we had taken the first two pregnancies, we followed the instructions diligently. However, this time, Caroline was a little hesitant, as she was not fond of taking pills. Moreover, an odd occurrence was happening around our home during Caroline's pregnancy. Things began to get complicated when we started experiencing events that went beyond the ordinary. It was natural for us to have countless questions. A strange occurrence happened almost every night - cats would come and lament and wail at our door. Even on nights when they did not cry, they would sit on the roof of our house, and their movements could be heard. At times, I would even wake up in the middle of the night with a catapult in hand, searching for them. While most people would be frightened by this, I remained unafraid, even when I knew they meant harm. I was willing to face them, even if it meant being eaten alive.

I started to feel bitter towards cats. Every time I set my eyes on a cat, I felt an overwhelming urge to kill it. One day, while I was on my way to work on a train so packed that we had to hang on to the door until we reached Bonteheuwel, where many people disembarked, leaving ample room for us. As the train moved, I accidentally banged my head against a steel pole. The impact was so intense that I almost fell off the moving train. However, I managed to cling on to the door. I gritted my teeth and screamed to cope with the excruciating pain that overwhelmed me. Luckily, the train was moving slowly and almost coming to a halt. If it had been moving faster, I might have lost my life. Despite the terrifying experience, I only required stitches on my ear. After that incident, I decided never to travel by train again and switched to using taxis.

Two days later, while I was on my way to work, my brother-in-law Frank, who was married to my sister Caroline, called me to deliver some sad news. He informed me that one of my cousins in Zimbabwe, Floria, had passed away. She was the daughter of my uncle. Floria simply collapsed, leaving behind her infant child who was only a few months old. I felt a strong urge to go and pay my respects, but Caroline was against the idea. She believed that only immediate family members should attend the funeral. Perhaps she was correct, or maybe she was mistaken, but I knew I had to go. So, I teamed up with my brother Khumbu, and we set off in my Volvo, which consumed a lot of fuel at 2.9 L. Despite most of its body being aluminium, the car was surprisingly heavy. As we prepared to leave immediately, something strange occurred.

It seemed as though someone or something was trying to prevent us from embarking on this journey. Caroline voiced her objections, and then, something happened to Khumbu that made us wonder why all of a sudden, we were encountering strange obstacles that seemed to be trying to stop us from going. I drove my car to a wheel alignment centre in Athlone, while Khumbu made his final preparations to join me on the trip. However, as he was getting ready at his house, something strange happened. The police arrived, accompanied by a man from Khayelitsha who was tracking a stolen iPhone. According to the tracking device, it led to Khumbu's place, but a search of the area yielded no results. Nevertheless, the man was convinced that Khumbu was the culprit. When they came up empty-handed, the man snatched Khumbu's precious passport and bolted with the police in tow. Just like that! When I returned, I was expecting Khumbu to be all set and ready to go, but instead, I was hit with some bizarre news. I felt utterly helpless. What were we to do? The mere thought of crossing the border without a passport, the key to unlocking two different worlds, made us second-guess our entire travel plans. We had no choice but to wait and pray that things would turn in our favour. With the clock ticking, we set a deadline of 6:00 pm and anxiously awaited as Khumbu made call after call in a desperate attempt to recover his lost passport.

Thank God the man finally returned the passport, and we were able to hit the road by 4:00 pm. The journey was, for the most part, alright. As always, it was a tiresome trek, but our hearts were resolute in reaching our destination. There were times when we had to push the car to a hundred and sixty km per hour, determined to make good time. Fortunately, we experienced little trouble with the car along the way. However, driving to Zimbabwe from Cape Town, especially for a funeral, is always a race against the clock. You're trying your best to arrive as quickly as possible, and every second counts. Thankfully, our trusty Volvo proved to be reliable, especially when well-maintained. In fact, I wouldn't hesitate to get another one if I could. The only drawback, of course, is the hefty price tag that comes with maintaining these cars. But hey, you get what you pay for, right?

I believe that it's a good practice to keep a low profile during gatherings. That's why I always pay close attention to my appearance and behaviour. I try to keep things simple and avoid creating the impression that I'm something special. After all, I'm just a regular guy dealing with life's challenges like anyone else. I'm the type of person who prefers to stay true to myself, even when I'm in a group setting. I don't enjoy being the centre of attention or having people gather around me, expecting me to paint a glamorous picture of life in South Africa. Instead, I prefer to remain the same person I am when I'm at home, sitting by the fireplace. That way, I can be sure that I'm not putting on a false front or pretending to be someone I'm not. Perhaps it's because I've never been one to lead an extravagant lifestyle, but I've never felt compelled to divulge much about my personal life. I staunchly refuse to fabricate or embellish details just to impress others or appear more impressive. I've observed that a significant number of individuals, both men and women alike, tend to engage in this type of behaviour, but it simply isn't my cup of tea. I prefer to maintain a low profile and preserve my privacy. I have no interest in seeking attention or allowing people to pry into my personal life. I'd rather let people speculate and form their own opinions about me, be it to elevate me as they did during my time in Mhondoro Ngezi or to diminish me as my woodwork instructor did back when I was a Form 1 student at Kenzamba. Ultimately, I leave it to others to determine how they perceive me. I don't lose sleep over what people think or say about me, as it's something that's beyond my control. What matters most to me is staying true to myself and living my life with integrity.

As we gathered with the mourners, I couldn't help but notice some of my cousins from Chiweshe. Swisdai, a vibrant man who grew up in rank to become a regional manager at Bain, was a man always on the go and he was leaving just as we arrived. Despite his hectic schedule, he's always been a pillar of support for our family, always ready to lend a helping hand when needed. Then there was Benson, who I've grown close to due to his frequent trips to Cape Town to purchase tires. It was great to see him there, and we chatted as we always do. The rest of the people gathered were relatives in some way or another, some of whom I hadn't seen in years. But when I spoke to them, it was as if no time had passed at all. I tried to interact with them in the same way I did ten or so years ago. I also knew that Benson was planning a trip back to Cape Town, so I pulled him aside for a brief chat. I tried to convince him to ride with me through Botswana on our way back, but unfortunately, he declined, as he wanted to catch a bus with some work colleagues. Nonetheless, it was great to catch up with him and see some familiar faces from home. I made it my mission to connect with as many people as possible within the limited time I had. Despite my desire to take a scenic drive through Mhangura with my siblings, who had also travelled to attend the gathering, I remained present at the moment.

As I prepared to depart, a realization hit me - this was the second time our family had gathered at this location to mourn the loss of a loved one. A surge of emotions rose within me as I remembered Actor, whose passing had left a profound impact on my life. Not only was he incredibly close to me, but he also entrusted me with the care of Fletcher. Now, as we gathered to lay his sister to rest, memories of Actor flooded back, reminding me of the importance of cherishing the time we have with family. Though the child lived with her mom, now married, I continually helped as much as I could afford in terms of fees and school-related things. The boy is very brilliant, closer to a genius.

When the time to leave came, I knew I had no option but to drive, though feeling tired because of the long drive from Cape Town. My two sisters and my brother Mandela came with me. In my mind, I had it registered that I had to drive, knowing consciously it was important to arrive early enough to catch some sleep to carry on to Harare the next morning.

Our roads required all mental alertness because of their ugly rugged state. Considering I did not have a spare tyre because one of my tyres had burst when Truther drove over a sharp iron while trying to move the car. But I was to sort that out once I get to Magaba Harare the next morning with Brother Benson's guys.

After spending the whole afternoon in Harare fixing my tyre issue, I made my way to Norton where I would sleep and fetch Khumbu, my nephew. The drive was long and tiring, but I felt a sense of accomplishment knowing that I had dealt with the tyre issue and was on my way to reunite with my family. Mind you, all along from the time I entered Zimbabwe, I had no internet. This meant no WhatsApp, which was a challenge for me, as I rely heavily on it to communicate with people. To overcome this, I had to hotspot with Truther, with whom I spent the whole day in Harare. This was my second time using a hotspot, having been introduced to it that very afternoon by my brother Mandela. It was a lifesaver for me, as it allowed me to stay connected with the world.

As soon as I got access to WhatsApp, a message from Caroline came. She tricked me into a mistake I would regret. Her message was misleading, but I blindly fell for it. Her eldest sister was in Zimbabwe, living there without a job, but her South African work permit was still valid. It was a tempting opportunity for me to help out, but I knew there were risks involved. Nonetheless, I couldn't help but feel a sense of responsibility to help out in any way I could. Caroline was persistent in trying to talk me into helping her again, but I stood firm and refused to be manipulated. However,

Caroline was never short of tricks, and she fooled me countless times, always seeming to be one step ahead of me. This time, Caroline simply said that Loveness, her other sister, had requested that she come and live with her. I didn't find any problem with this and didn't bother to check with Loveness if such a deal existed.

I took Clarisa with me to Cape Town, and we continued with our journey. From the moment I felt compelled to go and gather with family and mourn our beloved sister, to the time I arrived back to begin my normal routine of work and daily life, it was a rollercoaster of emotions. The experience reminded me of the fragility of life and the importance of family and friends. Despite the challenges and unexpected twists and turns, I was grateful for the opportunity to connect with loved ones and cherish the time we had together. My mind could not fathom the depths of misery that awaited me. Lady Life had brewed a potent concoction of woe and poured it mercilessly over my affairs.

It was only in the third week after my return from the funeral, when I was hoping to recover from the financial impact of that long trip, that I felt its full weight. Despite the chaos, we held on to hope, knowing that Caroline was pregnant with the promise of a new chapter in our lives. With each passing day, the anticipation grew, and I reminded myself of the beautiful life that awaited us after the birth of our twins. I pushed myself to the limit, determined to ensure that our future would be bright and full of joy.

Nature has a language of its own, and it often communicates with us in ways we fail to understand. Sometimes the signs are right before us, repeating themselves persistently, yet we still struggle to comprehend their meaning. In my case, I could see and hear the warnings of danger around our home, but I couldn't fathom their significance.

One strange occurrence stood out above all others. Night after night, since Caroline's conception, cats would gather outside our rented flat and wail. Their cries resembled crying babies or an argument in progress. This went on for seven months, driving me to the brink of annoyance and frustration as I wondered what it all meant. Despite my exasperation, I couldn't help but wonder if it was a sign of impending trouble, a foreboding that I couldn't decipher. All I could do was pray, hoping that one day my prayers would scare away the cats and chase the evil behind them. But the cats continued to wail, and when they grew tired, they would sit on the rooftop, a bad omen that filled me with dread. These were clear signs of an ugly and stinking soup brewing in the pot of misery, ready to be poured on us. I am not a prophet or a dreamer, and I had no idea what was coming. While I tried to focus on the future, life was about to take a drastic turn. It's a mystery how the cats seemed to know something about my fate, while I was completely clueless.

In the eighth month of Caroline's pregnancy, she was due for maternity leave. Little did we know that a dark, dark moment was about to descend upon us, and our lives would never be the same again. Caroline had just begun her maternity leave, and she planned to spend her first day submitting forms to claim some benefits at the Department of Labour. Everything seemed fine as we spoke through WhatsApp, and she updated me on the proceedings. But when the afternoon came, she messaged me to say that she saw blood slowly trickling down her legs. I asked how severe it was, and she replied that it wasn't too bad and that she wasn't in any pain, but she wanted my opinion. I told her to drop everything and head straight to Grote Schuur Hospital. Of course, I was going to see her after work and also ensure that our children at home, Blessing, and Mobi, were safe.

It was a moment of great concern for me, and I couldn't wait to be by her side and ensure that everything was alright. Little did I know that this was only the beginning of a long and painful journey, one that would test our strength and resilience beyond measure. But for now, all I could do was pray and hope that Caroline and our unborn twins would be safe. Caroline's first two pregnancies were smooth sailing, but this time around, it was a wild ride. She was transferred from hospital to hospital, starting at Mowbray Maternity before they whisked her away to Somerset Hospital when something unusual was detected. However, as her condition deteriorated, she was rushed to Groote Schuur where she stayed for two days. Four weeks before that, Caroline made her way to Somerset Hospital after picking up Blessing from school. I later had to dash home to collect Moreblessing from crèche before we headed to the hospital. Unfortunately, upon our arrival, we discovered that she had been transferred to Groote Schuur, leaving Blessing in the care of security guards. I quickly located Blessing, and together we journeyed to Caroline, my heart pounding in my chest as I wondered if something serious had happened. As we went our way, Blessing shared that Caroline had slept and fallen two days prior, but Caroline had not mentioned it to me. I didn't think it was related to her hospitalization. On the day she mentioned experiencing bleeding, I followed Caroline to the hospital after work, alone since I had arranged for my sister to take care of the children. When I arrived, I found Caroline waiting to be shown which bed she would occupy. I sat with her on a bench placed in the corridor, chatting and waiting until she was attended to. As we sat together, we all felt that she was entering early labour. I reassured her that by the following morning, she would be cradling her precious babies in her arms, and all would be well. I stood up, embraced her, and promised to be with her by 10:00 am the following morning with some clothes for preparation. Despite my anxiety and nervousness, the night passed slowly as I eagerly awaited good news. Unfortunately, my hopes were dashed. The cauldron of misery had simmered to its bitter conclusion, and all that remained was to serve it up and endure its bitter flavour. I dialled her number at the hour 7:30 a.m. from my workplace, and her voice was strained with agony. For a fleeting moment, I contemplated abandoning all tasks and racing to her side. But after consulting with Gary, it became apparent that it was wiser for me to lead my team to the work site, for she was surrounded by individuals who were better equipped to offer her aid than I was. We agreed that I would proceed to the hospital after dropping off my team at the site. This was a good arrangement since the site was close to the town, which meant my drive to the hospital would be quick compared to being at one of our sites in the southern suburbs. Accompanied by Simba, my assistant, and two team members, and I headed to the worksite. We wasted no time at the worksite, quickly setting everything up and preparing to leave. Just as we were about to depart, my phone rang. On the other end was a doctor from the hospital.

Suddenly, everything clicked into place. Something was definitely not right, and my heart urged me to leave immediately. My mind was consumed with worry, and I completely forgot about the sandwich I had prepared for breakfast. Sometimes, hunger is a state of mind, and our thoughts dictate how we operate. I never could have imagined that I would go three days without feeling hungry or even thinking about food, not until after the phone call. Despite the overwhelming feeling of worry after the phone call, adrenaline carried me safely to the hospital, although I was absent-minded during the drive. I was able to find a secure parking spot to protect my valuables.

Upon arriving at the maternity section, I expected to be greeted with smiles and happiness, undeterred by any pain. However, that was not the case. I was instructed to go directly to the theatre without any further information. I ended up waiting anxiously outside the theatre door for about an hour and a half, as no one told me what was happening.

The longer I waited, the more alarm bells rang inside me, and I began to feel restless. Calmness no longer seemed like the right thing to do, and I started to nag anyone who entered or exited the theatre door, desperate for information. After what felt like an eternity, a visibly shaken female doctor finally emerged to address me. She was direct and to the point. "Caroline had a cardiac arrest, and unfortunately, her daughter died due to lack of oxygenated blood in the brain. Her son was born alive, but he is unwell and has been taken to the nursery. We are doing our best to save Caroline, but we cannot guarantee her survival." I stood up from my seat without uttering a word, and with a heavy heart, I made my way out of the hospital. The events of the day had turned my world upside down in an instant, and I felt completely lost and unsure of what to do or who to turn to for comfort. As I drove calmly to the office, I couldn't help but feel the weight of the situation bearing down on me. Once I arrived at the office, I sought out Gary and shared with him the details of my predicament. Even he was at a loss for words as he listened to my story. I knew that I couldn't just sit around and do nothing, so I quickly left the office and headed back to the Hospital. As I merged onto the busy mid-morning M5 freeway, my thoughts and prayers were consumed with the hope that Caroline would pull through. I was so lost in my own thoughts that I missed the N2 off-ramp and found myself continuing straight on the M5 toward Milnerton. I had no choice but to take a turn in Maitland through Salt River, all the while replaying the words of the female doctor in my head and sending up prayers for Caroline's recovery.

Despite the chaos and confusion of the day, I couldn't help but feel a sense of resilience coursing through my veins. I knew that I had to stay strong and keep my faith, even in the face of such adversity. As soon as I parked my car, my feet led me straight to the Maternity section of the Hospital without any need for security clearance. The news of Caroline being alive upon my arrival felt like an immediate answer to the prayers I had been fervently offering while driving back to the Hospital. However, my mind could not shake off the thought of the deceased baby, so I requested to see her body before anything else. The hospital staff agreed to my request, and I was led to the room where I asked to sit on a bench while a lady disappeared behind a double door.

I sat waiting on a bench, feeling like the weight of the world was on my shoulders. As I waited, a middle-aged Coloured lady approached me, pushing a small trolley with a plastic tray containing the lifeless beauty, the body of what was meant to be my precious baby girl. I quickly got to my feet, taking the lifeless figure into my arms and sinking back down onto the bench. As I gazed at her, she looked peaceful, as if she were just asleep. It was hard for me to accept that there was nothing that could be done to bring her back to life. In her features, I saw glimpses of Blessing and Moreblessing, and my heart ached with the thought of what could have been. For a long moment, I remained glued to the bench, unsure of whether to prolong or shorten the process. The decision was mine alone to make, and even the lady who had brought the lifeless body in a trolley was in no rush to hurry me along. Tears streamed down my cheeks without restraint, as the weight of the reality set in. But resilience held me together, urging me to stay strong in the face of such catastrophe. The same lady who had brought my lifeless baby on the small trolley stood before me, holding out my phone. She asked if it would be alright to take some pictures using my phone, and I agreed. I knew that these pictures would be the only memories I would have of my baby, and they would serve as a memorial for her and for Caroline when she woke up. I planned to store them in my iCloud account for safekeeping. Afterwards, I made my way downstairs to the Nursery where they were monitoring the baby boy. As I entered the room, I was met with a sight that was both heart-wrenching and awe-inspiring. There were several little beds, each one surrounded by highly sophisticated medical machinery. And there he was, my baby boy, breathing heavily under the support of a ventilator, with countless sensors connected to him, monitoring every aspect of his body, especially his brain. I stood there, trying to process the reality of the situation, wishing that it was all just a nightmare. But the harsh reality soon set in, and I knew that I had to stay strong and keep my faith in God, even in the midst of such a tormenting nightmare.

As I stood there, with wide open eyes looking at what I hoped would be my baby boy, I couldn't shake the growing sense of despair within me. The machines were keeping him alive, but barely. The doctors delivered the news with their usual lack of diplomacy: my son was gravely ill and might not survive. Their words cut deep, leaving me longing for a glimmer of hope to cling to. But there was none to be found, only the dark reality of what lay ahead.

Despite the overwhelming sense of dread that gripped me, I knew I had to face the situation head-on. There was no other option. I hadn't even had a chance to see Caroline, who was in the ICU on the floor above. The doctors were waiting for me, eager to brief me on her condition before moving on to the next task. When I arrived, Caroline was hooked up to countless machines, with IV drips and blood transfusions hanging overhead. She looked so hopeless and fragile. The various machines were producing a cacophony of sounds that rang constant in my mind for days to come, accompanied by vivid images that stayed impressed in my mind.

As I stood there, my mind was consumed by a single question: Was this the same person I had shared a bed with day in and day out? I was transfixed, struggling to make sense of the senselessness that had unfolded before me. Suddenly, one of the doctors gently pulled me towards his colleagues, snapping me out of my daze. "She is very, very sick," Doctor Chambers carefully delivered the words. "Honestly speaking, we don't know which way things will go."

The doctors explained that her blood was not clotting, and their first priority was to stop the continual bleeding. They inserted packs into her stomach to absorb and prevent the blood from flowing uncontrollably. The hope was that the bleeding would stop, and she could undergo surgery to remove the packs from her stomach. I had witnessed sickness before, but what I was facing now was beyond anything I could have prepared for or imagined. I felt consumed by it as if all my wisdom, ego, and abilities had instantly diminished in the face of adversity. This sickness was of a different nature altogether. How could life demand so much from me, a mere me? I knew for sure that I had nothing in my arsenal that could tackle this kind of sickness.

Once again, I felt like I was being tossed between the horns of an angry bull. No matter what thoughts or images I conjured up, nothing seemed to make sense. I felt like collapsing and giving up or just dropping dead. I felt like I needed to speak to someone, anyone, who could help me escape from my nightmares. I tried to imagine what it would take to make the situation go away. So, I began making calls, reaching out to my relatives, Caroline's sister, and friends from church. The situation was messy and uglier than anything I had encountered before. It felt like a monster was swallowing me whole.

In the past, I had faced difficult moments, such as being shoved into a coffin alive, getting robbed at gunpoint, and experiencing other excruciating life events. But nothing had ever felt as overwhelming as this. As I stood alone in the hospital, consumed by overwhelming feelings of defeat and exhaustion, I sent a message to my cousin Benson, who happened to be in Cape Town at the time. I was desperate for a lifeline, but little did I know that this was just the beginning of an unforgettable journey that would change my life forever.

With one child already lost and another seriously ill, while my wife lay on the brink of death, I prayed, "Heaven I need a hug". But then, Prince Muchengi arrived. A friend, a brother, and an elder in the church, he may have been sent by heaven as an Angel wrapped in a familiar face to offer me a little embrace. Though he didn't have many words to offer, he did something even more significant. Before he left, he purchased R200 worth of airtime for me, a small but meaningful gesture that touched my heart.

As I waited in the hospital, I was visited by Pastor Dan Potgieter and Brighton, who spent some time with me, offering words of encouragement and support. But my mind was consumed by countless meetings with doctors, each one direr than the last. Both my child and wife were on the brink of losing their lives, and I felt powerless to do anything to stop it. It was a moment I felt my vigour, my faith and my will to survive diminishing and dissolving in the face of something mightier than I.

When I sent Loveness a brief message she immediately left work to rush to the hospital. When she arrived, she found Caroline motionless in a coma, and Loveness was struggling to hold back tears and keep her composure. I could feel the weight of the situation as I approached Loveness. Without an exchange of words, I placed my hand on her shoulder, and we stepped outside the ward. In the fading light of the sunset, we stood in silence, struggling to comprehend the gravity of the situation.

As we stood there, I couldn't help but think about the fragility of life and the importance of human connection. It was then that I saw my dear friend Grace, the only female member of our group Primitive Faith, arriving with a few other individuals, including her son Tafadzwa. Their presence was a much-needed source of comfort and support, reminding us that we were not alone in this difficult time.

This experience taught me the value of human connection and how it can bring light to even the darkest of moments. It is through these connections that we find the strength to face life's challenges, and I am grateful for the people in my life who have helped me through my own struggles. After gathering my thoughts, I stood in front of a small group of people and gave a brief speech. We formed a circle, holding hands, and I stood next to the wife of Tyson Baloyi, a brother from Malawi. As I spoke, I struggled to hold back my emotions, and she noticed. She let go of my hand and reached up to give my shoulder a gentle rub. At that moment, her simple gesture spoke volumes, offering me the comfort and support I desperately needed. It was a reminder that even in the midst of tragedy, there is still kindness and compassion in the world. Her action gave me the strength to remain calm and composed, even in the face of overwhelming grief.

Since the incident, I have tried my best to remain strong for my family and handle the situation to the best of my ability. The only time I allowed myself to cry was when the lady in the dark blue uniform brought me the lifeless body of my baby girl on a trolley. Since then, I have tried to stay calm and handle my emotions in a way that honours my daughter.

As we held hands, we calmly sang a hymn to prepare ourselves for prayer. This was just the beginning of the overwhelming support I would continually receive from the Church throughout the situation. Eventually, we went home, and my siblings in Cape Town were made aware of the situation. The following day, they all came to see for themselves. It was indeed a situation that could not be ignored. Although I couldn't personally call everyone, I was touched to see people like Brother Benson, who happened to be in Cape Town, coming to be with me. My long-time friend and uncle, Obert, also descended from Hermanus where he lives and works as an artist. Bamnini Simba, who lives in Gauteng, also made his way to see me. Lastly, my stepmom had to come all the way from Zimbabwe to spend more than a month with us. Overall, the support I received from my loved ones during this difficult time was truly heart-warming. Even though heaven couldn't send me winged beings, the human touch around me was compelling.

During this difficult time, the people around me were a source of strength. Some gave me assurance that with faith in God, things would be well. Others, like my friend Obert, took a more practical approach and prepared me for the worst. I remember one evening during prayer at my home, he wept bitterly.

On the third day, Caroline was transferred to the main ICU. The doctors were completely satisfied that her blood was clotting, and a second surgery was successfully performed to remove the packs in her stomach. Everything seemed to be alright, except for the fact that she was under life support and could pass away at any moment. Unfortunately, the boy did not make it. Despite his valiant effort to fight for his life for two days, it was deemed pointless to keep him on life support. The disconnection of the life support was a deeply painful moment for me. I was heartbroken when I saw the boy trying to cling to life, even after the life support was disconnected. I pleaded with the doctors to give him one more day, but they disconnected the life support anyway. They allowed me some time to hold him, and Benson was there with me during his last moments. I waited for the baby to pass away, but to my surprise, he continued to breathe through the day and into the night. I will never know if he had a chance to live if he had been given more time.

At midnight, someone called me to inform me of the passing of the child. I was devastated. I felt like they had cut his life short when he may have had a chance to live. But he was gone. I named him Israel, after myself. My parents had always called me Jacob since childhood, but I felt like there were too many things going wrong in my life. I wanted to change my name to Israel. So, it had always been in my heart that if I ever had a baby boy, his name would be Israel. I thought that it was my time to enjoy life with my son Israel, but heaven had other plans. Israel passed away, and I was left feeling utterly devastated. My name remained Jacob, but I felt like a broken man.

It's frustrating that common sense is not so common among the people around us. If only everyone subscribed to the simple idea of unity as a virtue, things would be so much better. But unfortunately, many people refuse to put aside their differences even when facing a common cause. To make things worse, Caroline's sister kept babbling about me, spreading rumours to family members far and wide. It's like a never-ending cycle of stress and disappointment. It's hard not to feel let down by heaven when everything around me seems to be falling apart. Although

Caroline's eldest sister continued to spread hurtful rumours about me, I chose to let them talk and considered their negativity a minor issue. I had a much greater situation to overcome - the memories of losing not one but two babies. I had no room for more pain and negativity in my life. This situation was unlike any other I had faced before. But in the midst of my struggle, my church-mates never ceased to offer their unwavering support. They showed up every day, sometimes straight from work, to be with me and help me through this difficult time. I was humbled by their willingness to sacrifice their time and energy for me. It was a testament to the power of community and the strength of faith.

One person who stood out among my church mates was an energetic young man who caught my attention from the very first day. It turned out that he was Grace's son, a small boy who showed a level of maturity beyond his years. One day, this young boy noticed something that everyone else had overlooked. He saw that I was hungry and brought me a plate of hot, well-cooked Sadza, which is a staple food in our culture. It was a simple gesture, but it meant the world to me. It's amazing how sometimes it's the smallest acts of kindness that have the biggest impact on our lives.

Even though Caroline's condition seemed hopeless, I found myself fixating on her eyes. From the moment I entered the

Labour ICU, they drew my attention from day one when they looked all white and lifeless. So, I continued to monitor them closely for any sign of change, even when everything else seemed to preach hopelessness. As I watched her lying motionless, I couldn't help but wonder if she was still the same person, I had shared a bed with. Despite these doubts, I refused to give up hope. I visited her regularly, hoping beyond hope that she would somehow recover.

But then came the day when the doctors called me to the family counselling room. As I made my way there, my heart sank. I knew what was coming: it was time to remove life support. The air in the room felt thick and heavy, and my mind was filled with a mix of emotions - sadness and fear. The doctors delivered the news with calm, clinical detachment, but their words landed like a heavy blow on my already battered spirit. I had been through so much already, and now this. Caroline had suffered severe brain damage due to lack of oxygen to the brain, and there was no hope for a meaningful recovery.

I could feel my heart pounding in my chest as the reality of the situation sank in. The doctors spoke with conviction, their words cutting through the air like a sharp knife. 'If we could force her to live,' they said, 'she will be bedridden, unable to talk or walk.'

The weight of their words hung heavy in the air, and I struggled to keep my composure. The thought of Caroline being trapped in a body that no longer functioned, unable to communicate or move, was almost too much to bear. I felt completely defeated, outnumbered, and outmatched by the medical experts. But I refused to give up without a fight. I searched for any last weapon in my arsenal to defend Caroline's life. After praying fervently and remembering the change I had noticed in her eyes, I finally spoke up. 'No,' I said firmly, surprising them all. 'Give her more time. She will be well. There are changes already.' I knew that the damage to her system was not visible externally, but it was intense, and recovery would be slow. Despite their objections, I convinced the doctors to let her remain on the life-support machine.

As I left the room, I felt a sense of defeat wash over me. I needed to get away, to clear my head and gather my thoughts. So, I began walking aimlessly, without a plan or a destination in mind. The weight of the situation was heavy on my shoulders as I walked, my mind consumed with worry and doubt. But still, I refused to give up hope. I knew that the road ahead would be long and difficult, but I was willing to do one more step every single day.

To my surprise, the very next day after giving Caroline some time to recover, I received a call from the hospital. "We told you, she's not improving," they said. I wasn't ready to give up on Caroline just yet. I knew I had to fight for her. This time, I pulled out what I thought was my last line of defence. "Caroline came into this hospital walking on two feet," I said firmly. "Before you pull the plug, I need to know how she collapsed while surrounded by doctors and medical staff, only to be found later." The room fell silent for what felt like an eternity. The doctors exchanged uneasy glances, clearly taken aback by my challenge. Finally, one of them spoke up. "We don't know," he admitted. "But we can arrange a meeting with the medical team who treated her, and they can explain what happened." I felt a sense of relief wash over me knowing that I had at least bought some time to give Caroline more time to recover. With my last line of defence, I had just delivered a crushing blow to the hospital staff. It was clear that they didn't have all the answers, and this was a major victory in our fight to save Caroline's life. But despite this triumph, the uncertainty and torment of our situation continued to weigh heavily on me every day. Thankfully, the church community rallied around me and offered unwavering support during this difficult time. And my sisters, Caroline, and Yvonne, were there with me every step of the way.

Together, we stood resolute and refused to give up on Caroline. We were determined to do everything in our power to bring her back to us, no matter what obstacles we faced along the way.

As we continued to fight for Caroline's life, I knew that each day would bring new challenges and setbacks. My prayer was that we become victorious in the end and defy the odds, and I cherished the support of my loved ones and the strength of our collective will. The day after our second meeting with the doctors, we returned to the hospital and headed straight to Caroline's bedside. As we approached her bed, we were greeted by a sight we never thought we'd see: her eyes were open, and she looked alive. One of the doctors who had previously doubted us simply said, "You were right." I resisted the urge to say; "I told you so" and instead focused on the fact that Caroline was showing signs of improvement. However, she was immediately placed in isolation to minimize the number of people visiting her. Despite the disappointment of many, particularly from our church community, we understood the importance of this precaution. Caroline remained in isolation for several weeks, but she continued to make significant progress. The machines that had been aiding her were slowly disconnected as her body began to function more and more on its own. We received the good news that her heart was now pushing blood constantly on its own. And soon, they began to reduce the assistance of the ventilator until there were days when she could go for an hour without it. It was a slow and steady process, but we were grateful for every bit of progress that Caroline made.

As Caroline battled through her illness, the medical team closely monitored her lung strength by observing the power of her cough. Most of the tubes had been removed, leaving only two - one by her throat, where they had made a hole due to an infection caused by the previous tubes passing through her mouth, and a second one that went directly to her stomach. It was a significant milestone in her recovery, but there was still a long way to go.

During all this time, I had to take time off work to be by her side. But as her condition started to improve, I knew it was time to go back to work. It was emotionally challenging to juggle work and visiting the hospital, but I was determined to make it work. The cost of living was high, and I was worried about how I would manage everything, but by the grace of God, things fell into place. My boss, Gary, was incredibly understanding and even paid me for the time I was absent.

Despite the challenges, I remained determined and resilient, just like my trusty car that carried me through the ups and downs of life. I was grateful for its steadfastness as I navigated through work and hospital visits. With each passing day, I held onto hope that my loved one would continue to make progress towards a full recovery. When my car hit a rough patch, I felt like my world was falling apart. But in the midst of my despair, something amazing happened. My friend Wellington came to the rescue and lent me his car. I was blown away by his kindness, and it gave me strength and took away worry. Despite the many challenges I faced, I remained determined to push through. Though there were moments when I felt like I had hit rock bottom, I refused to give up. I persevered with a brave face, even though deep down, I was struggling. It was an incredibly trying time, but the unwavering support from my friends and family gave me the strength to keep moving.

During our usual evening visit, when we least expected it, my sister Caroline was there, along with Yvonne and my Stepmom. Caroline was in the stage of learning to talk, and we were all gathered around her bed with the children present, including Moreblessing, who was hesitant to come closer to Mom. Caroline was trying to communicate something to us, but at first, we couldn't quite understand what she was saying. Eventually, we realized that she was asking for help to go to the restroom. This came as a surprise to us, but she was insistent until my sister helped her off the bed and slowly to her feet. Caroline balanced carefully with my sister and took cautious, baby steps towards the restroom, which was located in the general ward. We all went silent as we remain fixated on what we were just witnessing. The medical staff doing their usual things at the nurse station all turned their gaze to Caroline. At the nurse station, every head turned, this was surely newsworthy, and there was silence in the ward. Caroline had gotten up from the bed and walked on two. This was a recovery beyond what the Doctors had told me during the meetings. Just in time, as if by coincidence, while we were looking and trying to confirm we weren't in a dream. One of the Doctors entered, his attention immediately drawn towards what we were witnessing. He turned to me, and we looked each other in the eye. I remembered the words I had said to this same man. "Doctor do understand there's a lot you don't know about life and know that there's a power above the power of Medicine". Now, in my stare, I was saying "See, I told you" The Doctor's prediction was defied. Was there more recovery beyond this? Only time would tell. The attempt to walk, or rather Caroline's walk on this memorable evening was convincing enough for the Doctors to send her to the rehabilitation centre based in Mitchells Plain. Good news, good progress, but on the contrary, it meant an increase in the distance I was to cover daily while also limiting people that could visit her in my absence. Physically she was making slow progress, each time improving on speech and energy. But the biggest problem that resulted from the brain damage was memory loss, and memory recovery is a slow and painful process, especially for any caregiver. This became a great challenge for me, particularly from the days we started bringing her over home during weekends and returning her on Mondays. Our subject of discussion was the obviously painful ordeal in which the person is even surprised she was pregnant. She had lost the recollection of her pregnancy period. When I thought, I had narrated to her the things she wanted to understand, the subject would come back again as if we had never discussed it. She would cry over and again, it was also painful even more to me, having witnessed her sickness and the passing of the twins. This was happening after three months, at the same time I was now trying to accept everything and move on, kind of a natural way of seeing through hard times. We were at different stages; everything was brand new to her. Soon when she could steadily walk, she was released home to my care. I was hopeful, I felt like things were getting better.

When things aren't well at home, work becomes challenging. I was now at the centre of things; a recovering wife, whose sickness can be understood if you take a look at the depth of harm. When she got discharged her hands could not lift a cup of tea or a spoon. She wanted to try things, but she was still weak, and I wondered what it would take to see her energetic again. My kids were still quite young, and both girls needed a lot of care. My battle was just getting to another level, as Caroline was not released on any medication and required a lot of help. I had no choice but to shoulder the load, with a multitude of responsibilities, and finances that wouldn't allow me to hire someone. Once again, my sisters who lived closer did their best to help. This situation was so scary that each time we went to bed, I would wake up two to three times during the night to check if Caroline was still alive. During the day, she would sleep so much that I became scared and would wake her up just to make sure she was still breathing. It was a lot of sleeping, and the constant worry took a toll on me.

Chapter 39

My quest to know

I needed answers to things that weren't clear to me, so I turned to the doctors at Groote Schuur Hospital. I wanted to understand what had transpired on that fateful day of September 29, 2016. How did Caroline, who arrived at the hospital walking on two legs, suddenly collapse in the middle of countless medical staff?

To find answers, a series of meetings were set up between myself, Dr Aziz, and Professor Antony. We had long, extensive talks, but I found myself getting lost in their medical jargon. I refused to give up and requested that they put everything into layman's language so that I could understand.

I pushed hard for answers, and Professor Antony was more than willing to help or answer any questions I had. With his help, I was able to gain a better understanding of what had happened to Caroline and what her condition was. It was a difficult time, but I knew that I needed to keep pushing for answers to help Caroline understand what had happened.

I tend to ask questions, even if it annoys ill-prepared individuals. I was determined to find answers, so I continued to push for information. Eventually, the doctor requested my email and sent me a document explaining what they perceived had happened to Caroline.

The document detailed a subject called Amniotic Fluid Embolism (AFE), which is a leading cause of maternal death and a medical conundrum. They explained that this condition is very rare yet catastrophic, and research is still ongoing to understand it. Furthermore, they told me that the lack of understanding was compounded by the unavailability of animal models for testing.

When they saw how Caroline had survived, they told me that it could be classified as a miracle because the condition typically kills 99 out of 100 women. To make it simple for me, the doctor added, "If we were to take 99 more ladies going through the same experience, chances are that all 99 would die, leaving only your wife." I was grateful that I had sought answers to the questions that had been plaguing me for so long, and I knew that Caroline's survival was nothing short of a miracle.

As time went on, the challenges I faced became increasingly complicated, changing from stage to stage.

Initially, I had hoped once Caroline regains the ability to walk and talk, it would bring a sense of relief, but I soon realized that my struggles were more complex than I had anticipated. Despite this,

I remained composed and persistent in managing my responsibilities at home, with my children, Caroline, and work.

At home, I taught myself to tune out peripheral distractions and focus on what mattered most. At work, I maintained a calm demeanour and paid close attention to detail to avoid costly mistakes. My performance was so impressive that when one of the team leaders resigned, Gary approached me to help find a replacement. He specifically sought someone of my calibre, but it proved to be a challenging task

When it comes to my work, I take great care in everything I do, especially given the high stakes of the projects we work on. A small mistake could end up costing the company millions of Rands or even forcing it to close. Working under such pressure can easily impair one's concentration and lead to errors, but I am proud to say that I make mistakes in only 4% of my work. In contrast, I have observed other colleagues who always seem to have something to talk about on every job.

In the construction industry, when a project is completed, the main contractor compiles a snag list of things that require correction. The name of the company in charge of each task is noted on the snag list. My snag list would typically have only two or three items or none at all. It's no wonder that Gary sought someone like me when he needed to find a replacement for a team leader.

Despite the high-pressure environment at work, I am grateful that things have remained good for me. However, like everyone else, I am not immune to the normal problems that people face daily. Life is unpredictable and can throw mammoth problems our way, but it's important to remain resilient and focused, even in the face of all the troubles.

I am grateful that despite the significant stress I faced, things remained good for me. Life can be unpredictable, and we are not immune to the daily problems that people face. During this challenging time, Caroline was making good progress to the surprise of doctors. I did my best to take her to places where she could get help, but unfortunately, medication for brain recovery was not available. Therefore, my focus was on her diet, and I made sure to follow the recommendations of Obert, who was helping us.

Counselling was not effective due to Caroline's memory loss, but she was slowly improving in remembering things. As I monitored her progress, I noticed that her speech improved as her memory recovered. However, the financial burden of her medical care weighed heavily on me. I remembered that during the preparation for the upcoming project, I needed to keep this in mind and plan accordingly.

I wanted a second income and thought that since Gary had agreed to help me during my wife's pregnancy with buying a vehicle, I felt like changing the plan to a small truck would make a difference, I approached him again, and, upon hearing I have changed what I wanted, he quickly changed his mind and said he was no more in a position to assist me. I felt like I played my cards open, I should have been more cunning. Nevertheless, I had to carry on inching through my journey.

It took me more than a year of hard work and determination to finally save up enough money to buy a truck. It wasn't the newest or most glamorous vehicle, but I knew it would be a game-changer for me. Little did I know, my excitement was going to be short-lived. Instead of being a source of relief, the truck became a constant source of pain, stress, and expenses. It seemed like every time I turned around, there was another issue preventing me from hitting the road and making any money.

They say patience is a virtue, but in this case, it seemed like all of my patience was for naught. The truck was draining my resources instead of bringing in any income. It felt like I was slowly sinking, despite my resilience and never-say-die spirit.

But I refused to give up. I knew that the key to dealing with an old vehicle was to be proactive, so I decided to replace the engine and gearbox. I wasn't going to let a broken engine stop me from achieving my dreams. With a new clutch kit and a brake overhaul, I was determined to get this truck back on the road and earn the money I deserved. As they say, where there's a will, there's always a way!

Sometimes things will always find a reason not to work, life is like that at times. In life some things make no sense, especially things that defy logic, or rather should I say, if your journey home, to success or destiny has been predetermined to pass through barren land, in such circumstances your only choice would be no choice but to keep pushing.

Sometimes life can indeed be unpredictable, and things may not always work out the way we want them to. Despite facing numerous setbacks in my business ventures, I refused to give up on my dreams of creating a better life for myself.

One of my assistants, Simba, was a guy with great promise and an eagerness to learn. I saw the potential in him and decided to encourage him by imparting to him everything I could.

Simba was a lucky person, his luck was simply lying dormant, requiring a little provocation and that's what I did to him.

Eventually, Simba felt confident enough to venture out on his own. He started his own business and used the skills and knowledge most of which learned from me and he achieved great success. I was proud of him and happy to see him flourish, even though I was failing to succeed using the same methods and skills.

Simba's success taught me that sometimes the people we teach and mentor can end up surpassing us. But I didn't let that discourage me. Instead, I used it as motivation to keep pushing forward and striving for success.

I could not tire of knocking on doors of opportunity I was determined to find that open door and walk through it, no matter how many obstacles I faced along the way.

Simba struck gold when the experienced contractor Mendy took him under her wing. Despite having previously worked with our boss Gary, Mendy had become desperate, that's how she took Simba and brought him on as her plumbing subcontractor. Mendy's search for a reliable partner had left her feeling desperate, but Simba answered and quickly put her at ease.

As I searched for a breakthrough, my mind wandered back to 2016, just before Caroline fell ill. I had some ideas that I believed could take me places and propel me forward, but I knew I needed help to make it a reality. So, I gathered three friends and presented my idea to them. They agreed to give it a shot, but I soon realized that agreement alone wouldn't be enough to bring my vision to life. In business, even the smallest enterprises face challenges equal to the potential of their ideas, and trial and error are often necessary to achieve success.

What I've noticed in our African societies is that we often underestimate the power of unity. Without the necessary capital, it can be difficult to venture into profitable businesses with the potential to grow. In this age of apps, they have become the new gold mines, and every industry is searching for ways to digitize. However, the development and maintenance of apps can be costly, making it a difficult challenge for many entrepreneurs to overcome.

It's no secret that unity can lead to great achievements, but determination is the key to achieving any set goal. Sadly, not everyone sees things the same way in life. I had an app idea, but I couldn't afford to develop it on my own. Despite facing numerous obstacles, I persevered until only Prince remained. However, our efforts were in vain when the Chinese developer we contacted failed to deliver, leaving me devastated.

Despite all of these setbacks, one thing that had defined me throughout the years remained steadfast: my never-say-die spirit.

Something within me kept telling me that I still had enough fuel to keep inching forward and that my destiny required me to walk this path. I couldn't shake the feeling that a supernatural force was blocking all the avenues I tried to explore. But I refused to give up. I kept it in my mind that I had to keep pushing forward, no matter what obstacles lay in my way.

A nagging thought keeps resurfacing in my conscience. The hand blocking my path in life was undeniably a mighty one. And perhaps there was a reason why things were allowed to be so difficult in my life. Despite carrying the heavy burden of Caroline's illness and the other challenges I faced, I was still alive and relatively healthy. "Maybe God is trying to guide me towards a purposeful destination," I pondered.

Despite life's obstacles, I knew I only had one choice: to keep moving forward. Thankfully, the flames of hope still burned within me, refusing to be extinguished by ugly circumstances or negative talk. In life, some things are inevitable, no matter how hard you try to make things work. But I was determined to persevere, trusting that there was a greater purpose behind all the difficulties I faced.

Chapter 40

Marriage fails

It is a fact that when someone embarks on a journey, the intent is to make it to destiny unharmed and in time. The same is desired in institutions like marriage. A happily ever after is the desire of everyone that find a man or a woman and agree to journey together. When I got married in 2009, I told myself I will do all it takes to see myself sticking to one partner for the rest of my life. Once again, I was wrong in a way, sometimes you find yourself lacking the power and capacity to control things that keep a marriage union intact. There are things you can control and things you have no jurisdiction over.

Way before I thought of getting married, I used to stand before the mirror telling the man in the mirror how to work and better the man in the mirror. I had self-determination way before I even found a girlfriend, I felt it was paramount that I work to produce the best version of me and become that good person any person would enjoy being with. As far as I could judge myself, I was doing well. I had never cheated or slept around, and I had defied the odds. In fact, for a good period, as I transitioned into adulthood, I stayed without a relationship until I felt that it was time to commit. I chose my friends diligently, and I always behaved well in society, respecting people of all ages.

A few people who knew me even saw me as a role model. My stepmom even encouraged my brothers and her children to follow my example. Speaking of positive influence; I am reminded of a time in Mhangura when one family in the village had their niece sent home from Harare because she had fallen pregnant. When she came back to the area, very few people wanted anything to do with her. In the eyes of many, including her own family, she was an embarrassment and a bad example. But for some reason, I became her best friend. Being seen with this outcast regularly required some courage and thick skin, especially in a small village where gossip and judgment were rampant. However, I didn't let that stop me. I believed that everyone deserved to be treated with kindness and respect, no matter what mistakes they had made. I hoped that my actions would inspire others to do the same and to see that sometimes, being a positive influence means going against the grain and standing up for what is right.

During one of our casual conversations, she looked at me with admiration and told me that I had become a role model to her. I was taken aback and started to reflect on my life, especially the days when I lived in Mhondoro. I couldn't help but wonder, "Why would anyone choose me as their role model?" It was a valid question, considering that we were raised to look up to people who had achieved great things, received awards, and inspired others in some way.

As I pondered on what meaningful contribution I had made to earn the title of "role model," I couldn't come up with a definite answer. Nevertheless, I knew that I had to continue doing what I believed was right, regardless of whether it earned me any accolades or not.

My unwavering belief in the importance of having both parents present in a child's life stemmed from the undesirable experiences that marked my upbringing. Those ugly life experiences taught me valuable lessons and helped me distinguish between right and wrong, dos and don'ts. As a result, I made it my mission to create rules and vows that would bind my family together while avoiding anything that could potentially tear us apart. Always reminded myself if God ever blessed me with a family of my own, I would do everything in my power to provide them with the stability and love that I had longed for as a child.

When Caroline and I got married, the first year was filled with love and peace, and everything looked promising. We were happy every day of our lives, and it felt like we were invincible. We went an entire year without a single argument, content with what we had, even though we started from scratch without a bed. We never saw ourselves as poor and would share a laugh whenever someone pitied us. Our bond was unbreakable, and no matter how tough things got, we remained optimistic and grateful for each other's company.

When we first arrived at Thabisa's place to rent, we only had our bags with us. People watching us move in were expecting us to have more belongings, but when they realized that was all we had, Caroline couldn't help but burst into laughter. At that time, we were content with our simple life, never thinking that things would change. But change did come, and it came at a time when we started dreaming about a different life.

In life, there are things beyond our control. And when change finally arrived, it was a gradual process, taking more than just a day, month, or even a year. It all started with Caroline's sister coming to stay with us after Blessing was born. Within two days, a seed was planted, one that would slowly take root and transform Caroline into a new person. That seed caused a new person to begin to work in Caroline, bringing now and then negative surprises, and while I remained patient and hopeful, things soon became meaningless, especially after her illness.

Despite my efforts to keep things together, one by one, all my reasons for holding on began to crumble.

If there was ever a time I felt humiliated, it was during this period. People talked about me, saying negative things, but I learned to tune out the negativity and carry on. At times, I felt exposed and vulnerable, but I didn't care what others thought or heard. Through it all, I remained true to who I was.

Towards the end of our marriage, I turned to relatives and church elders for help, but even they were at a loss for words to encourage me. I even sought counsel and prayer from Pastor Tumpkin, but nothing seemed to work. Sadly, we eventually parted ways, and Caroline went to live with her father. When I sat down with him, everything was out in the open, but I refused to divulge to people outside her family the ultimate underlying details of what led to our separation. I knew people would be curious, but I reminded myself and let those curious to carry on being so, saying to myself if curiosity killed the cat, then let the cat die.

I spoke exclusively with Caroline's family, but decided to remain mum to everyone else, and they wondered in suspense. And let me tell you, the pressure from others to spill the juicy can be intense! But I stood my ground and kept the inner room locked tight. Why, you ask? Because Caroline is still the mother of two beautiful girls and deserves our utmost respect. Plus, as they say, life goes on. And for her too, that means taking a chance to build a new, exciting life. So let the rumours swirl and the speculation run wild - I'll keep the key to that inner room firmly in my grasp.

As much as we tried to move on, I feel compelled to lend a helping hand to her in any small way I can. It's hard to accept that despite all the hurdles we overcame together, life had other plans. Our experiences should have been the glue that held us together forever, but we can't control everything. Our memories are filled with both joy and darkness, but it's that dark moment that has left an indelible mark on both our lives - a pain that words can't begin to describe. I had hoped to live happily ever after, but it takes two to tango.

Separation or divorce leaves a person in a state of utter brokenness, regardless of gender. Contrary to popular belief, men feel the impact of a relationship's end just as deeply as women do. And let me tell you, my heart was shattered into a million pieces. It's tough to feel like you've been taken for granted by someone you thought was vulnerable and in need of your unwavering support during their weakest moments. Every breakup is unique, and mine was no exception. It tested me in ways I never thought possible. Mine left me as a single dad caring for 2 small girls.

Chapter 41

When little kids become your greatest teachers

As a single dad, I was now the sole caretaker of two beautiful girls - Moreblessing, who had just started grade R at Good Hope Junior, and Blessing was moving into fourth grade. These young girls needed the tenderness of a mother's touch, but without a Mom around, we were embarking on a new chapter. It wasn't going to be easy, but I was ready to step up to the challenge

Four years had passed from the time Caroline got sick, and now it was time for another upped level of my stamina, the test of my resilience, tenacity, love, patience and endurance. Could I handle it all? Would I be able to give delicate Moreblessing the care she deserved? These were the hard-life questions that plagued my thoughts.

I soon realized that words were meaningless without action. Life continued to be brutal, and I needed to be tougher than ever before. Work demanded my utmost dedication, and I refused to use my kids as an excuse for tardiness or sluggishness. I held onto my early-bird status by the skin of my teeth, but it wasn't easy. I had to develop a new way of doing things at home to maintain that coveted title.

For a brief moment, I had help from my brother's daughter, Shylet, but when she got pregnant, she left. Now, everything was on me. Sure, the girls didn't need me to bathe them, but cooking, dishes, and cleaning required my practical, patient leadership. I had to step up and be the ultimate multitasker to keep our home running like a well-oiled machine. Every evening, my routine goes into full swing. I become a culinary mastermind, whipping up supper while simultaneously packing lunch boxes for school and work. And, let's not forget about the next day's after-school hunger pangs that need to be satisfied with something freshly cooked or reheated. It's a challenging juggling act, but one that I quickly became a pro at.

But that's not all. As a parent, I began to see that it's the small details that matter. So, I kept my mind sharp and stayed alert to my girls' needs. From regular hairdos to other little things that only experience can teach me. I learned to take care of it all. It's a non-stop adventure, but I wouldn't have it any other way.

To be honest, in a typical family setup, I wouldn't have given much thought to when my daughters needed a new hairdo. But this experience demanded more than just throwing money at the problem. It was about making sure my girls looked presentable at church and school. I couldn't bear the thought of them looking anything less than perfect. Especially at church, where we spend a whole day on Saturday and have lunch with fellow churchgoers. in that set up it's tempting to shift the responsibility of feeding our family to those kind-hearted church moms. But I refused to do that, taking it upon myself to make sure my kids were well-fed and presentable, even if it meant sacrificing some of my own time and energy. It's just one of the many ways of standing up for my kids. As a father, I knew I couldn't be a superhero and do everything on my own, nor could I be in two places at once. So, I learned to be humble and ask for help when needed it. Friday afternoons were preparation days in Adventist households, where families would cook and prepare for the Sabbath. But with my busy schedule, I found myself strapped for time. That's when I turned to my sister Caroline for help. She graciously offered to buy and prepare our Sabbath lunch, taking some of the load off my shoulders. It was a relief to have someone to rely on, and it made our Sabbath meal all the more special, knowing that it was prepared with love and care by a family member. Learning to ask for help was just one of the many lessons I've learned on this parenting journey.

It was a blessing to have my sister Caroline help with preparing our Sabbath lunch. Not only did it make things more organized in terms of food, but Caroline also became my third set of eyes, along with Yvonne. They were able to spot things that I might have missed or things that were beyond my control. They took it upon themselves to ensure the well-being of my girls by arranging weekend sleepovers and even spending school holidays with them.But there's another person who deserves special recognition, Sheila. I have not met a lot of people so gifted in caring for and moulding children. She played a vital role alongside my sister, looking after my sister's kids, and always going the extra mile to make sure my girls felt loved and cared for. Her consistency in providing such exceptional care can only be described as a gift. It's not every day that you come across someone like Sheila, and I feel truly grateful to have had her in our lives.

As a dad raising young girls, I learned an important lesson that took me a while to figure out. It's easy to focus on all the things that make your kids look like they come from a well-to-do home. But it took me some time to realize that what mattered was the happiness of their hearts.

One day, while shopping with my daughter Moreblessing, I noticed her eyes light up when we walked past dolls and girl toys.

It was then that I realized how much she longed for these simple pleasures that she didn't have at home. It was a wake-up call for me, and it took me two years to truly understand what my daughter needed. But that day, I decided to make her day by picking up a doll and throwing it into the shopping trolley. The joy on her face was priceless, and it turned out to be the best shopping trip ever. It was a reminder that sometimes, it's the simplest things that can bring the most happiness to our children.

On weekends, specifically Sundays, as someone who believe it's crucial to instil in my children the values that will guide them in life. One of the most important of these is health, which is paramount to our overall well-being. Good health isn't just a happy accident; it requires effort and conscious decisions.

For instance, if I prioritise exercise and make it a part of my routine, I can't leave my kids out of the equation and expect them to figure it out on their own. As their parent, it's my responsibility to teach them how to take care of their health, including maintaining a healthy weight. In today's world of fast food, GMOs, and processed junk, it can be challenging to raise healthy children.

I made a commitment to ensure that my kids understand the importance of making healthy choices and how they can positively impact their lives. So, on Sundays, I would dedicate time to teach my children in practice.

To make learning about health and exercise fun for my kids, I decided to invite a few of their friends over and take them for a morning run in the park. This experience was not only a great way for them to get some exercise, but it also provided plenty of learning opportunities.

As someone who tends to be quiet and focused on my thoughts or reading, I realized that I needed to be more attentive to my children's needs and concerns. In particular, my daughter Moreblessing taught me the importance of paying attention to the little incidents that happen at school, on the playground, and even while playing in the park. I learned to pause from my pursuits and listen to what my children had to say, especially when it came to reports of pain, injuries, and bruises.

Through this experience, I discovered that being an attentive and engaged parent is not only important for my children's well-being but also a rewarding and fulfilling experience for me. Ultimately, by taking the time to teach my children about health and exercise, and by being present and attentive to their needs, I was able to provide them with the tools and support they need to live happy, healthy lives. I also discovered how it is important and never wasteful to sometimes awaken the toddler in me to connect with my children. I've made a conscious effort to laugh with them at the things that make them laugh and to find stories that entertain them. This has been especially important for my daughter Blessing, who is a gifted talker. She could talk nonstop, and in every sentence, seeking my affirmation and approval. And I made sure to follow everything she said and give her the attention she deserves. But sometimes she's quiet, and that's when I knew she's deep in thought, processing the world around her. It's during these moments that I would try to create a safe space for her to express herself, to share her ideas, and to ask questions. Being a parent is not just about providing for your children's physical needs; it's also about creating an environment where they feel seen, heard, and understood.

In general, my kids have been healthy and attending school regularly. They've only experienced the occasional cold, fever, or sore throat. Blessing has even taken her passion for music to the next level by taking violin lessons. It's been amazing to see her grow and develop her skills.

Being present-minded and engaging in my children's lives is essential. By taking the time to connect with them, listen to their thoughts and ideas, and support their passions, I'm able to provide them with a strong foundation to build their lives. And in return, they bring me immeasurable joy and fulfilment.

Whenever one of my children caught the flu or a cold, I had to take time off work to take them to the doctor. On several occasions, the doctors would complement me, saying; "You are a great father, and we would love to see more parents like you." My motive was simple: I did not want to leave anything to chance, nor did I want to burden others by asking for their assistance. I believed that the responsibility to care for my children was entirely mine.

I grew up in a household where we were taught not to inconvenience others for anything. Ensuring my children's health and well-being not only put me at ease but also brought comfort to their mother, despite the distance. She always loved hearing about their progress.

Along the way, I almost forgot this vital lesson instilled in me by my upbringing. All of a sudden, my daughters and I developed a habit of singing together. But unlike the days when my mother taught us melodies from her childhood, my girls' upbringing in the church made it easy and acceptable for us to embrace the singing mentality. Blessing, in particular, loved using the Advent Hymnal App on my gadget, which led us to pitch and tune as we sang.

Before we knew it, we had a compilation of our favourite hymns. This reminded me of the days when we would sit around the fire, singing, clapping, and playing tambourines-- a skill my sisters learned from our mother.

Despite all the activities I can do with my kids now, I'm not ashamed to admit that we still have a long way to go before we can recreate the same vibe and environment that surrounded our family in the past. The harmony and unison we shared fooled us into thinking that one day, our singing could earn us a spot in the celestial choir. As I looked back on those moments, I realized that the experience of singing with my daughters was not just about creating beautiful music but also about keeping our family's traditions alive. As I engaged in these activities with my daughters, everything seemed to be going well. The kids were happy, and I was pleased with their positive response to our new challenges.

At school, my daughters were consistently earning good grades. Maria Botha, who teaches violin to Blessing, was also pleased with her progress. I encouraged Maria to find a teacher for Moreblessing as well, and we planned to enrol her in violin classes in January 2022. Although Blessing's progress was slow, it was steady, and the good news came that she was now qualified to play in the orchestra. These kids were being groomed to join well-organized orchestras in Cape Town. I was thrilled to see Blessing's hard work paying off, despite her being a slow learner. As we continued with our daily routine, we woke up each day brimming with hope and enthusiasm. Our hearts were focused on a brighter future, and we prayed daily with the assurance that better things were on the horizon.

Chapter 42

A challenge like I never thought

Amidst the hustle and bustle of everyday life, it never appeared like a tempest was brewing inside my beloved daughter, Blessing.

It was a normal Sunday afternoon when the first signs of trouble began to emerge. Initially, it was a persistent small cough that lasted a few days and didn't seem to be anything to worry about. However, as the Sunday wore on, her condition began to change, and I knew I had to take action. Taking precautions, I decided to keep her home from school the following day. I could tell that she was not herself. As the day progressed, I became increasingly concerned about her well-being, so I decided to keep a closer eye on her.

That night, I brought her into my room to keep a watchful eye over her as she slept. But as the night wore on, it became increasingly apparent that something was seriously wrong. Blessing's condition rapidly deteriorated, and she was soon writhing in pain, clutching her stomach and struggling to breathe.

At that moment, I knew that I had to act fast. Without hesitation, I rushed her to the hospital, praying for a miracle. As we made our way to the emergency room, I still felt the doctors will find the problem and we will go back home and carry on with our lives. But I was wrong, something serious had been growing inside her and we were soon to find out. This was a different sickness. My heart was cut as I watched my daughter, Blessing, struggle through an illness unlike any she had ever experienced before.

Now we were at the Red Cross War Memorial Children's Hospital, where the doctors conducted a thorough examination. What they found was both rare and serious: Blessing had a dilated heart, also known as Cardio Myopathy. This condition causes the heart to grow bigger and weaker and can lead to heart failure and damage to other vital organs.

I was devastated by this news. Just when I thought I had adjusted to the challenges of my life, this more complicated illness suddenly appeared on the scene, demanding that I summon every ounce of strength and stamina I possessed to manage and cope with it. As I sat there, grappling with the news of my daughter's condition, it felt like a spiritual war more than anything else. I was overwhelmed, unsure of how to face this challenge head-on.

In moments like these, I couldn't help but think back to all the other struggles we had faced in the past. It seemed like life was constantly lining up obstacles our way, and I couldn't help but wonder why. It was all too big for me, so huge beyond my stamina and I felt discouraged and defeated. Sometimes, it takes a personal experience to truly understand the severity of a situation. And even when it hits close to home, it can leave you reeling and gasping for air. Some circumstances refuse to let up, relentlessly hammering at your doorstep and leaving you with questions that only God himself can answer.

Cardiomyopathy is a complicated and dangerous condition, not easy to manage at all costs. As a father trying to raise kids on my own, I thought I was rising to the challenges, copying well, trying to absorb the situation, going back to normal life, making a juggle many things that makes life normal.

Blessing's illness came to pose a challenge beyond my imagination. There was a point when I felt taking a day off or a few hours from work to go see a doctor was too much of a juggle among other things. Not until a time came when my child's hospitalization called for me to be with her for days in the hospital, many days she stayed in the ICU, I had to be there and also find a way to pop up at work.

One ugly experience of being in a foreign land as an immigrant under a temporary resident permit is that bills never relent, the more particular situations call for your attention, the more you need to attend to such with money, while any time taken from work is time unpaid. Many times, you try to put on your thinking cape trying to see a way that leads to quick relief from your circumstances. Such times call you also to offer sincere prayers, fasting, asking, and pleading with God to see you out of your situation. Blessing was diagnosed in October 2021, and before long, while I felt the situation was demanding a lot from me, experiencing a few quick admissions, not long as we moved midway through November did the cardiology team begin to suggest a heart transplant.

In the blink of an eye, my vibrant child, once full of life and energy, was forced to miss the last term of grade five in 2021. As November approached, she was briefly discharged from the hospital, only to be readmitted a week later. This time, it happened during the busiest season at work, as we were preparing to shut down for the December holidays. I found myself spending my holiday at the hospital, watching helplessly as my child's condition deteriorated before my eyes.

During that trying time, I witnessed my child's body wasting away as she struggled to eat, constantly vomiting and rejecting anything that came near her mouth. It was a heart-wrenching experience, one that left me feeling helpless and overwhelmed.

As I sat by my child's side, feeling helpless and overwhelmed, all I could do was pray. I reached out to a few close friends, asking them to pray in a specific manner, and was touched to find that many others offered to pray as well. Even as I struggled to remain hopeful, my heart aching with uncertainty, I found solace in the support of my community.

Meanwhile, Caroline was dealing with her challenges, battling aching feet and trying to stay informed from afar. Despite the distance we maintained constant contact, offering each other support and encouragement during this difficult time.

As I spent more and more time in the hospital, I found myself becoming accustomed to the rhythms of life there. I saw children come and go, some left healed and whole, while others succumbed to their illnesses. I watched doctors rush to attend to emergencies, their faces etched with the strain of long hours and constant stress. Sometimes they would succeed, while other times I witnessed a child dying, followed by the cries and agony of a mother who has just lost a kid, turning the whole environment sombre. Doctors and nurses carrying dejected faces after losing a patient, I sat there observing how they try to put on a brave face to move to the next task awaiting.

The image that captivated me was that of a young child in the ICU, surrounded by an array of tubes resembling a colossal spider ensnaring the little one's forehead. Some of the tubes extended to the child's tiny nose, while others were slim and flexible, snaking their way through the nostrils and down into the stomach. The overwhelming sight evoked a deep sense of empathy within me for the child and their family, who were undoubtedly enduring a difficult and trying time.

Moving from the ICU to the cardiology ward, was a frequent sight to witness young children adorned with adhesive bandages on their chests, the aftermath of invasive surgeries that had ripped open their tiny chests. The cacophony from beeping monitors and the mechanical whirring of ventilators filled the air, calling for constant attention from the medical staff. As I observed these scenes, I couldn't help but reflect on our own experiences. Blessing, in particular, had endured countless blood draws, to the point where the medical staff struggled to find an unused vein for administering medication or drawing blood. Some doctors demonstrated a lack of expertise, repeatedly pricking her in search of a vein. However, Blessing held a special fondness for a young, energetic female doctor named Yolanda, who had an uncanny ability to locate and hit the vein on her first attempt.

As Christmas and the New Year came and went, I found myself pacing the beautifully decorated, wide corridors of the Red Cross Hospital. The festive decorations were intended to lift the spirits of the hardworking staff, the devoted parents, and, most importantly, the young patients. Often, I would walk along the gleaming, silent floors of corridor E1, making my way to the benches near the elevators where I could access reliable Wi-Fi on my phone. There, I would browse through the latest updates on Facebook, reading through the gossip, the boasts, and the fabrications that were constantly being shared. At other times, I would delve into various YouTube publications, avidly following NASA's latest space adventures and the latest technological advancement.

Whenever I grew weary from pacing the hospital corridors, I would join Blessing at her bedside and patiently answer her countless questions. Other times, when Blessing drifted off to sleep, I would stay by her side, taking out my computer to write. And all the while, we never forgot about little Moreblessing, who was staying with my sister. Despite the distance, my children share a strong bond, and Moreblessing has a remarkable way of getting what she wants. Despite being a tall girl, she never hesitates to draw closer to me, taking my hand and making her requests known without hesitation.

One remarkable quality of Moreblessing is her self-sufficiency. She never asks anyone for anything, instinctively knowing where to turn to solve her problems. Despite being physically apart, we maintained daily contact through video calls, which became a routine during our stay at the hospital. After the first week of January 2022, we were finally discharged and returned home, but our respite was short-lived.

It was then that I came to understand the term "revolving door patients," referring to those who are frequently admitted and discharged from the hospital. From October 2021 to January 2022, Blessing had been admitted eight times, an experience that underscored the challenges faced by families with chronically ill children.

Our stays would not have been lighter without the relentless support and presence of my sister Caroline who sacrificed many nights in my absence. To be at the hospital, by the bedside is not small talk. Not forgetting the many trips also made by her husband and son bringing food, sometimes daily. Of course, the support would have been more than that, but hospital protocols had changed during the Covid lockdown period to only allow one person by the bedside, no swapping, no visiting, but they listened to circumstances around me and allowed my sister to come and relieve me. Yvonne as always made sacrifices also, that can only be made from the heart.

Chapter 43

A passion from the past

Although life is filled with problems that threaten to consume us whole, we learn to smile in the face of adversity. Even when life-threatening problems stare us down with a menacing grin, we find a way to summon the strength to keep going and strive for fulfilment and purpose.

Apart from my problems, both good and bad, I have always felt a deep-seated energy within me that whispers encouragement and motivates me to make a difference in the lives of others. My heart is naturally drawn to children and youth, and I feel a special connection to rural communities. Perhaps it is my upbringing that instilled in me a sense of belonging to these communities. Perhaps it is the memories from moulding during the gatherings around the fireplace, the roam around the fields in search of venison, and the memorable moments in the grazing fields.

Many times, I visit Zimbabwe, I find it hard to spend any significant amount of time in the city, so I only make a stopover in Harare or Norton, and thereafter I find myself heading to rural Mhangura. It is here where my crucibles began to work in me a work of shaping and sharpening me for the more challenging circumstances life would later throw at me. However, there is one thing that I cannot help but notice - a persistent and ever-present sign of dying hope in the children that reminds me of my own childhood. These children are going through experiences that are reminiscent of my own, and every time I look at them, I am reminded of the years of toil and grinding that I endured. Despite their varying circumstances, I can see an unvoiced passion, a desire and a willingness to do great things in most of these kids. Behind their silence and unspoken words, I can read unvoiced ambition and attributes of greatness. Like my own days of toil, the environment, atmosphere, and status of the people we looked up to forbade us from vocalizing our dreams or expressing ambitious goals. The surroundings set limits and barriers that require a daring attitude to attempt to break free from the status quo. The eloquence in silence is so powerful that one can only whisper to oneself about any desire to break free. Nevertheless, in a greater number of them, I see potential and talent in abundance, such talent and whatever manner of potential they house within their hearts, if remain unharnessed will surely perish and get buried. Something needs to be done. Already I see a generation of a group of boys that I used to teach football at Richmond school, despite them being talented and having a burning desire to play sport for a living and if possible, reach the skies.

A few years later, upon my return, I was surprised to see how almost all of them were now married with a child or two, I mean, that was so early and quicker than my anticipation. Despite the fate of the then generation of talented little, not so little anymore, I have within me a burning passion of wanting to see one or two youngsters doing well in any field they feel passionate and talented in.

Each time I feel like I am being compelled by a force from within. I felt like doing something to brighten my little corner. So, I looked at many people who end up helping or uplifting others, the difference between them and me being many of those people seem so well up with many doing well and being financially well-positioned. But here I was, still having achieved nothing, only a job that pays my bills, yet something within me kept nagging me saying there is no better time to begin.

As I thought back on my journey, characterized by failures and mistakes, it seemed like these experiences were the motivation behind my willingness to help others. But I asked myself, can one truly achieve success if their point of motivation is driven by a desire to see others succeed in the things they failed at? I have walked the road of failure, and I have stared fear in the eye. I know the obstacles that stood in my way, and I know what could have been done differently if I were to succeed. I am acutely aware of the mistakes, impatience, and frustration that led to my past failures. But what if I can now, in some small way, help a soul and entrust the rest to the Almighty? What if I have reached the pinnacle of my abilities and am now the best version of myself? What if God is still counting on me to reach out to those in need, even those I may not be aware of? These thoughts led me to have a conversation with my brother, Mandela, about launching Shamwari Projects, which aims to scour remote areas for hidden talent and cultivate diversity. We wholeheartedly embraced the idea and decided that soccer, despite its expense, would be the ideal sport to run and coordinate owing to its popularity and our familiarity with it since childhood. While we discussed the logistics, my old friend Oliver, who was in Harare pursuing his own ventures, expressed his desire to establish an under-16 soccer team. This led to further discussions between Oliver, my brother, and me, where we brainstormed and deliberated on the name of the academy. We unanimously agreed on the name Gute Soccer Academy and proceeded to take action. I wasted no time in sending Oliver funds to purchase soccer balls in Harare while I began saving for soccer boots. By December, I was thrilled to be in the sporting shop purchasing 16 pairs of soccer boots, with plans to purchase more in the near future. We delivered the boots to the club, and the excitement amongst the players and coaches was palpable.

In January, we registered with the Sport and Recreational Commission and ZIFA, the football governing body, knowing that the real work had just begun. Our next order of business was to acquire more boots and jerseys, which I tried my best to make look professional within the limits of my budget. Adding also some training equipment as per the requirement of football. For training, we also began to gather a lot of coach-assist material to help us go ahead. Surely, we did set ourselves on a journey that seems to be a thousand miles journey.

The true challenges that require resilience and character are often the ones that catch us off guard. While we initially thought that our primary task was to teach kids how to play soccer, we soon realized that we had to address the mentality of parents and guardians as well. Some parents were willing to learn and gladly supported our involvement with their children, while others opposed us for no apparent reason. Some of the most vocal naysayers were those whose kids were not participating, while others felt slighted after being screened out, despite the fact that some of their children were not cut out for soccer or required extensive training to grasp the basics.

Another group of individuals saw the academy as an opportunity to profit from it even before we had laid the foundation. These challenges required us to remain steadfast and maintain our focus on the primary goal of nurturing young talent and promoting the game of soccer in rural areas.

The rural economic environment posed yet another set of challenges. Unlike the urban setting, where businesses operate interdependently and within certain hours, rural farming communities allow individuals to work at their own pace and on their own schedules. This independence presented unique obstacles for us, as we had to find a way to work around the farmers' schedules while also accommodating the kids' responsibilities. While kids were excused from certain responsibilities during school hours, any other commitments were considered obstacles that had to be navigated delicately.

Finding arrangements that satisfied parents while also allowing the kids enough time to practice required careful planning and flexibility. We had to adapt to the unique circumstances of the rural setting and find creative ways to ensure that the kids were able to attend practice sessions while also fulfilling their other responsibilities. Despite the challenges, we remained committed to our goal of uplifting soccer talent in rural areas.

One of the most common responsibilities of growing up in a rural setting is the task of tending to livestock. It's a job that can prove challenging, particularly when it comes to negotiating with parents who may have other plans for their time. It can be difficult to convince an adult to abandon their daily routine for the sake of a child's playtime. But as a rural boy, I learned to improvise and turn adversity into opportunity.

I scoured the grazing fields for a second training ground, determined to turn this chore into a win-win situation. With careful planning and a bit of creativity, I managed to find a solution that satisfied parents, allowing kids to pursue their passion for sports. It wasn't always easy, but we persevered, determined to make the most of every opportunity.

Of course, my journey is far from over, and I know that there will be challenges along the way. But I face each obstacle with a sense of purpose and a willingness to adapt and overcome. The road ahead may not be smooth, but I'm confident that with perseverance and determination, I'll continue to make strides towards achieving my goals.

The great work of setting foundations has been done over the years through rough times. I and others around me consider the starting of the Gute Soccer Academy as an inspired move. When the stringent rules on Covid 19 began to lift, just like everyone we began to try and emerge from our hibernation like those resilient animals we watch on National Geographic from the uttermost cold place on this earth. Tough for a person like me who was trying to come to terms with handling the sickness of my daughter while at the same time trying to involve myself in things that mattered in my life. Tough as I found myself operating, we still managed to make some movements, to show there are still signs of life in the projects we have embarked on. Our kids have been to a few places, and one of the programs we sent a few determined ones was a college connect program in Harare which gives kids a chance to showcase their skills with the hope of finding a placement into a US college with a scholarship offered.

We took a bold step and managed to register and send three of our boys from the soccer academy. They went and fared well, two got selected while one could not make it because he fell sick during the trials. It was a very exciting moment for the kids, their parents and also us. Even though in the end we could not afford the high fees those agents ask for, we still felt it was the right thing to do. The boys got a chance to meet some of the premier league coaches that got hired to conduct the trials. An exciting moment for the boys to dream that these things are possible. It indeed takes a leap of faith to do something new. Upon entering an initiative, one does not know how people will receive it. It may not be entirely a new thing like re-inventing the wheel. In our case, the idea of introducing a soccer academy in one of those forgotten areas was received by the community with mixed feelings. Some, failed to see the significance of such a thing while another bunch never cared or paid attention.

Nevertheless, a handful of parents loved it and some were more than willing to assist in whatever small way possible. After sending the three boys to Harare for the college connect program, a new chapter like we never anticipated began to unfold. Remember when we began this initiative, we only wanted to cater to the rural marginalized because we felt that kids in the cities have vast avenues that they can pursue and pursue careers in whatever way they desire.

Even though this ideology sounded good, we did not know that destiny will steer this initiative in a way that would surprise us all.

Soon after my friend returned from Harare, we began to receive calls from parents living in cities and towns asking if we could host their children during school holidays and teach them a thing or two about modern football. We gladly said yes, so kids began to come from Harare, Chegutu knowing they are going to a rural remote place. Feels like defying the odds in a small way. Normally children would seek a way to the city where opportunities are always available. Also, thanks to Oliver and his wife for welcoming these kids. Now seeing that our soccer program is spreading its wings trying to fly, we do not intend to limit it but instead, follow where it leads. Also we cannot help but think of how to have good facilities to be able to host more kids in the future. Not forgetting to mention that more kids will be catered for during school holidays when we host training camps giving the youngsters the kind of training that can afford them to play anywhere. Already kids from Harare went back with a good report after they became surprised by our training methods, and coaches alike from the premier league in our country have expressed surprise with our methods of training.

Let me remark that my involvement in the Gute Academy is just a slice of the pizza, Shamwari Projects if pursued to its potential is life-changing, not only for a few individuals but the community, and societies can benefit. So, we will take it one step at a time. For now, dear friends, let me go back and climb over a few little life obstacles.

Chapter 44

The chapter I hate to write

While I tried to appear normal and face life's daily routine, it's ups and downs. There was an ugly chapter that had imposed itself on me and my family, even though I wished it away and no matter how hard or what efforts I exerted.

The health of my dearest daughter continued to weigh heavily on me. Day and night, I and Blessing prayed fervently to the Almighty in whose enigmatic presence we relished. Pleading for Blessing's heart to be healed. Hoping to avoid the much-feared transplant.

In addition to the fight against this dreaded monster that intruded our lives, taking away the joy and health of a vibrant, talented genius in the making,

Life did not stop, and as life happened around me, I had to face it and picture and prepare for a tomorrow beyond problems at hand. These problems did not cause me to forget the things I held dear, such as the need and determination to expand my work and fulfil the cardinal commitment of my life which is to help others in what smaller way I can.

Despite these unrelenting struggles I faced, I have come to accept that my life is a nomadic journey, filled with constant challenges and daily battles. But through it all, I have learned to build up a fierce resistance and to face every obstacle head-on, refusing to be overwhelmed by the weight of adversity. Yet, each time I think I've overcome one hurdle, life never fails to throw another one in my way, a challenge that stares me down with a sly grin. But determination seems to be now in me a natural attribute.

Many challenges they are of course, but I tried to keep pushing forward, fighting the good fight, and to live each day as though everything was normal, to behave, talk and engage in a normal way without giving out a hint how life was threatening to throw us tumbling into the abyss.

As my daughter continued without complaining, courageously fighting against a life-threatening heart condition, I found myself faced with a daunting decision in January 2023: to travel to Australia to complete my skills assessment as part of my process to migrate to Australia with the girls.. Despite the overwhelming sense of fear and uncertainty that threatened to consume me, I summoned all my courage and resolved to act against the odds. And against the word and warnings of doctors not to step away from Blessing.

On a crisp February morning, after making up my mind, I found myself seated tightly on my seat as the plane stood on the tarmac at the Cape Town International Airport. Then I listened, to a thunderous roar of the twin giant turbine engines as they whirred to life, their powerful thrust pushing the massive Boeing metal bird forward, to speed along the tarmac until that moment with a jolt and a tilt upwards as the front wheels lost contact with the ground, and we were airborne, losing gravity, soaring towards the heavens, feeling rest assured the twin engines will continually strive against the air and carry us through until we touch the ground on the other end of the ocean.

As we ascended higher and higher, I couldn't help but marvel at the sheer power of the plane, the way it cut through the air with effortless grace. With each passing moment, I felt my spirits lift, my heart buoyed by the sense of possibility and adventure that lay ahead.

As I sat during the journey, my mind kept playing a see-saw between my problems and working a remedy. Despite the trials and tribulations that lay in my path, I felt like I was capable of facing them head-on, armed with the strength and resilience that had carried me through so many challenges before.

Other instances my mind raced with thoughts of the long journey I had embarked on while leaving behind two special girls who had sent me off with overflowing hope and love. It was this same hope for a brighter future, and unwavering aspiration that burned fervently as well within my heart.

For the whole journey I felt I was in emotional turmoil, driven by love and an unyielding commitment to a better present and a tomorrow filled with joy, wellness, and harmony. I couldn't help but feel a surge of different kind of emotion, a sense of excitement coursing through my veins.

My route took me via Qatar. So, while I sat on the plane from Qatar to Brisbane, I fell asleep and found myself sinking deep into a nightmare where I was under attack and had to fight back. Now in my efforts to fight back in my sleep, I kicked against the legs of a lady sitting next to me and had to apologise. That nightmare I never knew would repeat during my entire stay in Queensland.

After a long and tiring flight, we touched down at the Brisbane airport. Before we knew it, we were getting through security checks in which I was singled for a search. I wondered if appearing different among the rest of the travellers drew interest from the officers at the airport, nonetheless, in no time I was out and reading messages from Aaron who instructed me to take a train to Helensvale.

Before long I was in the company of my diminutive buddy in the person of Aaron. From Helensvale into the G-Link buses to Labrador, a good neighbourhood near a small river, this is where I first encountered a river that changes direction of flow time and again. I later learnt the name of the river as Bigerra Creek.

The two months I spent in Australia was a time Characterised by much prayer and fasting, mainly for the health of my daughter and as well pleading for success to also consider my efforts and repay me with good for the relentless determination.

During this time my daughter held on to a time out of the hospital, an impressive moment to our liking, the doctors also spoke with me and expressed much joy. This was a moment that brought relief and much needed chance and I pushed with every bit of energy to navigate through this new environment. Much thanks also to a compassionate friend in the person of Aaron for the priceless help, playing host together with his wife Dr Joy whom we teasingly called Dr Amai after her achievement in bagging her PHD in ecology. Despite her achievements, she is never once carried away and seems not to badge but remain steadfast in character and humility.

I would have loved to push myself a little more, seeing how my efforts to navigate Australia were seemingly beginning to get responses. But that wish of carrying on pushing was not to continue because fate had called Blessing back to the hospital.

When I enquired over the phone, Yvonne urged me to carry on as this hospitalisation seemed like nothing that would last for many days, however something kept whispering into my ears to drop all things and return to see off the trouble.

I listened to the voice of conscience, returning back to Cape Town to a delightful surprise first to Moreblessing and my sister's kids at home. Then the following day I strolled through the hospital corridors to stun Blessing who for a moment froze with a grin the moment she laid her eyes on my figure.

At last, I was by my daughter's bedside. Each time she gets hospitalised, I considered everything secondary, I felt the willingness to stand up for her with an unwavering determination. Blessing in turn always repeated. "Daddy, each moment you come from work to be with me, I feel half my pain and my worries flying away."

Of course, the relationship and the journey between my kids and I had always been characterised by an unmistakable emotional bond. This bond became escalated by Blessing's sickness. Then there arose also a bond between the two kids, Moreblessing quickly learned how to guard after Blessing with a caring heart beyond her age. I watched many times with teary eyes even the days Blessing pushed to be at school. The care from Moreblessing and in turn Blessing returning the same, what an unbelievable pair my children were.

From the time Blessing began attending school, she became unbelievable, her intellectual intelligence, her willingness to volunteer and serve other kids, not to mention her involvement in music, bringing home countless certificates of achievements. Her level of respect at home, church and in the neighbourhood, she was always in the league of her own, always exuding positivity even from the hospital bed. A friend to any doctor she became, continually doing art with those hands bruised by the numberless pricking by needles to put drips. From the hospital bed she would knit scarfs for people at home, always starting with me, even the time I travelled to Australia, she handed to me a handkerchief embroidered I LOVE YOU DADDY.

From the hospital bed she always expressed her longing to be home and plant vegetables and experiment with bean seeds. I have not seen such hope and positivity, such faith in God from a little girl, always writing me something to encourage me even as she grew weaker. Many times I withdrew myself to go and cry privately, especially those moments I saw her growing weaker and there was negative talk and vibe from the doctors. I would find a way to lift my spirit when I came before her, seeing how much faith she had and how she planned for the future. Being that weak she caused me to weep bitterly in private when she spoke of the time in future when she would have kids. I looked at her and listened to her plans, her hope, enthusiasm, and unwavering faith. My heart felt shattered when I prayed for a miracle to save my child.After giving so much to the fight, only one thing made sense – we looked for healing of our broken hearts, a healing that could only come with the restoration of my daughter's health.

Despite our fighting, our hope and tenacity, we watched the little girl slowly slipping away. Her energy, intelligence, ambitions to become a doctor and build her own hospital was slipping away from me as she weakened.

What was I to do? I watched her in agony, offered her comfort, even weeks before she became very weak, I watched her getting more emotional, wanting me closer than before, I would allow her to leave her bed, dragging her drips to come and spent the night in my arms. Nurses looked at this and were speechless. She continually grew weak, swelling all over and I watched in pain as doctors began to care less until the day, they decided to sedate her during my absence.

I was heartbroken to say the least, and I confronted the whole team of doctors, beginning with the senior professor who made it clear it wasn't him who had anything to explain but instead pointed out he prefers I see his team at once because he wants his team to speak with one voice. After that decision I returned in the evening, and Theresa, Blessing's cousin from her mom's side told me "she could not eat because she is weak." So I thanked her for the days she spent with Blessing during the afternoons. I tried talking to Blessing as much, but she was too sedated to remain awake for a minute and I remember her last meaningful words as she signalled me closer; "Daddy, I love you so much" from that time I watched on together with my two sisters as she fought for every second breath.

Just like that, the night of June 24 2023 heralded a stark reality that my heart had refused to even imagine. Blessing left us having just turned 13 the previous month.

I felt like just ending my life to see off such misery, however, one thing, only one, stopped me – Moreblessing – a complete replica of her sister in deeds and character. What would her life be if I could leave her just like that? So, I resolved that for her sake, let me bear the pain, the shame and agony. People, friends, and family came forward with words of encouragement, telling me it shall be well. However, I am of the opinion that our lives will never be the same again. **Even if God was to give me Africa to rule, I would always say. "It could have been better Lord if Blessing was here!"**

Epilogue

"Daddy I am sorry that you have to go through all this and see things you aren't supposed to see." These words, to say the least, were heart-rending to me.

Blessing as always would speak after many thoughtful moments in a situation so demanding of every bit of energy. In trying to cope, we saw ourselves drawing closer, physically, and emotionally. Knowing my child, I understood the deeper meaning behind the few words, words from a troubled 12-year-old girl. In short, my daughter was saying "Daddy we all understand I am now grown up to deserve privacy but please forget all of it and be here for me."

Besides these indelible remarks, my daughter had always been resilient beyond the eloquence of my words. I have not seen a time when a young lady would give so much to life, hoping and trusting in faith and prayer, and continually so when the odds were pushing her into the abyss. These events around us kept my mind in a constant race to keep up with an avalanche of thoughts bombarding me relentlessly.

As a person of faith, watching a child born in faith, succumbing to an illness that seemed to require more spiritual intervention when science was falling short. I felt duped by faith and religion, I felt like

I didn't know God. Was I introduced to the wrong side of God? And was this God now falling short to address our problems in practice? Did I not possess enough faith to see the child delivered? How about the hundreds that were in fervent intercessory prayer? What more could one ask from a little girl? Was she not a wellspring of positivity in her most trying moments? What does life really require from me?

Despite the myriad of questions, we kept on praying and hoping. As a constant reminder my daughter would say "Daddy pray for me." So, in prayer, we carried on and when she felt too unwell, she added on. "Daddy please keep waking up to check on me." She was worried that she might pass away in her sleep and because she felt my presence was paramount to her making it.

By this time, she was turning very emotional, wanting me to hug her often, sometimes asking me; "Daddy can you please hug me." Many times, she would simply ask to hold my hand and talk out her wishes and future plans, but repeatedly remarking; "Daddy each moment you come in to be with me, I feel half my pain getting lifted."

All my life, I have walked a rugged pathway. From the early days when I looked up to guardians to shape my destiny, to the time I felt like I now hold in my hands the tools to chart my path and shape my destiny. Rugged as the pathway was, filled with little goodness and an overwhelming amount of pain and fruitless toil. I can attest, nothing has ever prepared me for the next chapter at every turn of the page.

About the Author

Sifelani Masamba was born and raised in Zimbabwe. Because of uncertainties that plagued his family, he didn't grow up in one town or village; together with his mom and siblings they found themselves shifting from place to place in search of a better life. Through hardships, Sifelani managed to build a resilient character, a believer of progress who has managed to stand resolute in the face of adversity. When he became an adult, he took matters into his hands and has traveled and lived in various countries in Africa and has travelled abroad in relentless efforts to change the narrative around him. His attitude towards life is a testimony to the resilience of the human spirit in the face of adversity. Against many odds, he lived soberly, calmly and handled difficult life situations with grace and composure while remaining on track in pursuit of a better life.

Acknowledgements

It takes a village to raise a person. I value the presence of many friends and relatives in whose love I bask and flourish, friends too numerous to mention each by name. I am grateful for the role that each one has played in shaping and sharpening me. I love you all.